NEW
MATHS
IN ACTION

S4²

Members of the
Mathematics in Action Group
associated with this book:

D. Brown
M. Brown
R.D. Howat
G. Meikle
E.C.K. Mullan
K. Nisbet

Published in 2005 by:
Nelson Thornes Ltd
Delta Place
27 Bath Road
CHELTENHAM
GL53 7TH
United Kingdom

07 08 09 / 10 9 8 7 6 5 4 3

A catalogue record of this book is available from the British Library

ISBN 978 0 7487 9043 2

Illustrations by Oxford Designers and Illustrators
Page make-up by Tech-Set Ltd

Printed and bound in Croatia by Zrinski

Acknowledgements
Jean Ryder (DHD Multimedia Gallery): 40; Corel 768 (NT): 65; Joe Cornish/Digital
Vision LL (NT): 74; Joe Cornish/Digital Vision LL (NT): 74; Alamy RF (NT): 76; Greek
postal service Jeff Miller: 90; Stuart Sweatmore: 111; Corel 667 (NT): 125; Digital
Vision 7 (NT): 133; Corel 760 (NT): 137; Corel 467 (NT): 153; Photodisc 17 (NT):
162; Corel 308 (NT): 168; Gerry Ellis/Digital Vision JA (NT): 177; Digital Vision 9
(NT): 195; Corel 797 (NT): 210; Eyeware (NT): 216; Corel 62 (NT): 216; Corel 328
(NT): 228. This product includes mapping data licensed from Ordnance Survey®
with the permission of the controller of Her Majesty's Stationery Office, © Crown
copyright. All rights reserved. Licence no. 100017284.

The publishers have made every effort to contact copyright holders but apologise if
any have been overlooked.

COVER ILLUSTRATION BY THE STUDIO DOG, PHOTODISC 26B (NT)

Contents

Introduction

This book has been specifically written to address the needs of the candidate following the Standard Grade mathematics course at General Level. It is the second part of the course, completing the syllabus and complementing the coverage in Book S3[2].

The content has been organised to ensure that the running order of the topics is consistent with companion volumes S4[1] and S4[3] aimed at the Foundation and Credit Level candidate respectively. This will permit flexibility of dual use and facilitate changing sections during the course if necessary.

Following the same model as in S3[2], each chapter follows a similar structure.

- A review section at the start ensures the knowledge required for the rest of the chapter has been revised.
- Necessary learning outcomes are demonstrated and exercises are provided to consolidate the new knowledge and skills. The ideas are developed and further exercises provide an opportunity to integrate knowledge and skills in various problem solving contexts
- Challenges, brainstormers and investigations appear throughout to provide an opportunity for some investigative work for the more curious.
- Each chapter ends with a recap of the learning outcomes and a revision exercise which tests whether or not the required knowledge and skills addressed by the chapter have been picked up.

The final two chapters in the book are devoted to revision.

- Chapter 12 contains revision for each chapter, revisiting each of the eleven chapters in this book. This complements the equivalent chapter in Book S3[2], together providing a topic by topic revision of the whole course.
- Chapter 13 provides an opportunity to prepare for assessment and contains questions covering both S3 and S4 topics. The revision exercises here give the student a chance to select strategies. Where, before, questions on Pythagoras were encountered in the Pythagoras chapter and trigonometry could not be confused with it, being in the trigonometry chapter, the student now encounters mixed revision in the form of six two-part tests. Part 1 of each test contains non-calculator and calculator neutral questions; part 2 provides the questions where a calculator may be used.

A Teacher Resource Pack provides additional material such as further practice and homework exercises and a preparation for assessment exercise for each chapter.

To assist with final revision, in association with Chapter 12 a revision checklist is included, and in association with Chapter 13 there is a 'prelim exam' laid out in a similar fashion to the final exam. A marking scheme is also included.

1 Area

Calculating area is one of the most common calculations in everyday life.

- Farmers must know the area of their fields so that they can calculate amounts of seed and fertiliser.
- Carpet fitters must know how to work out the area of carpet needed for floors.

Do you always work out the area of the carpet correctly?

Aye. I've a flair for it.

1 Review

◀◀ **Exercise 1.1**

1 Which of these units would be used to measure area?

a cm   **b** m²   **c** cm³   **d** m   **e** mm²   **f** cm²   **g** m³   **h** km²

2 Find the area covered by each of these tilings.
Assume each tile is 1 cm².

a 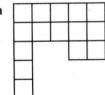   **b**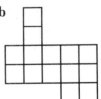

3 a Write each length in centimetres:
    i 70 mm   **ii** 93 mm   **iii** 6 mm   **iv** 5 m   **v** 7·82 m

   b Convert each length to millimetres:
    i 87 cm   **ii** 23·1 cm   **iii** 0·3 cm   **iv** 6 m   **v** 15·64 m

   c Write these lengths in metres:
    i 700 cm   **ii** 638 cm   **iii** 35 cm   **iv** 8000 mm   **v** 78 mm

   d How many metres are there in:
    i 4 km   **ii** 9·5 km   **iii** 7·515 km   **iv** 32·63 km?

   e Write each distance in kilometres:
    i 8000 m   **ii** 3500 m   **iii** 7482 m   **iv** 85 m

4 Calculate the area of each rectangle.

a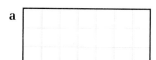

b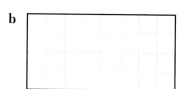

5 By first working out the area of each rectangle, find the area of each right-angled triangle.

a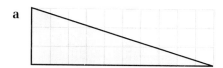

b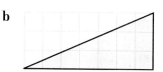

6 The rule: | **Only count squares that are at least half-used.** |

Estimate the area of:

a the letter M

b the euro coin.

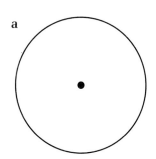

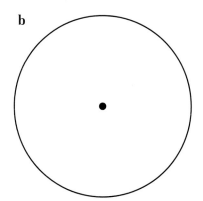

7 Measure the radius and the diameter of each circle.

a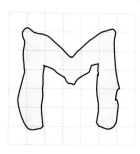

b

2 The rectangle formula

Example   What is the area of a rectangle which is 4 cm by 6 cm?

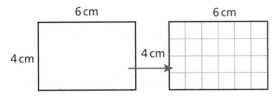

6 cm

4 cm

6 cm

4 cm

Area = 4 rows of 6 squares = 24 squares

$A = lb$

$A = 6 \times 4 = 24 \text{ cm}^2$

Exercise 2.1

1 Use the formula $A = lb$ to help you calculate the area of this rectangular wall.

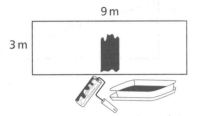

9 m

3 m

2 Calculate the area of each rectangular stamp.

a

7 cm

5 cm

b

8 cm

7 cm

c

15 cm

4 cm

d

200 mm

60 mm

e

175 mm

50 mm

3 A farmer has some rectangular fields.
   a Calculate each area in square metres.

i

200 m

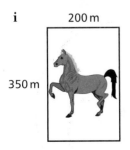

350 m

ii

550 m

475 m

iii

610 m

425 m

b   A hectare is equal to 10 000 m².

Give the areas of these fields in hectares.

4 The top surface of Mrs Ramsay's kitchen table is rectangular.
Its length is 1·8 metres and its breadth is 1·1 metres.

Calculate its area.

5 Sam's desk-top is 87 cm long and 62 cm broad.

Calculate its area.

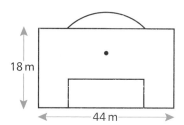

6 The penalty box on a football field is
18 metres by 44 metres.

Calculate its area.

18 m

44 m

7 Measure the length and breadth of each sticker in millimetres and then calculate
each area in square millimetres.

a   **b**

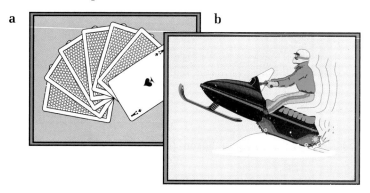

Exercise 2.2

1 Calculate the area of the front cover of the book.

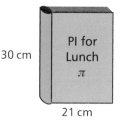

30 cm

Pl for
Lunch
π

21 cm

2 A rectangular garden has four rectangular flower beds.
The rest of the garden is covered by gravel.
The garden is 32 metres by 24 metres and the beds are as follows.
Bed A: 16 m by 9 m   Bed B: 16 m by 4 m
Bed C: 10 m by 5 m   Bed D: 8 m by 11 m
Calculate:
a the area of each flower bed   **b** the total area of the flower beds
c the area of the whole garden   **d** the area covered by gravel.

3 Mrs Bremner is buying carpet for her L-shaped living room.
  a Calculate the area of A.
  b Calculate the area of B.
  c What is the total area of the living room?
  d The carpet costs £11·99 per square metre.
     How much will it cost?

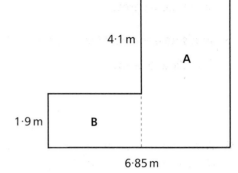

4 Below is a plan of Billy's kitchen. He wants to cover the floor in vinyl.

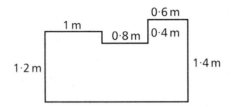

  a Break the plan into suitable rectangles.
  b Calculate the area of vinyl needed.

5 George needs to buy veneer for the top of his desk.
   The top is a rectangle 75 cm by 1·35 m.
  a Work out the area of veneer needed in cm².
  b Work out the same area in m².
  c Once the veneer has been glued on top he needs to put a trim round the outside of
     the desk top.
     What length of trim is needed?

---

3 The square – a special type of rectangle

A square is a special type of rectangle which has all four sides the same length.
This means that we can use the formula $A = l^2$ for squares (since $b = l$).

Example

5 cm

$A = l^2$
$\Rightarrow A = 5^2$
$\Rightarrow A = 25$ so the area of the square is 25 cm²

Exercise 3.1

1 Use the formula to calculate the area of each of these square tiles.

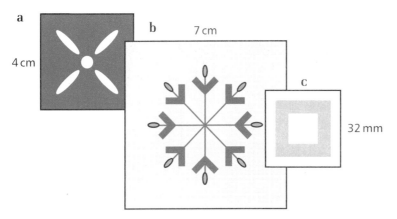

2 Annabelle's dance mat is square.
The sides are 86 cm long.
What is the area of the dance mat?

3 The Thorne family have a large rug for picnics.
The rug is square and has sides of 3·1 m.
Calculate the area of the rug.

4 Tourists are getting fed up of crazy golf.
The park keeper decides to build a giant draughts board
using black and white square paving slabs.
The manufacturers say that the slabs have sides of length
650 ± 2 mm.
This means that the side of every slab might be 2 mm too big
or 2 mm too small.

  a What is the maximum length of the side of a slab?

  b What is the minimum length of the side of a slab?

  c What is the maximum and the minimum length of side of the draughts board?

  d What is the maximum and the minimum area of the board?

5 A square metre measures 1 metre by 1 metre (100 cm by 100 cm).

  a Calculate the area of this square metre in square centimetres.

  b How many square centimetres are in a square metre?

Investigation

Mr McGregor is having trouble with rabbits in his vegetable patch. He decides to fence off a rectangular patch using some rabbit proof netting. He has 36 metres of rabbit netting.

Here are two rectangles that he could make:

A

13 m

5 m

B

15 m

3 m

Which one has the larger area?

Investigate other rectangles that can be made using 36 metres of netting.
Find the dimensions of the rectangle that has the largest area.

4 Triangles

In each case the green triangle has an area half that of the rectangle ABCD.

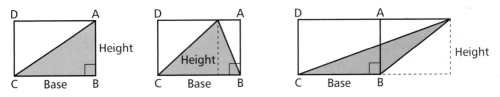

Note the **altitude**, or height, of the triangle is labelled, and equal to AB.
Note that the base equals BC.
The area of the rectangle is AB × CD = altitude × base = ab.

> So the area of the triangle is found using the formula $A = \frac{1}{2}ab$
> where a is the altitude and b is the base, both in the same units.

Example   Calculate the area of this triangle.

$A = \frac{1}{2}ab$

$\Rightarrow A = \frac{1}{2} \times 8 \times 5$

$\Rightarrow A = 20$

so the area of the triangle is 20 cm².

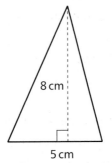

8 cm

5 cm

Exercise 4.1

1 Use the formula $A = \frac{1}{2}ab$ to calculate the area of each triangle.

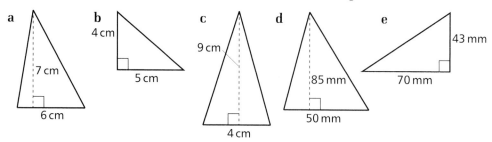

a 7 cm, 6 cm
b 4 cm, 5 cm
c 9 cm, 4 cm
d 85 mm, 50 mm
e 43 mm, 70 mm

2 Work out the area of these triangles using the formula $A = \frac{1}{2}ab$.

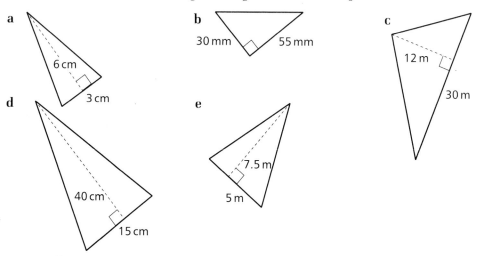

a 6 cm, 3 cm
b 30 mm, 55 mm
c 12 m, 30 m
d 40 cm, 15 cm
e 7.5 m, 5 m

3 Some panes of glass on the front of this greenhouse are triangular.
Calculate the area of each pane of glass.

a 15 cm, 46 cm
b 150 mm, 400 mm

Sometimes the altitude (AB) lies outside the triangle.
The formula still works in these cases.

Example   Calculate the area of this triangle.

$$A = \frac{1}{2}ab$$
$$\Rightarrow A = \frac{1}{2} \times 6 \times 5$$
$$\Rightarrow A = 15$$

So the area of the triangle is 15 cm².

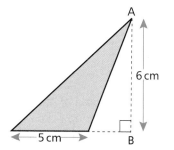

4 Calculate the area of each triangle.

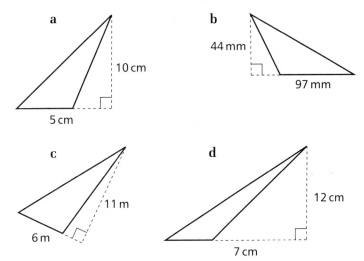

a 10 cm 5 cm

b 44 mm 97 mm

c 11 m 6 m

d 12 cm 7 cm

5 The main entrance to Glenellachie Castle has an 'archway'.
When viewed from the front it looks like
two triangles sitting on top of two rectangles.

Calculate the area of one triangle.

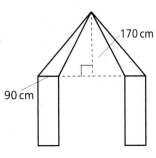

170 cm

90 cm

Exercise 4.2

1 Calculate the area of each triangle.

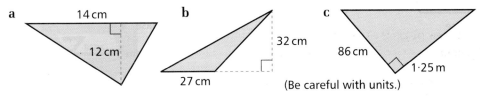

a 14 cm 12 cm

b 32 cm 27 cm

c 86 cm 1·25 m

(Be careful with units.)

2 The Maths Magyars Football Club is ordering new corner flags.
The flags are pentagonal and look like an isosceles triangle fixed to
a rectangle.

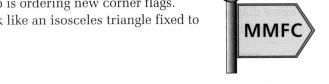

MMFC

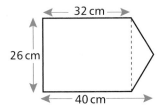

32 cm
26 cm
40 cm

a Calculate the area of the rectangle.
b Calculate the area of the triangle.
c What area of material is needed for one flag?

2 a The side of the plane gangway is a parallelogram.

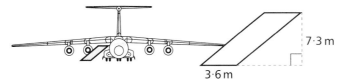

3·6 m   7·3 m

Calculate its area.

b The side of a staircase also has a parallelogram shaped panel.

Calculate its area.

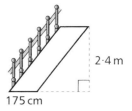

2·4 m

175 cm

3 Sarah's duvet cover is rectangular and has a parallelogram printed on it. The diagram shows what the top looks like.
a What is the area of the top of the duvet cover?
b What is the area of the parallelogram?
c What area is coloured green?

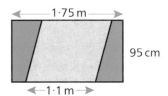

1·75 m

95 cm

1·1 m

4 The club badge of the Vikings ice-hockey team is shown.

The V is made from two congruent parallelograms.

Calculate the total area of the V.

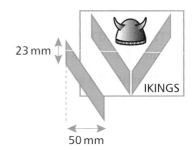

23 mm

IKINGS

50 mm

6 The kite and the rhombus

A kite is a quadrilateral with one axis of symmetry passing through a pair of vertices.

The axis means …   … diagonals intersect at right angles …   … so it can be surrounded by a rectangle …   … and we see the kite is half of this rectangle.

> **The area of a kite = half of the area of the surrounding rectangle.**

In the example above we see
 i the breadth of the rectangle is equal to the short diagonal
 ii the length of the rectangle is equal to the long diagonal.

Area of kite $= \frac{1}{2} \times$ area of rectangle $= \frac{1}{2} \times$ length $\times$ breadth

$= \frac{1}{2} \times$ short diagonal $\times$ long diagonal

The area of a kite = half of the product of the diagonals.

$$A = \frac{1}{2}d_1 \times d_2$$

The rhombus is just a special kite. It has a second axis of symmetry.
So the same formula will work for it.

Example

Calculate the area of this rhombus.

$A = \frac{1}{2}d_1 \times d_2$

$\Rightarrow A = \frac{1}{2} \times 10 \times 4$

$\Rightarrow A = 20$

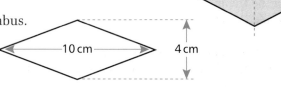

so the area of the rhombus is 20 cm².

Exercise 6.1

1 Calculate the area of each rhombus and kite.

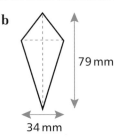

a 7 cm, 3 cm

b 79 mm, 34 mm

c 4 cm, 5·6 cm

d 10·5 cm, 7·3 cm

2 The sign for the Little Diamonds Nursery is in the shape of a rhombus.
The diagonals of the rhombus are 80 cm and 96 cm long.

What is the area of the sign?

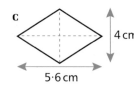

The Little Diamonds Nursery

3 Scott is entering a kite flying competition.
The rules of the competition state that the area of the kite must be no more than 9500 cm².
A diagram of Scott's kite is shown here.
a Calculate its area.
b Say whether he will be allowed to enter the competition.

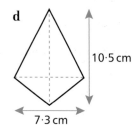

98 cm, 188 cm, *Scott*

4 The blade of a bricklayer's trowel is kite shaped.
Its diagonals are 305 mm and 178 mm.

Work out the area of metal needed to make it.

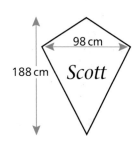

7 The trapezium

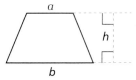 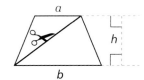 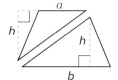

A trapezium ...   ... cut along one   ... gives two triangles.
                         side of the diagonal ...

Area of the trapezium = sum of the areas of the triangles

$$= \tfrac{1}{2}ah + \tfrac{1}{2}bh$$

$$= \tfrac{1}{2}h(a + b)$$

For a trapezium $A = \tfrac{1}{2}h(a + b)$

This is often considered as:

half the sum of the parallel sides × the distance between them.

Example   Work out the area of this trapezium.

$$A = \tfrac{1}{2}h(a + b)$$

$$= \tfrac{1}{2} \times 8 \times (5 + 9)$$

$$= 56$$

so the area of the trapezium is 56 cm².

Exercise 7.1

1 Calculate the area of each trapezium.

a 9 cm / 14 cm / 11 cm

b 14 cm / 8 cm / 4 cm

c 85 cm / 4·4 m / 2·6 m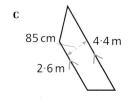

d 70 mm / 120 mm / 110 mm

2 A chimney stack has a side which is a trapezium.

Calculate the area of this side.

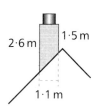

2·6 m / 1·5 m / 1·1 m

3 When viewed from the side, a swimming pool, with its deep end and its shallow end, is a trapezium.

Calculate the area of this trapezium if the shallow end is 1 metre deep, the deep end is 4·2 metres deep and the distance between the ends is 18 m.

4 This is a podium for prize winners at the school sports.
The front of the podium is a trapezium.

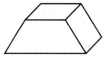

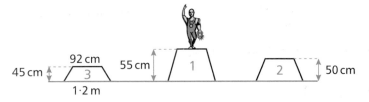

Each of the podiums has the same sized base and top.
Calculate the area of the front of each podium.

8 The circle

For thousands of years mathematicians have been fascinated by the circle.

The diameter is twice the radius. $\boxed{D = 2R}$

By measuring as accurately as possible, mathematicians found that there was also a simple relationship between the diameter and the circumference.

$$\boxed{C \approx 3D}$$

As they developed methods to measure more accurately, mathematicians discovered

that the factor was closer to 3·141 593. $\boxed{C \approx 3\text{·}141\,593D}$

The actual factor is an unending decimal. We use the Greek letter π (read as 'pie') to

represent this number. $\boxed{C = \pi D}$

Using 3 for π gives us a rough estimate.
Using 3·14 for π gives a reasonably good answer (to 3 significant figures).
Using the π button on the calculator gives a more accurate answer.

(Hint: If you don't have a calculator then $\frac{22}{7}$ can be easier to use than 3·14.)

Example
Calculate the circumference (to 3 significant figures) of a circle:
a diameter 4 cm, using 3·14 for π
b radius 12 cm, using the calculator
c radius 21 cm, without using the calculator.

a $C = \pi D \Rightarrow C = 3 \cdot 14 \times 4 = 12 \cdot 56$. Circumference is 12·6 cm (to 3 s.f.)
b $C = \pi D \Rightarrow C = \pi \times 2 \times 12 = 75 \cdot 398\ 223\ 6 \dots$ Circumference is 75·4 cm (to 3 s.f.)
c $C = \pi D \Rightarrow C = \frac{22}{7} \times 42 = 42 \div 7 \times 22 = 132$. Circumference is 132 cm (to 3 s.f.)

Exercise 8.1

1 Calculate the circumference of a circle with diameter:
    a 16 cm   **b** 38 mm   **c** 6·4 m

2 Calculate the circumference of a circle with radius:
    a 7 cm   **b** 4 m   **c** 15 cm

3 Using $\pi \approx \frac{22}{7}$, calculate the circumference of a circle:
    a with diameter   **i** 7 cm   **ii** 35 m   **iii** 49 mm
    b with radius   **i** 14 m   **ii** 28 mm   **iii** 63 m

4 Divide by π to calculate the diameter (to 3 s.f.) of a circle with circumference:
    a 100 cm   **b** 250 m   **c** 23·5 mm

5 How far apart do you need to set the ends of a pair of compasses to draw a circle of circumference:
    a 20 cm   **b** 250 mm   **c** 15 cm?

6 Florence wants to make a trundle wheel which travels 1 metre in one turn of the wheel.
What radius of circle must she make the wheel?

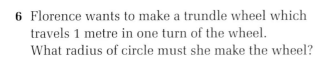

7 A cow is tied to a post. The length of the rope is 4·6 metres.
The cow can only eat the grass within a fixed circle.

Calculate the circumference of the circle.

8 The centre circle on a football pitch has a diameter of 20 metres.

Calculate its circumference.

9 The Earth has a radius of 4000 miles.
A satellite orbits the Earth 100 miles up.
a What is the radius of the satellite's orbit?
b How far does the satellite go in one orbit?
c A second satellite orbits 120 miles up.
How much further will it travel in one orbit?

10 A race track is as shown.

Calculate the distance travelled by a runner who does one lap of the circuit.

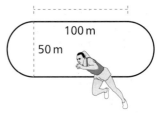

9 The area of a circle

A circle is divided into thin sectors (in this example 36 sectors each of 10°).

10° sectors laid down alternately

Half the circumference

Radius

If these are cut out and rearranged they form a shape very like a parallelogram. The thinner the sector, the closer the shape is to a parallelogram.

Area of the circle ≈ area of the parallelogram ≈ base × height
= half circumference × radius = $\pi r \times r$

> **The formula for the area of a circle:** $A = \pi r^2$

Example   Calculate the area of a circle of: **a** radius 7 cm   **b** diameter 18 cm.

a $A = \pi r^2 = \pi \times 7^2 = \pi \times 49 = 153 \cdot 9 \text{ cm}^2$ (to 4 s.f.)
b $D = 18 \Rightarrow r = 9$. $A = \pi r^2 = \pi \times 9^2 = \pi \times 81 = 254 \text{ cm}^2$ (to 3 s.f.)

Exercise 9.1

1 Work out the area of a circle:
  a of radius   **i** 2 cm   **ii** 3·7 cm   **iii** 25 mm
  b of diameter **i** 32 mm   **ii** 1·8 m   **iii** 15 cm

2 Using $\pi \approx \frac{22}{7}$, calculate the area of a circle:
  a of radius   **i** 7 cm   **ii** 1·4 cm   **iii** 21 mm
  b of diameter **i** 14 mm   **ii** 49 m   **iii** 70 cm

3 A golfer predicts that he can get his ball closer to the hole than his opponent.

His opponent's ball is 12 metres from the hole.

What is the area of the part of the green he must land in to make his prediction true?

4 Colin and Ruth are looking for a new house.

They are both doctors and need to live within 20 km of the hospital so that they can get there quickly.

What is the area (in km²) in which they should look for a house?

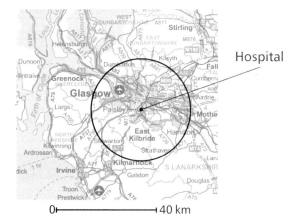

Hospital

0⊢————————⊣40 km

Exercise 9.21

1 Calculate the area of each shape. (Each is a fraction of a circle.)

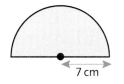

a

7 cm

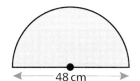

b

48 cm

c

3 m

2 A goat is tethered by a rope 3·7 m long.
The rope is fixed to a point on a wall.
What is the area of grass that the goat can graze?

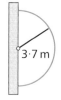

3·7 m

3 This road sign is in the shape of a rectangle and a semi-circle combined.

a Calculate the area of the rectangle.

b Calculate the area of the semi-circle.

c Calculate the total area of the sign.

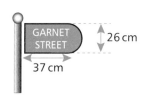

GARNET STREET

26 cm

37 cm

4 The sign for 'The Target' amusement arcade is shown here.
   a What is the area of the whole sign?
   b What is the area of the smallest circle?
   c What is the area of the middle ring?
   d What is the area of the outer ring?

The Target

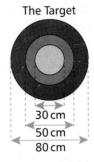

30 cm
50 cm
80 cm

5 A plumber uses washers to make joints watertight.

The outer diameter is 25 mm.
The diameter of the hole is 10 mm.

Calculate the area of the top of the washer.

25 mm

10 mm

6 Jamie's jacket had buttons as shown.

They were of diameter 2 cm.
Each of the holes for thread was 2 mm in diameter.

Calculate the area of one side of a button.

7 What is the radius of a circle whose area is 1 m²?

Give your answer in centimetres.

8 a Calculate the diameter of a wheel which has an area of 350 cm².
   b How far will the wheel travel in ten turns?

9 A circular rug covers 8 m².
   a What is the radius of the rug?
   b What is the circumference of the rug?

Challenges

1 Find a formula for the area of a washer with outside radius R mm and inside radius r mm.
2 Find a formula for the radius, r, of a circle given the area, A.
3 Find a formula for the circumference, C, of a circle given the area, A.

RECAP

Area of a square

$A = l^2$

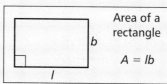

Area of a rectangle

$A = lb$

Area of a triangle

$A = \frac{1}{2}ab$

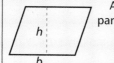

Area of a parallelogram

$A = bh$

Area of a kite

$A = \frac{1}{2}(d_1 \times d_2)$

Area of a rhombus

$A = \frac{1}{2}(d_1 \times d_2)$

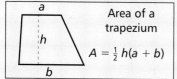

Area of a trapezium

$A = \frac{1}{2}h(a + b)$

Circumference of a circle

$C = \pi D$

$C = 2\pi r$

Area of a circle

$A = \pi r^2$

1 Calculate the area of each quadrilateral.

a
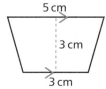
6 cm
4 cm

b
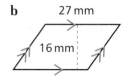
27 mm
16 mm

c
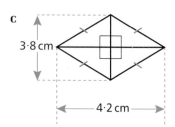
3·8 cm
4·2 cm

e
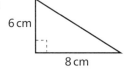
5 cm
3 cm
3 cm

f
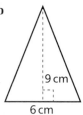
kite   4·5 cm
8·2 cm

g
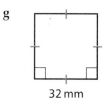
32 mm

2 Calculate the area and circumference of a circle:
  a with diameter 7 m
  b with radius 37 mm
  c with radius 4·5 cm.

3 Work out the area of each triangle.

a
6 cm
8 cm

b
9 cm
6 cm

c
59 mm
46 mm

4 Mrs Henderson is painting a picture of a pixie on the
  wall of the Nursery Class. The pixie's face is a semicircle.
  a What is the area of the pixie's hat?
  b What is the area of the pixie's face?
  c What is the total area of the painting?

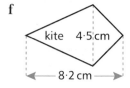
38 cm
19 cm
38 cm

5 Mrs Henderson's next task is to paint the lid of a
  puzzle box.
  The lid is circular and has holes (square, circle and
  triangle) for different shaped objects to pass through.
  a Calculate the area of the lid.
     (Ignore the holes for the moment.)
  b Calculate the area of the holes.
  c Calculate the area that requires painting.

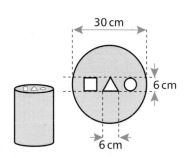
30 cm
6 cm
6 cm

REVISE

2 Surface area and volume

The relationship of surface area to volume is very important.

If there are two boxes with the same volume then the one with the smaller surface area will usually cost less to produce.

1 Review

◀◀ Exercise 1.1

1 **a** Which of these units would be used to measure area?
   b Which of these units would be used to measure volume?
   i   ml   **ii** km^2 **iii** cm^3 **iv** cm^2 **v** mm^2
   vi m^2 **vii** m^3 **viii** cm   **ix** litres

2 Each of these containers holds 1 litre when full.
   How much water is in each one? Give your answer in millilitres.

   a   **b**   **c**   **d**   **e**   **f**

3 Convert these volumes to litres (1 litre = 1000 ml).
   a 4000 ml   **b** 5500 ml   **c** 3750 ml   **d** 8325 ml   **e** 250 ml

4 Convert these volumes to millilitres.
   a 6 litres   **b** 2·225 litres   **c** 0·75 litre   **d** 3·5 litres   **e** 0·412 litre

5 What is the volume of each shape? (Count the cubes. Assume each cube is 1 cm^3.)

   a 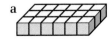   **b**   **c**   **d**

6 Convert each weight to kilograms (1 kg = 1000 g).

   a 4000 g   **b** 7000 g   **c** 3425 g

   d 2750 g   **e** 7200 g   **f** 9850 g

7 Convert each of these weights to grams.

   a 8 kg   **b** 6·458 kg   **c** 27 kg

   d 9·3 kg   **e** 18·7 kg   **f** 2·43 kg

8 Calculate the perimeter of each shape.

   a
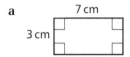

   b
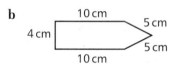

9 Which of these are the nets of cubes?

   a   **b**   **c**   **d**   **e**

10 Which of these are the nets of cuboids?

   a   **b**   **c**

2 Volume of a cuboid

The volume of a cuboid is the number of cubic centimetres (cm³) that can fit into it.

This cuboid is 6 cm long, 4 cm wide and 3 cm high.

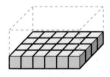   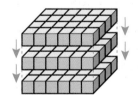   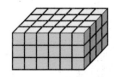

To fill the bottom layer of the cuboid we need 6 rows of 4 cubes. (6 × 4 = 24)
We need 3 layers to completely fill the cuboid. (24 × 3 = 72)
The cuboid has a volume of 72 cm³.

We can see from this example that

> **Volume of a cuboid = length × breadth × height**
>
> or $V = lbh$

Example   Calculate the volume of this cuboid.

$$V = lbh$$
$$\Rightarrow V = 3 \times 5 \times 4$$
$$\Rightarrow V = 60$$

So the volume of the cuboid is 60 cm³.

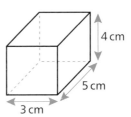

Exercise 2.1

1 Calculate the volume of each cuboid.

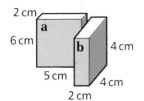 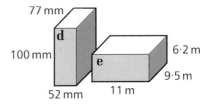

2 Calculate the volume of each box.

a
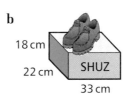
b

3 When a container is to be filled the volume is usually given in **litres and millilitres**. The amount a container can hold is called its **capacity**.

Reminder   1 cm³ = 1 ml and 1000 ml = 1 litre

Find the volume of each carton in   **i** millilitres   **ii** litres.

a

b
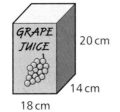

4 This fish tank is 80 cm by 56 cm by 50 cm.
It is filled to a depth of 45 cm.
Calculate: **a** the capacity of the tank
b the volume of water in the tank in litres.

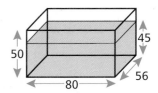

Exercise 2.2

1 The Glendinnings are installing a new central heating system.
The size of radiator required for a room depends on the volume of that room.
Here are the dimensions of their rooms. They are all cuboids.

Living room: 3·8 metres long by 3·5 metres wide by 2·7 metres high

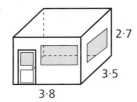

Dining room: 3·8 metres long by 2·35 metres wide by 2·7 metres high
Kitchen: 6 metres long by 2·6 metres wide by 2·35 metres high
Bedroom 1: 3·95 metres long by 3·9 metres wide by 2·3 metres high
Bedroom 2: 3·75 metres long by 2·5 metres wide by 2·3 metres high
Bathroom: 2·2 metres long by 1·6 metres wide by 2·3 metres high

There are three sizes of radiators.
Size A: for rooms under 10 m³
Size B: for rooms over 10 m³ and under 30 m³
Size C: for rooms over 30 m³

a i What is the volume of the living room?
ii What size of radiator do they need for the living room?
b What size of radiator do they need for the bathroom?
c How many of each type of radiator do they need?

2 An interior designer is doing a make over on a living room
for a TV show. He decides to have a cuboid shaped piece of
wood as a coffee table.
The table is 55 cm high, 105 cm long and 70 cm wide.
a Calculate the volume of this piece of wood.
b 1 cm³ of pine weighs 0·53 g.
Calculate the weight of the piece of wood if it is pine.
Give your answer to the nearest kilogram.

3 Mr Keegan is packing for a school trip.
Cornflake packets are 8 cm by 20 cm by 30 cm cuboids.
a How many such packets can he pack in a bigger
container which is 20 cm by 60 cm by 40 cm?
b How many could he fit in a box which is 25 cm
by 60 cm by 32 cm?

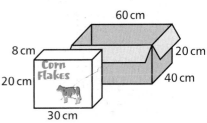

3 Volume of a cube

A cube is a special cuboid with length, breadth and height equal.

$$\text{Volume of a cube} = \text{length} \times \text{breadth} \times \text{height}$$
$$= \text{length} \times \text{length} \times \text{length}$$
$$= (\text{length})^3$$

$$\boxed{V_{\text{cube}} = l^3}$$

Example   Calculate the volume of this ice cube.

$$V = l^3$$
$$\Rightarrow V = 6^3$$
$$\Rightarrow V = 6 \times 6 \times 6$$
$$\Rightarrow V = 216$$

So the volume of the ice cube is 216 cm³.

Exercise 3.1

1 Calculate the volume of a cube of side:
   a 3 cm   **b** 25 cm   **c** 4·7 cm   **d** 25 mm   **e** 3·2 m

2 A stock cube has sides of 12 mm.
   Calculate its volume.

12 mm

3 Carol has bought a container for her patio. The container is a cube of side 40 cm.
   What volume of earth is needed to fill the container?

4 Imagine a cube of water of side 10 cm.
   a What is the volume of this cube in   **i** cm³   **ii** litres?
   b What is the volume of a tank which is a cube of side 1 metre?
        Answer in   **i** cm³   **ii** litres.
   c How many of the 10 cm cubes of water would fit inside the tank?
   d Scientists decided that 1 gram would be the weight of 1 cm³ of water.
        What is the weight of   **i** the 10 cm cube   **ii** the water in the tank?
   e Scientists also decided to call 1000 kg one tonne.
        Give the weight of water in the tank in tonnes.

5 A fish tank is a cuboid and comes with a stand. The
   manufacturers say that it is only safe when the combined
   weight of the tank and the water does not exceed 35 kg.
   a Calculate the volume of the tank.
   b The empty tank weighs 950 grams.
     i Calculate the total weight of the tank and water.
     ii Is it safe to completely fill the tank with water?
   c What is the maximum allowable depth of the water?
        Give your answer to the nearest appropriate centimetre.

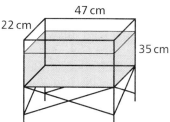

4 Surface area

The surface area of a solid is the total area of all its faces.
The best way to calculate the surface area of a solid is to consider a net of the solid.

Example 1   Calculate the surface area of a cube with edge 5 cm.

We can see from the net that the surface of the cube is
made of six squares of side 5 cm.

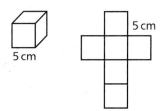

Area of one face $= l^2$

$\qquad = 5^2 = 25 \text{ cm}^2$

Surface area $\quad = 6 \times 25 = 150 \text{ cm}^2$

So the surface area of the cube is 150 cm².

Example 2   Calculate the surface area of a cuboid which is 5 cm by 2 cm by 12 cm.

We can see here that the net of a cuboid is made from
six rectangles.
Two of these rectangles are 5 cm × 2 cm;
two are 5 cm × 12 cm; and two are 2 cm × 12 cm.

The front and the back are the same, the right side and
the left side are the same, and the top and the bottom
are the same.

Area of front (back) $\quad = 12 \times 5 = 60 \text{ cm}^2$

Area of right (left) side $= 2 \times 12 = 24 \text{ cm}^2$

Area of top (bottom) $\quad = 2 \times 5 = 10 \text{ cm}^2$

Total surface area $\qquad = 2 \times (60 + 24 + 10)$

$\qquad\qquad\qquad\qquad = 188 \text{ cm}^2$

So the surface area of the cuboid is 188 cm².

> **Surface area = 2 × (area of front + area of side + area of top)**

Exercise 4.1

1 Calculate the surface area of each cuboid.

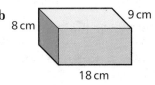

a 7 cm, 7 cm, 7 cm

b 8 cm, 9 cm, 18 cm

c 15 cm, 3·3 cm, 2·7 cm

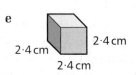

d 35 mm, 62 mm, 43 mm

e 2·4 cm, 2·4 cm, 2·4 cm

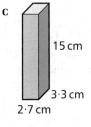

2 An office stores lots of records in boxes like the one shown. In order to make records easier to find it is decided to colour code the boxes.
They are to be covered with brightly coloured vinyl. What area of vinyl is required to completely cover one of these boxes?

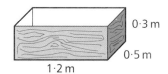

35 cm
40 cm
62 cm

3 A cardboard box, 40 cm by 70 cm by 90 cm, is used for transporting books. What area of cardboard is needed to make it?

4 A window box like the one shown here is a cuboid without a top.
Calculate the area of wood required to make it.

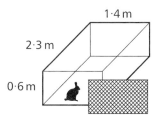

0·3 m
0·5 m
1·2 m

5 The diagram shows the frame for a run for a rabbit. All the sides need netting put onto them except the bottom.
Calculate the area of netting required.

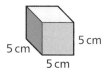

1·4 m
2·3 m
0·6 m

Exercise 4.2

1 A set of child's building bricks consists of 64 bricks.
The bricks are cubes of side 5 cm.
The bricks are to be coated in vinyl.
How much vinyl will be required for
a one brick   **b** the whole set?

5 cm
5 cm
5 cm

2 The manufacturer of the bricks in question **1** states that the cubes have sides of 5 ± 0.2 cm. This means the sides might be as big as 5·2 cm or as small as 4·8 cm.
Calculate:
a the largest area of vinyl   **b** the smallest area of vinyl
that might be needed to cover the set of bricks.

3 The solids in the diagram below are all stuffed toys from a crèche.
For each toy calculate:
i the volume of filling required   **ii** the area of material needed to make the covering.

a
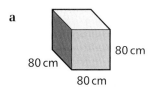
80 cm
80 cm
80 cm

b
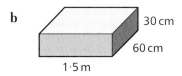
30 cm
60 cm
1·5 m

c
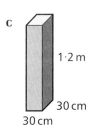
1·2 m
30 cm
30 cm

4 These two wooden crates have the same volume.
The wood costs £3·50 per square metre.
Calculate the difference in the cost of the wood required to make the two boxes.

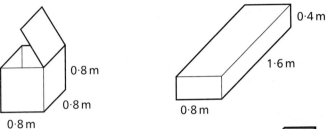

5 The volume of this cuboid is 320 cm³.
   a Calculate the height of the cuboid.
   b Calculate the surface area of the cuboid.

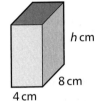

Investigation

A manufacturer wants to produce cartons with a capacity of 1·728 litres.
The three cartons shown here have a volume of 1·728 litres.

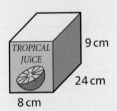 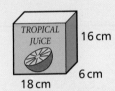 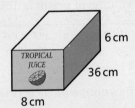

a Which one costs least to make (the one with the smallest surface area)?
b Can you find a better solution for the manufacturer?

---

5 Volume of a prism

A prism is a solid which has a constant cross-section.
Wherever you cut it, parallel to the base, you get a shape congruent to the base.

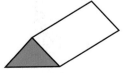 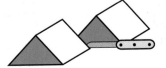

This diagram shows a triangular prism but there are many types of prisms. Each prism takes its name from the shape of the base.

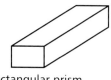 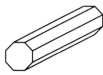 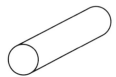

Rectangular prism   Octagonal prism   Circular prism
   (cuboid)   (cylinder)

For every type of prism, its volume is the product of its base and its height (the height being the distance between its ends).

$$V = Ah$$

where A is the area of the base/cross-section and h is the distance between the ends.

Example   A pentagonal prism has a base of area 25 cm².
             It is 6 cm long.
             Calculate its volume.

   $V = Ah$

   $\Rightarrow V = 25 \times 6 = 150 \text{ cm}^3$

Volume of prism is 150 cm³.

Exercise 5.1

1 Calculate the volume of each prism.

a 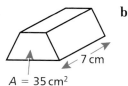   b 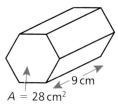   c 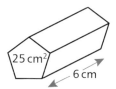   d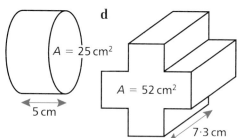

$A = 35\,\text{cm}^2$ 7 cm
$A = 28\,\text{cm}^2$ 9 cm
$A = 25\,\text{cm}^2$ 5 cm
$A = 52\,\text{cm}^2$ 7·3 cm

2 Calculate each volume.

a 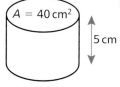   b 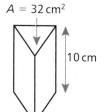   c 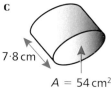   d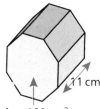

$A = 40\,\text{cm}^2$ 5 cm
$A = 32\,\text{cm}^2$ 10 cm
7·8 cm $A = 54\,\text{cm}^2$
11 cm $A = 102\,\text{cm}^2$

6 Volume of a triangular prism

We often have to work out the cross-sectional area before we can calculate the volume.

Example   Calculate the volume of this triangular prism.

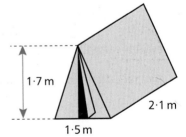

Cross-sectional area (triangle) $= \frac{1}{2}bh$

$$= \frac{1}{2} \times 4 \times 7$$

$$= 14 \text{ cm}^2$$

$V = Ah$

$\Rightarrow V = 14 \times 11$

$\Rightarrow V = 154 \text{ cm}^3$

Exercise 6.1

1 Work out the volume of each triangular prism.

a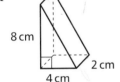

b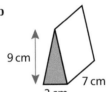

c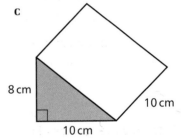

2 Calculate the volume of this tent in cubic metres.

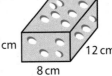

3 Which cheese has the biggest volume?

a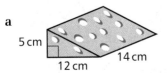

b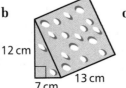

c

4 This patio plant container is a triangular prism.
Calculate:
a its cross-sectional area
b its volume.

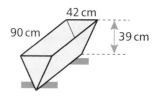

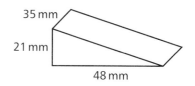

5 This triangular prism is a ramp for model cars.
The cross section is a right-angled triangle.
Calculate its volume in mm^3.

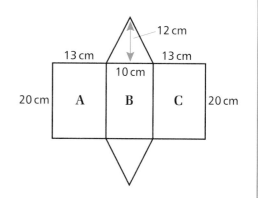

7 Surface area of a triangular prism

The net of a triangular prism has two congruent triangles and three rectangles.

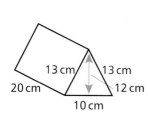

Area of triangle $\quad = \frac{1}{2}bh$

$\qquad\qquad\qquad\quad = \frac{1}{2} \times 10 \times 12$

$\qquad\qquad\qquad\quad = 60 \text{ cm}^2$

Area of rectangle A $= lb \qquad\qquad$ Area of rectangle B $= lb$

$\qquad\qquad\qquad = 20 \times 13 \qquad\qquad\qquad\qquad\qquad = 20 \times 10$

$\qquad\qquad\qquad = 260 \text{ cm}^2 \qquad\qquad\qquad\qquad\qquad = 200 \text{ cm}^2$

Area of rectangle C $\;=$ Area of rectangle A

Total surface area $\quad = 2 \times 60 + 2 \times 260 + 200$

$\qquad\qquad\qquad\quad = 120 + 520 + 200$

$\qquad\qquad\qquad\quad = 840 \text{ cm}^2$

Exercise 7.1

1 Calculate the surface area of each triangular prism.
The first three have isosceles triangles as bases.

a

5 cm 4 cm
12 cm
6 cm

b

26 mm 24 mm
35 mm
20 mm

c

25 mm 24 mm
14 mm 5 mm

d

2·8 cm 4·49 cm
5 cm
3·51 cm

e

31 cm 28 cm
20 cm 29 cm
5·6 cm

2 This chocolate bar is sold in a box which is a triangular prism.
Calculate the surface area of the box.

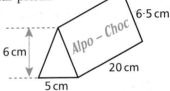

6 cm
5 cm
6·5 cm
20 cm
Alpo – Choc

3 This paperweight is in the shape of a triangular prism.
Calculate its surface area and its volume.

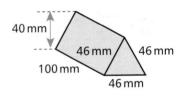

40 mm
100 mm
46 mm
46 mm
46 mm

Exercise 7.2

1 This plant container is designed to be mounted on a wall.
It is a triangular prism and the cross-section is a right-angled triangle.
It is made from timber and has no top.
   a Calculate the area of timber that is needed to make the
      container.
   b Calculate the volume of the container.
   c Compost is sold in litres.
      How many litres of compost are required to fill the container?

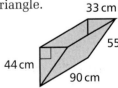

33 cm
55 cm
44 cm
90 cm

2 The base of this vase is an equilateral triangle with sides of 20 cm.
   a Calculate the area of this triangle.
   b Calculate the surface area of the vase.
   c Calculate the volume of the vase.
   d What is the weight of the water in the vase when it is full?

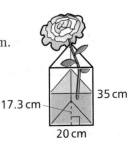

35 cm
17.3 cm
20 cm

3 A triangular prism has a volume of 1440 cm³.
Its length is 20 cm.

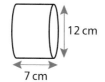

a What is the cross-sectional area of the prism?
b The base of the triangle (the end) is 12 cm.
Can this prism be stored, without turning, on a shelf
which is 7 cm below the shelf above?

---

8 Volume of a cylinder

A cylinder is a circular prism.

So its volume can be found using the same formula as for all prisms:

$$V = Ah$$

but since its cross-section is a circle, $A = \pi r^2$

so $\boxed{V_{\text{cylinder}} = \pi r^2 h}$

Example

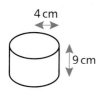

$V = \pi r^2 h$

$\Rightarrow V = 3 \cdot 14 \times 4^2 \times 9$

$\Rightarrow V = 452$ (to 3 s.f.)

So the volume of the cylinder is 452 cm³ (to 3 s.f.)

Note: For π use either 3·14, or the π button on the calculator, or
the fraction $\frac{22}{7}$ if no calculator is available.

Exercise 8.1

1 Calculate the volumes of these cylinders.

a 2 cm
10 cm

b 7 cm
5 cm

c 15 mm
40 mm

d 0·9 m
1·2 m

e 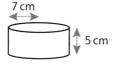 12 cm
7 cm

f 8 cm
27 cm

2 The Southburn Caravan Park has two drums
at its entrance. These two drums have been
filled with concrete and a flag has been put
in the middle of each one.

Calculate how much concrete is needed to
fill both drums.
Give your answer in cubic metres.

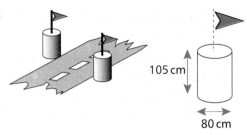
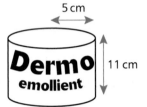

105 cm

80 cm

3 Kirsty uses ointment for her eczema.
It comes in a cylindrical tub.
Calculate the capacity of the tub.

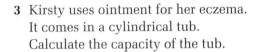

5 cm

Dermo
emollient

11 cm

4 Fiona makes coffee in her cafetière.
The base of the cafetière has a radius of 5 cm and it has a height of
22 cm.
  a Calculate the volume of the cafetière.
  b Her coffee mugs have a base with diameter 7·5 cm and
height 9·5 cm.
Calculate the volume of one mug.
  c How many of these mugs can be filled from this cafetière?

9 Surface area of a cylinder

Consider the net of this cylinder:

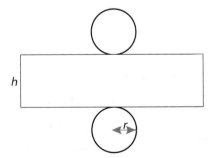

h

h

r

The curved surface of the cylinder opens out to a rectangle.
The breadth of this rectangle is the same as the height of the cylinder.
The length of the rectangle is the same as the circumference of the lid of the tin.

Area of rectangle $= lb$

$\Rightarrow$ Curved surface area of a cylinder $= 2\pi rh$

Example
Find:
a the curved surface area
b the total surface area of this cylinder.

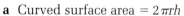

4 cm

12 cm

a Curved surface area $= 2\pi rh$
$$= 2 \times 3 \cdot 14 \times 4 \times 12$$
$$= 301 \text{ cm}^2 \text{ (to nearest cm}^2)$$

b Area of top $= \pi r^2$
$$= 3 \cdot 14 \times 4^2$$
$$= 50 \cdot 2 \text{ cm}^2 \text{ (to nearest cm}^2)$$

Total surface area of cylinder = top + bottom + curved surface
$$= 301 + 2 \times 50 \cdot 2$$
$$= 401 \cdot 4$$

So the total surface area is 401 cm² to the nearest cm².

Exercise 9.1

1 Calculate the curved surface area of each cylinder.

a
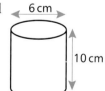
3 cm
9 cm

b
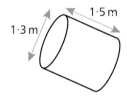
8 cm
14 cm

c
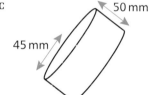
50 mm
45 mm

d
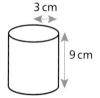
6 cm
10 cm

e

1·5 m
1·3 m

2 A napkin ring is open at both ends.
Calculate the surface area of this napkin ring.

2·5 cm
Dad 4 cm

3 Calculate the total surface area of each of these cylinders.

a
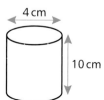
4 cm
10 cm

b
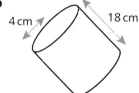
4 cm
18 cm

c
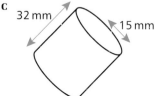
32 mm
15 mm

4 Calculate the total surface area of this tin of fruit.

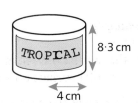

8·3 cm

TROPICAL

4 cm

5 All of this cake is iced except the bottom.
The cake is a cylinder with radius 15 cm and
height 14 cm.

Calculate the area that is iced.

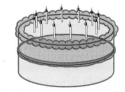

Exercise 9.2

1 Guttering is made by bending a rectangular
piece of plastic to form half a cylinder.
The radius of this piece of guttering is 5·5 cm
and the length is 5 m.

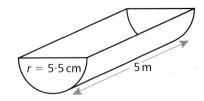

$r = 5·5$ cm   5 m

Calculate:

  a the area of plastic required to make the
  guttering (including the semi-circular ends)

  b the capacity of the guttering.

2 Workers at an agricultural show mark off a
parking area with metal drums.
In order to make the drums impossible to
move they are going to fill them with concrete.

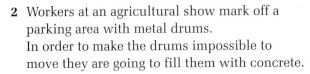

P A R K I N G

  a Calculate the volume of one drum.

  b They need fifty to mark off the parking area.
  What volume of concrete do they need?

  c Concrete weighs 2403 kg per cubic metre.
  Give the total weight of concrete required in
  tonnes.

  d The drums need to be painted to make them
  look presentable.
  Calculate the area that needs painted.
  (Remember there are fifty drums and the
  bottoms won't need painting.)

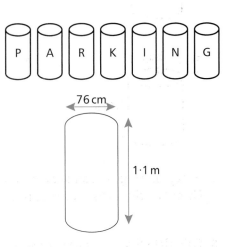

76 cm

1·1 m

◄◄ **RECAP**

Volume of a cuboid

$$V = lbh$$

where l is the length and b is the breadth and h is the height of the cuboid, measured in the same units.

Volume of a cube

$$V = l^3$$

where l is the length of the edge of the cube.

Surface area of a cuboid $S = 2($area of top + area of side + area of front$)$

$$S = 2(lb + lh + bh)$$

where l is the length and b is the breadth and h is the height of the cuboid, measured in the same units.

Surface area of a cube $S = 6 \times$ area of one face

$$S = 6l^2$$

where l is the length of the cube.

Volume of a prism $V =$ Area of the base $\times$ height

$$V = Ah$$

for a *triangular prism*

$$V = \tfrac{1}{2}abh$$

where a is the altitude of the triangle and b is the base of the triangle and h is distance between the ends, measured in the same units

for a *cylinder*

$$V = \pi r^2 h$$

where r is the radius of the base and h is the distance between the ends, measured in the same units.

Surface area of a triangular prism
   $S = 2 \times$ area of triangular base + areas of the three rectangular faces

Surface area of a cylinder
   $S =$ curved surface area + $2 \times$ area of circular ends
   $S = 2\pi rh + 2\pi r^2$
   where r is the radius of the base and h is the distance between the ends, measured in the same units.

1 Calculate the volume and surface area of each of these cubes and cuboids.

a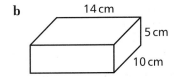
7 cm
7 cm
7 cm

b
14 cm
5 cm
10 cm

c
3·2 cm
3·2 cm
9 cm

2 Calculate the volume and surface area of these triangular prisms.

a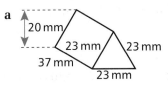
20 mm
23 mm   23 mm
37 mm
23 mm

b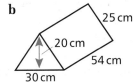
25 cm
20 cm
54 cm
30 cm

c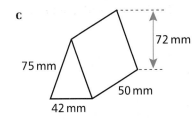
72 mm
75 mm
50 mm
42 mm

3 Calculate, for each cylinder:
  a the volume **b** the curved surface area **c** the total surface area.

POPZI COLA
11 cm
3 cm

Baked Beans
10·5 cm
8 cm

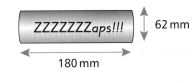
ZZZZZZZaps!!!
62 mm
180 mm

4 This vase is an octagonal prism.
The area of its base is 220 cm².
Its height is 34 cm.
  a Calculate its volume in litres.
  b The vase is filled with water.
    What is the weight of the water?

5 A big sculpture is to be erected in the centre of Juiceville.
The sculpture is solid bronze and is in the shape of a cylinder to
signify man's struggle to find the perfect soft drink receptacle.
  a Find the volume of the sculpture.
  b One cubic metre of bronze weighs 8500 kilograms.
    Give the weight of the sculpture in tonnes.

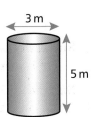
3 m
5 m

3 Money

In 1799, Prime Minister William Pitt the Younger introduced income tax to fund the war against Napoleon.
The rate was 10% of a person's total income above £60 per year.
Later in this chapter you will learn more about income tax and how to calculate it.

In 2003–04 the average wage for all full-time employees was £476 per week. The average credit card debt was £1100 for each adult in the UK.

1 Review

◄◄ Exercise 1.1

1 How many: **a** months **b** weeks **c** days are there in a non-leap year?

2 Write these 24-hour clock times as am/pm times:
    a 09 00   **b** 23 00   **c** 07 45   **d** 20 30

3 How long is it from:
    a 8.30 am to 1 pm   **b** 8.45 am to 2.00 pm
    c 09 30 to 12 00   **d** 12 45 to 06 30?

4 Write these times as hours. (Use decimals.)
    a 4 hours 30 minutes
    b 3 hours 15 minutes
    c 5 hours 45 minutes

5 How much should be put in the meter to park for:
    a 25 minutes   **b** 50 minutes
    c $1\frac{1}{2}$ hours   **d** $1\frac{3}{4}$ hours?

PARKING
First 30 minutes 50p
Each additional
10 minutes 20p

6 Calculate   **i** 1%   **ii** 2%   **iii** 10%   **iv** 50% of:
    a £2   **b** £30   **c** £400   **d** £5000

7 Find: **a** 6% of £82 **b** 9% of £524 **c** 17% of £4500

8 This is Kay's bill for decorating materials. Copy and complete the bill.

> *12 rolls of wallpaper at £8·27 per roll* = £......
> *18 m of border at £1·35 per metre* = £......
> *2 packets of paste at £2·38 per packet* = £......
>
>   *Total* = £......

2 Money calculations

Look for quick methods.

Example 1 Calculate £5·55 + £8·97 + £7·45.
Answer = £5·55 + £7·45 + £8·97 = £13 + £8·97 = £21·97

Example 2 Calculate £14·95 × 8.
£15 × 8 = £120 and 5p × 8 = 40p
Answer = £120 − 40p = £119·60

Example 3 Calculate £5·45 × 50.
Answer = £5·45 × 5 × 10 = £27·25 × 10 = £272·50

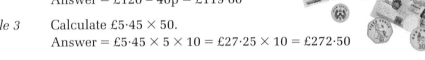

Check answers by estimating.

Example 4 Estimate £38·75 × 52.
£38·75 rounds to £40 and 52 rounds to 50.
Estimate is £40 × 50 = £2000.

Exercise 2.1

1 Calculate:

  a £51·75 + £24·25 **b** £6·18 + £8·59 + 82p **c** £263 + £78·70 + 98p

  d £90 − £53·75 **e** £90·25 − £68·99 **f** £63·17 − £7·99 + £28·33

2 Calculate:
  a 49p × 8 **b** £2·99 × 6 **c** £12·95 × 4 **d** £4·62 × 10 **e** 85p × 100
  f 96p ÷ 4 **g** £17·46 ÷ 3 **h** £56·16 ÷ 9 **i** £84·70 ÷ 10 **j** £73 ÷ 100

3 Calculate:
  a 85p × 20 **b** £6·50 × 30 **c** £7·25 × 40 **d** £87·50 × 60
  e £70 ÷ 20 **f** £84 ÷ 40 **g** £280 ÷ 50 **h** £6300 ÷ 90

4 a Round these amounts to the nearest 10p:
    i 69p **ii** £3·92 **iii** £52·75 **iv** £4·829
  b Round these amounts to the nearest 1p:
    i 82·7p **ii** £5·881 **iii** 66·666...p **iv** £99·875

5 Estimate:

  a £3·99 × 12   **b** £6·09 × 28   **c** £29·87 × 49   **d** £409·50 × 67

  e £79·43 ÷ 4   **f** £902·99 ÷ 12   **g** £584·92 ÷ 31   **h** £9099 ÷ 19

6 Copy and complete this bill.

> *400 g cheese at 39p per 100 g*   = £.....
> *600 g ham at 58p per 100 g*   = £.....
> *1·5 kg salmon at £2·80 per kg*   = £.....
>   *Total*   = £.....

7 Meera checks the price of a CD in several shops.
The prices are £8·99, £9·49, £8·49 and £7·99.
Calculate the average (mean) price.

8 Rosie buys a camera on HP. Calculate:

  a the total cost of buying on HP

  b the difference between the cash price and
    the HP cost.

DIGITAL CAMERA
CASH PRICE £190
or HP terms 10% deposit +
6 payments of £29·99

9 a Calculate the cost of 100 g of each
    type of coffee.

  b Which is the better buy?

BEST BUY
COFFEE
£4·50
contents 300g

KOOL
COFFEE
£3·20
contents 200g

3   Wages and salaries

Example 1

  Alan gets the job.
  How much will he earn in:

  a a week   **b** a year?

CUSTOMER SERVICE ADVISOR
£6 per hour   37·5 hours per week

  a Weekly wage = £6 × 37·5 = £225

  b Total for a year = £225 × 52 = £11 700

Example 2

  Ann applies for the post and is successful.
  How much will she earn per month?

  £10K p.a. means £10 000 per annum (per year).
  Monthly salary = £10 000 ÷ 12 = £833·33
  (rounded to the nearest penny)

Audio Typist
WANTED
£10k p.a.

Exercise 3.1

1 a Trevor earns £250 per week. How much does he earn in 4 weeks?
  b In 6 months Nicola earns £8220. How much does she earn per month?

2 a Tom's weekly wage is £195. How much does he earn in a year?
  b Tina's monthly salary is £1168. How much does she earn in a year?

3 Kate applies for the job.
  If she is successful how much will she earn per month?

SHORTHAND
SECRETARY
100 W.P.M.
£18K PER YEAR

4 Colin gets a job in a shop.
  How much will he earn
  a per week   **b** per year?

SHOP ASSISTANT
£5 PER HOUR
40 HOUR WEEK

5 a How much does this job pay for a 37·5 hour week?
  b Calculate the total amount earned in a year.

LEGAL
SECRETARY
£10·80 PER HOUR

6 Calculate the salary if it is paid:
  a monthly
  b weekly, correct to the nearest penny.

SALES
PEOPLE
WANTED

£13K P.A.

7 How much would the attendant earn in:
  a a week   **b** a year?

Car Park Attendant
4·5 hours per night
£6·50 per hour
6 nights a week

Example 3
Clare is interested in an administration post.
a Calculate her monthly salary if she was to
  start on the lower limit of the pay scale.
b How much more per month would she
  earn if she started at the top of the scale?

SENIOR ADMINISTRATOR
salary £19,185 – £24,069 p.a.

a Monthly salary on lower limit = £19 185 ÷ 12 = £1598·75
b Monthly salary on upper limit = £24 069 ÷ 12 = £2005·75
  Extra on top scale = £2005·75 − £1598·75 = £407

Exercise 3.2

1 Ms Wright earns £37 440 in a year.
  a Calculate her monthly salary.
  b On average she reckons she works a 45 hour week.
    How much does she earn per hour? (Ignore holidays.)

2 Calculate the monthly salary of the successful applicant using:
a the lower
b the upper limit of the salary scale.

> **Head Of Personnel**
> £24,000 to £28,200
> per year

3 Calculate the total yearly salary of the successful applicant, before bonuses and incentives, using:
a the lower   b the upper limit of the salary scale.

> **PART-TIME VACANCIES**
> **TELESALES STAFF**
> £440 - £650 PER MONTH
> + bonus + incentive

4 Jane gets a job as a clerical assistant.
a She starts on the lower limit of the pay scale. Calculate her monthly salary.
b How much more does a person on the top of the scale receive per month?

> Clerical Assistant
> £10,719 - £11,805
> per year

5 Duncan sees two cleaning jobs advertised.
a Which is the better paid?
b By how much a week?

> **CAPITAL CLEANERS**
> £5·67 PER HOUR
> 36 HOURS PER WEEK

> **CITY CLEANERS**
> £215 PER WEEK

6 How much would Sam earn in a week for working 37·5 hours:
a in the daytime
b at night?

> **DRIVERS WANTED**
> Hourly Rate
> £7 during day   £8 at night

7 Wendy applies for this computer post. She starts on the bottom of the pay scale.
a Calculate her monthly salary.
b How much does someone at the top of the scale get on average per week?

> **WEB EDITOR**
> TOP SALARY
> £29,946 - £35,750 p.a.

8 Hillary and Henry work in a travel agency. Hillary is paid £7·75 per hour. Henry is less experienced and earns £6·30 per hour. They both work 37·5 hour weeks.
a How much does
  i Hillary   ii Henry earn in a week?
b Over a year how much more does Hillary earn than Henry?

Investigation

The table lists the minimum hourly wages in 2004.

Age	Minimum wage per hour
16–17	£3
18–21	£4·10
over 21	£4·85

a Calculate the minimum weekly wage for a person over 21 working a 36 hour week.

b Have the minimum rates increased since 2004? If so, how much are they now?

4 Pay rises

Example

Sue works for the local authority.
Her annual salary is £13 200.
She receives a 3% pay rise.
Calculate: **a** the pay rise
b her new **i** monthly **ii** annual salary.

a pay rise = 3% of £13 200 = 3 ÷ 100 × 13 200 = £396

b i new annual salary = £13 200 + £396 = £13 596

ii new monthly salary = £13 596 ÷ 12 = £1133

Exercise 4.1

1 Tania is paid £6·95 per hour. She gets a 35p per hour increase.
How much does she earn per hour after the increase?

2 Mark earns £195·60 a week. He is awarded a rise of £4·89.
What is his new wage?

3 Millie's annual salary is £16 878. Her annual rise is worth £675·12.
Calculate her new annual salary.

4 Kelly earns £400 a week. She gets a 5% increase in wages.
Calculate her: **a** pay rise **b** new weekly wage.

5 Kevin's monthly salary is £1860. He receives a 3% pay rise.
Calculate his: **a** pay rise **b** new monthly salary.

6 Copy and complete the table.

Old hourly rate	Percentage pay rise	Actual pay rise	New hourly rate
£5	4%		
£8	3%		
£10	2%		
£18	5%		

7 Joe works as a joiner. He is paid £9·50 an hour and works
a 36 hour week.
He is given a 6% pay rise.
a How much more will he earn per hour?
b What is his new hourly rate?
c Calculate his weekly wage after the increase.

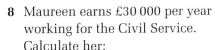

8 Maureen earns £30 000 per year
working for the Civil Service.
Calculate her:

CIVIL SERVANTS
GET A 4% PAY RISE

a pay rise   **b** new annual salary   **c** new monthly salary.

9 At Enterprise Estates, Fred earns £380 per week and Freda £316.
All the employees are given a 5% pay rise.
a Calculate the pay rise for   **i** Fred   **ii** Freda.
b What is   **i** Fred's   **ii** Freda's new weekly wage?
c How much more than Freda does Fred earn, per week,
   i before   **ii** after the rise?

10 Phil applies for an office job.
A rise of 3% is to be added to the
advertised pay scale.
Calculate the new:
a lower limit
b upper limit of the pay scale.

MAGIC MARKETING
Office Junior

£9k — £10k p.a.

5 Time-sheets and overtime

Example 1

		TIME-SHEET			
Sharon Smith		Employee No. 152			Week No. 48

	In	Out	In	Out	No. of hours worked
Mon	08 00	12 00	13 00	17 00	8
Tue	08 30	12 00	13 00	17 30	8
Wed	08 00	12 30	13 15	17 00	8·25
Thu	08 15	13 00	14 00	16 45	7·5
Fri	08 30	12 30	13 15	16 00	6·75
				Total =	38·5 hours

Look at Friday. Sharon worked from 08 30 to 12 30 before lunch.
That's 4 hours. After lunch she worked from 13 15 to 16 00.
That's a further 2 hours 45 minutes (2·75 hours).
Total hours worked on Friday = 4 + 2·75 = 6·75 hours.

Exercise 5.1

1 Sanjeev starts work at 8.30 am and works until 5 pm.
  He has an hour off for lunch. He works from Monday to Friday.
  How many hours does he work:
  a each day
  b in a week?

2 From Monday to Friday Mrs Watson starts work at 9 am and finishes at 4.45 pm.
  She gets 45 minutes for lunch.
  On Saturday she works from 9 am until midday.
  How many hours does she work in a week?

3 Eric works a night shift. He clocks on at 22 30 and finishes his shift at 07 00.
  He has a break of 45 minutes during the night. He works five nights a week.
  Calculate the total number of hours he works in a week.

4 The time-sheet shows when Bob Holmes clocked in and out of work one week.
  a Write down the number of hours he worked each day.
  b Find the total number of hours for the week.

```
                    TIME-SHEET
Bob Holmes            Employee No. 205                    Week No. 32

          In     Out     In      Out     No. of hours worked
Mon     09 00   13 00   14 00   18 00           ...
Tue     08 30   12 30   13 30   17 00           ...
Wed     08 30   13 00   13 30   17 00           ...
Thu     08 15   12 30   13 30   16 30           ...
Fri     08 45   13 00   14 00   16 30           ...
                                        Total = .... hours
```

Example 2

Patrick's basic rate of pay is £6·40 per hour.

In one week he works 35 hours paid at the basic rate plus 3 hours of overtime.

The overtime is paid at time and a half.

Calculate his total pay for the week.

(Note: time and a half means that for each hour the rate is increased by a half.)

Basic pay = £6·40 × 35 = £224

Each hour of overtime at time and a half = £6·40 + $\frac{1}{2}$ of £6·40 = £6·40 + £3·20 = £9·60

For 3 hours his overtime pay = £9·60 × 3 = £28·80

Total pay for week = £224 + £28·80 = £252·80

Exercise 5.2

1 Terry is paid double time when he works overtime at weekends.
His basic rate of pay is £6·50 per hour.
How much is he paid for each hour of overtime?

2 The table shows some basic hourly rates.
Copy and complete it, filling in the overtime rates at double time.

Basic rate	£5·50	£6	£6·25	£7·80	£8·85	£9·68
Double time	£11					

3 Calculate the overtime pay per hour at time and a half for these basic rates.
   a £4   b £5   c £5·60   d £8·70   e £11·50

4 Calculate the overtime pay per hour at time and a quarter for these basic rates.
   a £4   b £6   c £8·40   d £7   e £10·60

5 Calculate the overtime pay per hour at time and a third for these basic rates.
   a £6   b £4·50   c £5·70   d £8·10   e £11·40

6 On Sundays Steve is paid double time. His basic rate of pay is £5·75 per hour.
   a How much is he paid for each hour on a Sunday?
   b How much does he earn for working 5 hours on a Sunday?

7 Marie's basic rate is £6·80 per hour. Overtime is paid at time and a half.
   On Monday she works 7 hours at the basic rate plus 1 hour's overtime.
   a How much does she earn at the basic rate?
   b How much is she paid for the overtime?
   c What is her total pay for the day?

8 Michael's basic week is 35 hours. His basic rate of pay is £9·20.
   Overtime is paid at time and a quarter.
   For a week when he works 40 hours calculate his:
   a basic pay for the 35 hours
   b overtime pay
   c total wage for the week.

6 Piecework and commission

Not everyone is paid by the hour.
Some people are paid for the number of items made or tasks completed.
This is called piecework.
People in selling jobs are often paid according to the value of the goods sold.
This is called commission.

Example 1
Stella knits special jumpers. She is paid £24 for each one.
How much is she paid for producing eight jumpers?

She is paid £24 × 8 = £192

Example 2
Harry sells cars. He is paid a commission of 2% of the value of his sales.
How much commission does he earn for selling a sports car for £9900?
Commission = 2% of £9900 = 2 ÷ 100 × 9900 = £198

Exercise 6.1

1 Ged clears the roof gutters of houses. His standard charge is £35 per house.
  How much does he earn for doing three houses?

2 Kimberley works as a driving instructor. She is paid £26 for each lesson she gives.
  How much is she paid for a day when she gives five lessons?

3 Sheila sells electrical goods. She earns a basic wage plus commission of 1% of the
  value of her sales.
  How much commission is she paid for selling goods to the value of £350?

4 Vic works for a van hire company. He is paid a
  commission of 2% of the value of the hire sales he
  makes.
  How much commission does he make in a week when
  the value of his hire sales is £4000?

5 Tariq telephones house owners to try to interest them in building and contents
  insurance. For every customer who asks for a quotation he is paid £4·25.
  How much is he paid for 20 quotations?

6 Walt, a window cleaner, charges £5·50 per house.
  On average it takes him 30 minutes to clean the
  windows of a house.
  a If he works an 8 hour day how much should he earn
    in a day?
  b He reckons to work for 46 five-day weeks in the year.
    How much should he earn in the year?

7 Diamond Double Glazing pay their sales force a commission of 5%.
  How much commission is paid on a contract worth:
  a £2000   b £3500?

8 The Target Ticket Agency is paid £2·80 for each ticket they sell.
  How much are they paid when they sell 3000 concert tickets?

Example 3   Ellie stamps and addresses envelopes for a promotion company.
She is paid £2·50 for every 10 she processes.
How much is she paid for processing: **a** 50   **b** 700 letters?

    a For 50 letters pay = 50 ÷ 10 × £2·50 = 5 × £2·50 = £12·50
    b For 700 letters pay = 700 ÷ 10 × £2·50 = 70 × £2·50 = £175

Exercise 6.2

1 Carrie delivers free newspapers. She gets 30p for every ten papers.
How much does she get for delivering papers to a street of 80 houses?

2 Perfect Printers charge £8 per 100 for printing leaflets.
Lee orders 2000 leaflets. How much does it cost him?

3 Easysell Estate Agents charge a commission of 0·5% for selling a house.
How much do they get for a house sold for: **a** £60 000   **b** £185 000?

4 Fergus hand-paints crockery.
The table gives his rates of pay.
How much is he paid, in total, for painting
8 plates, 8 mugs and 8 saucers?

PLATES	£1·50
MUGS	£1·10
SAUCERS	75p

5 Diana works in a furniture store. She is paid a basic wage of £5·80 per hour
for a 37·5 hour week. She is also paid commission of 3% of the value of her sales.
Calculate: **a** her basic weekly wage
              b her commission for selling £4200 worth of furniture
              c her total wage for the week.

6 Ernie and his school friends decide to raise money for charity by washing
cars and cleaning their interiors. They charge £4·50 per car.
    a How much do they raise by cleaning 20 cars?
    b Their target is £200. How many customers do they need?

7 Kevin is a salesman for Sleepsound
and Keith travels for Soundsleep.
In March each of them sells £18 000
worth of goods.
Who earns more from his pay plus
commission, and how much more?

SLEEPSOUND
Pay £1020 per month
+ 7% of sales

SOUNDSLEEP
Pay £1170 per month
+ 6% of sales

7   Payslips

Workers receive payslips which show all their earnings for the latest week or month.
This includes any overtime, commission and bonuses (extra payments, possibly for
reaching set targets).
Most workers pay income tax and National Insurance (NI) to the government.
Also many workers contribute a weekly or monthly amount to a pension fund.
Pensions provide an income when a worker is retired.

Make sure you understand the following terms.

- Gross pay: total earnings including basic pay, overtime, bonuses, commission
- Deductions: money paid out of your earnings, including income tax, National Insurance and pensions
- Net pay (take-home pay) = Gross pay − Deductions

Example 1   This is Mr Plumber's payslip.

Name A. Plumber	Employee number 703	NI number YM12378A	Week number 17
Basic pay £408·40	**Overtime** £52·70	**Bonus** £30	**Gross pay**
Income tax £82·90	**NI** £30·10	**Pension** £23·80	**Total deductions**
			Net pay

Personal information → (Name row)

Basic pay and extras → (Basic pay row)

Deductions → (Income tax row)

Take-home pay → (Net pay row)

Calculate his:
- **a** gross pay
- **b** total deductions
- **c** take-home pay.

a Gross pay = £408·40 + £52·70 + £30 = £491·10
b Total deductions = £82·90 + £30·10 + £23·80 = £136·80
c Net pay = Gross pay − Total deductions = £354·30

Exercise 7.1

1 Calculate the gross pay in each case.

a Basic pay   £184·00
   + Overtime   £38·00
   Gross pay   _____

b Basic pay   £246·30
   + Bonus   £45·50
   Gross pay   _____

c Basic pay   £374·57
   + Overtime   £64·85
   + Bonus   £25·70
   Gross pay   _____

2 Calculate the total deductions in each case.

a Income tax   £24·00
   + NI   £7·00
   Total deductions   _____

b Income tax   £184·60
   + NI   £75·80
   Total deductions   _____

c Income tax   £258·69
   + NI   £124·83
   + Pension   £74·83
   Total deductions   _____

3 Calculate the net pay (take-home pay) in each case.

a Gross pay   £283·00
   − Deductions   £ 67·00
   Net pay   _____

b Gross pay   £348·00
   − Deductions   £ 86·00
   Net pay   _____

c Gross pay   £402·58
   − Deductions   £104·83
   Net pay   _____

4 Mr Thatcher works for an electronics company. This is his payslip for one week.

Name A. Thatcher	Employee number 96	NI number YM74585A	Week number 17
Basic pay £374·92	Overtime £36·75	Bonus £31·50	Gross pay
Income tax £73·57	NI £22·78	Pension £19·04	Total deductions
			Net pay

Calculate his: **a** gross pay
                b total deductions
                c take-home pay.

5 Ms Baker is employed by a hydro-electrics company.
This is her payslip for June.

Name A. Baker	Employee number 230	NI number YM83293B	
Basic pay £2048·68	Overtime £0	Bonus £65·75	Gross pay
Income tax £385·63	NI £146·49	Pension £124·62	Total deductions
			Net pay

Calculate her: **a** gross pay
                b total deductions
                c take-home pay.

6 Mrs Parker works for an insurance company.
This is her payslip for one week.

Name N. Parker	Employee number 104	NI number YM80388B	Week number 36
Basic pay £......	Overtime £40·39	Bonus £17·75	Gross pay £
Income tax £......	NI £9·52	Pension £12·95	Total deductions £82·24
			Net pay £228·19

Calculate her: **a** income tax
                b gross pay
                c basic pay.

8 Income tax

If your income in a tax year is below a certain amount you do not pay tax.
This amount is called your tax allowance.
The tax allowance is made up from a personal allowance plus any other special allowances.
(Other tax allowances include expenses such as special clothing or equipment needed for work, and membership of professional bodies.)

In the tax year 2004–2005 the personal allowance was £4745.
Income above the tax allowance is called taxable income.
Income tax is paid on your taxable income.

Income includes earnings, pensions, interest from savings and most other sources of money.

Example 1   Omar is single. His total income for the year is £21 000.
His tax allowance is £4745. Calculate his taxable income.

Taxable income = total income – tax allowance
= £21 000 – £4745 = £16 255

This table shows the income tax rates for the tax year 2004–2005.

Taxable income	Rate of tax
£0–£2020	10%
£2020–£31 400	22%
over £31 400	40%

Example 2   Mr Yates earns £26 000 in the tax year. His tax allowance is £4745.
a Calculate his taxable income.
b How much of his income is taxed at   **i** 10%   **ii** 22%   **iii** 40%?

a Taxable income = £26 000 – £4745 = £21 255
b i Amount taxed at 10% = £2020
ii Amount taxed at 22% = £21 255 – £2020 = £19 235
iii Taxable income is less than £31 400 so none of it is taxed at 40%.

Exercise 8.1

1 Jessica works part-time. Her total earnings in the tax year come to £3000.
Her tax allowance is £4745.
a Does she have to pay income tax?
b What is her taxable income?

2 Ali's total income for the tax year is £14 800.
His tax allowance is £4745.
a Does he have to pay income tax?
b What is his taxable income?

4 Pete's bank book shows his deposits, withdrawals and interest.

Date	Details	Receipts	Withdrawals	Balance
01/04/03	Cheque	£250·00		£250·00
01/04/04	Interest	£11·25		....
15/08/04	Cheque	£160·00		....
27/12/04	Cash		£175·00	....

Calculate the balance of his account on:

a 01/04/04   **b** 15/08/04   **c** 27/12/04

5 Calculate the balance of Janis's account on:

a 04/04/04   **b** 24/06/04   **c** 04/04/05

Date	Details	Receipts	Withdrawals	Balance
04/04/03	Cheque	£3875·00		£3875·00
04/04/04	Interest	£232·50		....
24/06/04	Cash		£850·00	....
04/04/05	Interest	£186·45		....

6 Lewis is given £200 for his birthday. He puts it in a deposit account which pays 6% p.a. How much interest is there after a year?

7 Mr Foster invests £4000 in an account which pays 7% p.a. interest. How much interest does the account earn in one year?

8 Calculate the interest in a year on these amounts invested with Rock Solid Bank.

a £30   **b** £700

c £3500   **d** £15 000

> **ROCK SOLID BANK**
> Interest 5% p.a.

9 Dylan's savings account pays 4% interest. He has £90 in the account.

a How much interest does the bank pay him for one year?

b How much interest will he be paid in total if he leaves the £90 in for 5 years? Note: He takes out the interest at the end of each year.

10 Marilyn opens an account with the Toprate Building Society. She deposits £720 in the account.

a Calculate the yearly interest.

b How much interest will she earn in 8 years? Assume that she withdraws the interest when it is paid each year.

> **TOPRATE BUILDING SOCIETY**
> Interest 3% p.a.

Example 3   Mr Banks invests £25 000 at 3·5% p.a.
After 9 months he closes his account.
Calculate the interest earned.

Interest for 12 months = 3·5 ÷ 100 × 25 000 = £875
Interest for 1 month = £875 ÷ 12
Interest for 9 months = £875 ÷ 12 × 9 = £656·25 (to the nearest penny)

Exercise 10.2

1 Mrs Adams has £600 in an account. The interest rate is 4% p.a.
How much interest is earned each year?

2 Joan deposits £4000 in a savings account which pays 3% p.a.
Calculate the annual interest.

3 Mr Jackson opens an account with the Trusty
Building Society.
He deposits £7800 at an interest rate of 5% p.a.
How much interest will the account earn in:
a 1 year
b 3 years? (Assume it earns the same amount each year.)

4 Ryan's bank account pays 6% p.a. interest.
He has £90 in the account.
Calculate the interest earned in: **a** 1 year   **b** 8 years.
(Assume it earns the same amount each year.)

5 Calculate the yearly interest paid on deposits of:
a £100   **b** £5000
c £6250   **d** £24

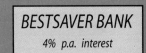

6 Zoe invests £100 at 6% p.a. Zak invests £110 at 5%.
Who earns more interest in a year? How much more?

7 Ms Connor puts £18 000 in the Mushroom Building
Society.
a How much interest will she earn in one year?
b Calculate the total interest for 6 years.
(She takes out the interest at the end of each year.)

8 Imran invests £12 500 at 4·5% p.a.
a Calculate his annual interest.
b Each year he withdraws his interest and puts it towards the cost of a holiday.
What is the total amount paid towards his holidays after 4 years?

9 Martina deposits £3600 with the Rapid Growth Bank.
   How much interest will she receive in:
   a 1 year   **b** 1 month   **c** 8 months?

10 Calculate the interest on:
   a £600 at 5% for 6 months
   b £80 at 4% for 3 months
   c £9000 at 6% for 4 months
   d £48 000 at 6·5% for 8 months

 RECAP

Money calculations
You should be able to carry out calculations involving money, including finding
percentages of amounts. You should also be able to round amounts of money to
suitable accuracy and estimate answers to calculations.

Wages and salaries
You should be able to do calculations involving wages, salaries, piecework,
commission, overtime, time-sheets and pay rises.

Payslips and deductions
You should be able to do calculations involving gross pay, net pay, income tax,
National Insurance, bonuses and pensions.
Net pay = gross pay – deductions
Taxable income = total income – tax allowance

Savings
You should be able to understand cheques, bank statements, savings accounts and
interest. You should be able to calculate simple percentages without a calculator,
for example: 1%, 2%, 4%, 5%, 10%, 15%, 20%, 25%, 50%. You should be able to
use a calculator to carry out more difficult percentage calculations.

1 Fred earns £2145 per month. He receives a monthly pay rise of £62.
  a Calculate his new monthly wage.
  b How much will he earn, in total, in the next 6 months?

2 a Karl, who is self-employed, installs bathroom suites. He charges £125 per suite.
  How much does he earn in a week when he installs five suites?
  b Dorothy is paid 2% commission on her carpet sales.
  How much commission does she earn in a week when her sales total £4500?

3 On Sundays Sean is paid double time. His basic rate of pay is £7·86 per hour.
  a How much is he paid for each hour on a Sunday?
  b How much does he earn for working 3 hours on a Sunday?

4 This is Viv's time-sheet.
  a Write down the number of hours she worked each day.
  b Find her total hours for the week.

TIME-SHEET				
Viv Sharp		Employee No. 274		Week No. 18
	In	Out	In	Out	No. of hours worked
Mon	09 00	12 30	13 00	18 00	...
Tue	08 30	12 30	13 00	17 30	...
Wed	08 30	13 30	14 30	17 30	...
Thu	08 15	12 15	13 00	16 15	...
Fri	08 45	13 15	14 00	16 45	...
				Total = ... hours

5 Complete the balance column for this bank statement.

STATEMENT			
Date	Paid out	Paid in	Balance
2 Oct			£435·50
6 Oct		£96·75	
13 Oct	£495·80		
20 Oct	£100·00		

6 Chris deposits £8000 in a savings account which pays 5% p.a.
  Calculate: **a** the annual interest **b** the total interest earned over 6 years.
  (Assume the same amount of interest is paid each year.)

7 Emily is employed as a painter.
  How much will she earn per week?

PAINTER
£8·50 per hour
38 hour week

8 Alice's annual salary is £23 610. She is given a 4% pay rise.
   a How much is the pay rise worth?
   b Calculate her new   i annual   ii monthly salary.

9 Mrs Piper works for an insurance company.
   This is her payslip for one week.

Name N. Piper	Employee number 95	NI number YM63791B	Week number 28
Basic pay £483·57	Overtime £30·48	Bonus £8·50	Gross pay £......
Income tax £88·37	NI £25·84	Pension £19·26	Total deductions £......
			Net pay £......

Calculate her: a gross pay
                  b total deductions
                  c net pay.

Use this table of tax bands and rates for questions 10 and 11.

Taxable income	Rate of tax
£0–£2020	10%
£2020–£31 400	22%
over £31 400	40%

10 Amy earns £21 600 in the tax year. Her tax free allowance is £4745.
   a Find her taxable income.
   b How much of her income is taxed at the   i 10%   ii 22% rate?

11 Richard's taxable income is £23 700.
   a Calculate the tax payable at 10%.
   b How much of his income is taxed at the rate of 22%?
   c How much tax is paid at the 22% rate?
   d Calculate the total tax payable.

REVISE

4 Similarity

Architects and engineers drew many scale drawings of the Space Shuttle before the first test model was built.

In this chapter you'll learn how to make scale drawings of your own.

1 Review

◄◄ Exercise 1.1

1 a Copy the compass and fill in the missing cardinal points.
  b Write down the three-figure bearing of each cardinal point.

2 Measure these angles.

a    **b**   **c**

3 For each of the following, measure:
  i the bearing of the boat from the port   **ii** the bearing of the port from the boat.

a   **b** 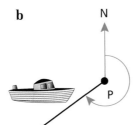   **c**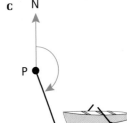

4 Illustrate each of the following with a simple sketch.
  a A ship left port and sailed on a bearing of 030°.
  b A ship left port on a bearing of 175°.
  c A ship left port on a bearing of 240°.

7 Mr Smith is planning his garden.
The actual garden measures 8 m by 12 m.
What is the scale of the diagram?

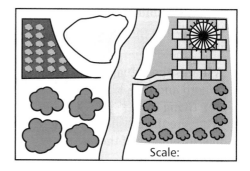

8 The actual height of the Eiffel Tower is 320 m.
What is the scale of the diagram?

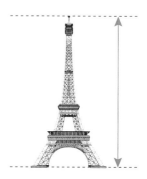

3 Scales as ratios

A scale can be represented as a ratio.
'1 cm represents 100 cm' can be written as **1 : 100**.
This is called a **representative fraction** (RF).
This means any **one unit on the map represents 100** of the same **units on the ground**.

1 cm represents 100 cm or 1 m represents 100 or 1 foot represents 100 feet.

Example 1   The scale of a map is 1 : 50 000.
The distance between two hills on the map is 3 cm.
What is the actual distance expressed in kilometres?

1 cm represents 50 000 cm
so 3 cm represents 50 000 × 3 = 150 000 cm
$$= 1500 \text{ m}$$
$$= 1 \cdot 5 \text{ km}.$$

Example 2   Express 1 cm represents 150 m as a representative fraction.
1 cm : 150 m = 1 cm : 150 × 100 cm = 1 cm : 15 000 cm = 1 : 15 000

Exercise 3.1

1 Using a scale of 1 : 200, work out the actual distances in metres given by:
   a 3 cm   **b** 5 cm   **c** 8 cm

2 Using a scale of 1 : 50 000, calculate the actual distances in kilometres given by:
   a 3 cm   **b** 7 cm   **c** 5·5 cm

3 Fill in the missing entries in the table. The first column has been done for you.

Length on map	2 cm	5 cm	3 cm	5 cm	4 cm
Actual length	6 m				
Representative fraction	1 : 300	1 : 500	1 : 1000	1 : 15 000	1 : 50 000
Scale of map	1 cm to 3 m				

4 Find the representative fractions and scales from the information given.

Distance on map	2 cm	1 cm	3 cm	1 cm	2 cm	4 cm
Actual distance	10 m	15 m	12 m	300 m	500 m	1 km
Representative fraction	1 : 500					
Scale	1 cm to 5 m					

5 Find the distance on the map from the information given.

Distance on map				
Actual distance	400 m	2 km	5 km	20 km
Representative fraction	1 : 1000	1 : 10 000	1 : 50 000	1 : 500 000

6 Joe and Margo walked for 10 km. On the map this was represented by 5 cm.
What is the scale of the map written as a representative fraction?

7 The actual engine is 8·1 metres in length.
  a Measure the length of the drawing.
  b What is the scale of the drawing?

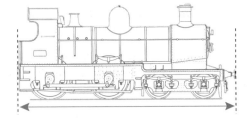

8 An archaeologist measures the ruins of a temple.
The actual length was 8 m. On his plan the length is 5 cm.
What is the scale of the plan?

9 A model of the *Titanic* measures 20 cm.
The actual length of the ship was 270 metres.
What is the scale of the model?

4 Making scale drawings

You must first choose the scale.
This will depend upon the measurements involved and the size of paper.

Remember: the larger the scale drawing, the more accurate the measurements that we take from it will be.

Example Tim lives in Paisley, 3 km south of the airport.
Liz lives in Glasgow, 4 km east of the airport.
How far apart are Tim and Liz?

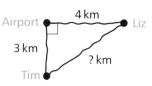

Make an accurate drawing of the triangle.
Use a scale of 1 cm to 1 km (1 : 100 000).

Step 1 Draw AL = 4 cm.
Step 2 Draw ∠LAT = 90°.
Step 3 Draw AT = 3 cm.
Step 4 Measure TL (5 cm).
Step 5 Scale up: 5 × 100 000 = 500 000 cm = 5 km.

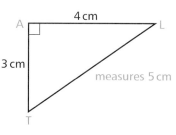

Tim and Liz are 5 km apart.

Exercise 4.1

1 Using the scales given, make an accurate drawing of each sketch.

a
4 km
5 km
1 cm represents 1 km

b
4 km
6 km
1 : 50 000

c
5 m
1 m
5 m
1 m
1 cm represents ½ m

d
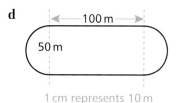
100 m
50 m
1 cm represents 10 m

e
80 m
120°
A regular hexagon
1 : 1000

For each of the following, choose the scale carefully.
Remember to draw a sketch before making the scale drawing.

2 A ship sails south for 6 km and then west for 4·5 km.
   a Make an accurate drawing of the route.
   b Measure the distance in centimetres between the starting point and the end point.
   c How far has the ship to travel to get back to where it started?

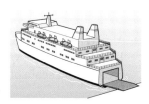

3 A mountain rescue team walked in a north-easterly direction for 2 km.
They then turned and walked south-east for 1·5 km.
  a Make an accurate drawing of their route.
  b How far have they to travel to get back to their starting point?

4 Here is a sketch of an orienteering map.
  a Make an accurate drawing of the map.
  b Once the competitors reach checkpoint 3,
    how far are they from the start?

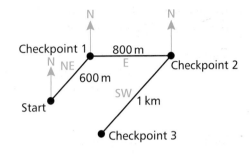

5 In a triathlon event, the competitors first swim north-west for 800 metres, then
south-west for 500 metres before swimming back to the starting line.
  a Make an accurate drawing of the course.
  b The competitors have to swim round this course three times.
    How far do they swim in total?

6 A helicopter left Prestwick to pick up a casualty from the hills.
It flew 140 miles in a north-easterly direction to the casualty site.
With the casualty on board, it flew 40 miles north-west to a hospital.
After refuelling, it flew back to Prestwick.
  a Make an accurate drawing of the route flown by the helicopter.
  b How far did it fly in total?

Exercise 4.2

1 From each of the diagrams below, work out the bearing and the distance travelled.

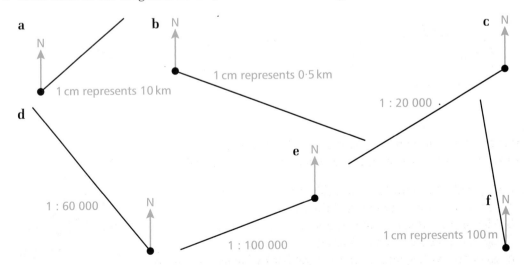

2 a Work out the bearing and distance for each part of these scale drawings.

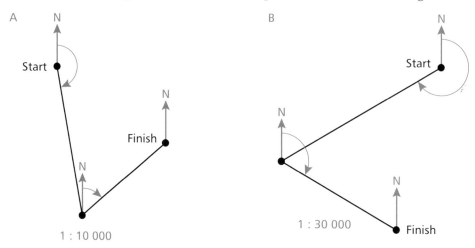

b Find the bearing of:
   i the finish from the start   **ii** the start from the finish.

3 The diagram shows the flight path of a plane as it flew over some hills.

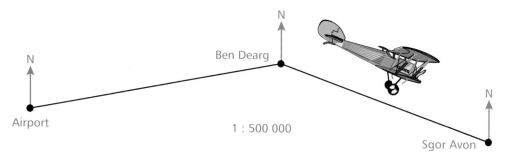

  a Once the plane reached Sgor Avon, what bearing had it to take to get back to the airport?
  b The plane then flew back to the airport. How far had it flown in total?
  c What bearing did the plane take to fly from Ben Dearg to Sgor Avon?

4 Below is a scale drawing of a course laid out for a sailing regatta.

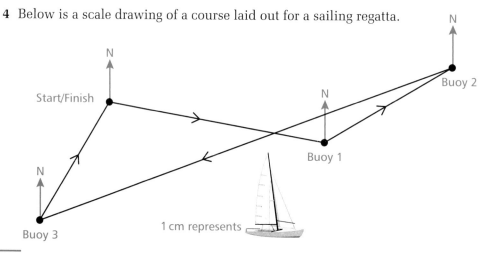

a Copy and complete this table.

b The actual distance of leg 1 is 2 km.

   i What is the scale of the map?

   ii Calculate the lengths of the other legs.

Leg	Description	Bearing	Measure
Leg 1	from start to buoy 1	100°	6 cm
Leg 2	buoy 2 from buoy 1		
Leg 3	buoy 3 from buoy 2		
Leg 4	the finish from buoy 3		

5 This scale drawing shows the route that Richard and his friends walked.

  a Give the bearing of each part of the journey.

  b How far did they walk from start to finish?

  c On the top of Sgor Geal, Richard realised that he had left his camera on the top of Carn Hope.

   What bearing should he follow to get back to the top of Carn Hope?

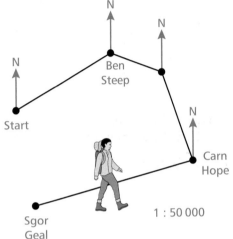

6 A ship sails for 8 km on a bearing of 080°.
It then turns and sails on a bearing of 145° for a further 6 km.

  a How far is it from where it started?

  b What bearing must the ship take to get back to where it started?

7 From an airport, a plane flew for 60 km on a bearing of 325° then for 100 km on a bearing of 170°.

  a How far was it from the airport at this point?

  b It then flew straight back to the airport. What bearing did it follow?

8 Two fishing boats leave the harbour at the same time.
One sails for 30 km on a bearing of 176° and the other for 40 km on a bearing of 259°.
How far apart are they at the end of their journeys?

9 Two ships are visible on a radar screen. One is 27 km away on a bearing of 015°.
The second ship is 33 km away on a bearing of 173°.

  a How far apart are the ships?

  b What is the bearing of the second ship from the first ship?

10 A lighthouse is 1·5 km away from a car ferry on a bearing of 010°.
The docks are only 0·8 km away from the ferry on a bearing of 079°.

  a How far is the lighthouse from the docks?

  b What is the bearing of the docks from the lighthouse?

5 Enlarging and reducing

These are two photographs of the same hill.

Picture 1

←— 3 cm —→

Picture 2

←————— 6 cm —————→

The second one has been enlarged. It is 2 times the size of the first one.

It has been enlarged using a scale factor of 2 … an enlargement factor of 2.

Each length on picture 2 is double the same length in picture 1.

Example

Picture 1

←—— 4 cm ——→

Picture 2

←——— 6 cm ———→

a Find the enlargement factor from picture 1 to picture 2 .
b State the reduction factor from picture 2 to picture 1.

a Enlargement factor $= \dfrac{\text{enlarged size}}{\text{smaller size}} = \dfrac{6}{4} = 1 \cdot 5$

The length of each line on picture 2 is 1·5 times its length in picture 1.

b Reduction factor $= \dfrac{\text{reduced size}}{\text{larger size}} = \dfrac{4}{6} = \dfrac{2}{3}$

The length of each line on picture 1 is $\frac{2}{3}$ of its length in picture 2.

Note that:
- an enlargement factor is greater than 1
- a reduction factor is less than 1.

Exercise 5.1

1 Draw each shape twice as large.

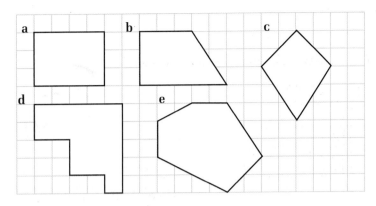

2 Reduce these using a factor of 0·5.

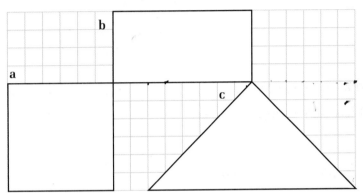

3 By measuring the marked lengths calculate:
  i the enlargement factor   **ii** the reduction factor.

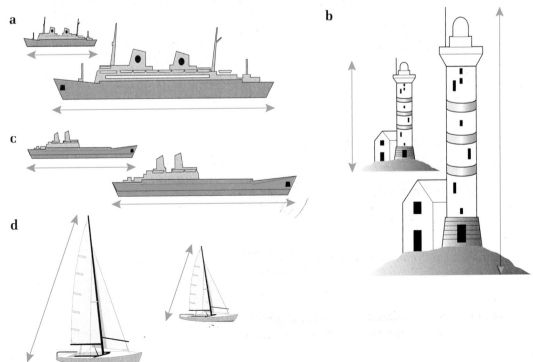

4 Enlarge each shape using the scale factor given.

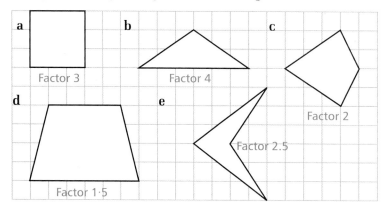

5 Draw each shape using the reduction scale factor given.

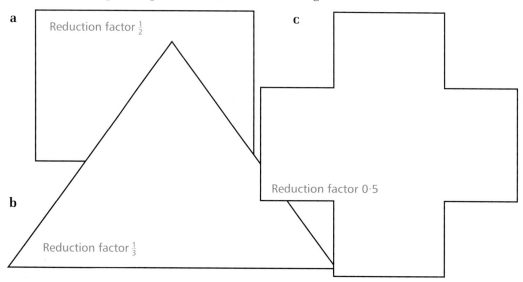

6 Using scale factors

Scale factors can be used to find missing lengths.

Example   A photograph shows the Angel of the North.
The height of the image in the photograph is 5 cm.
The wingspan measures 14 cm.

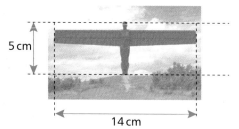

The actual statue is 20 m high.
What is the actual wingspan?

We want to enlarge a drawing to 'real life'.

$$\text{Enlargement factor} = \frac{\text{actual height}}{\text{height in photo}} = \frac{20\,\text{m}}{5\,\text{cm}} = \frac{2000}{5} = 400$$

Actual wingspan = wingspan in photo × scale factor
$$= 14 \times 400$$
$$= 5600\,\text{cm}$$
$$= 56\,\text{m}$$

Exercise 6.1

1 A model of a Spitfire is 10 cm in length.
The enlargement factor for the actual plane is 95.
a What is the actual length of the plane?
b The model has a wingspan of 10·7 cm.
What is the actual wingspan?

2 The living room on an architect's plan measures 7·2 cm by 6·6 cm.
The enlargement factor is 60.
What are the dimensions of the living room?

3 From the pictures and scale factors, work out the actual lengths or heights of these animals.

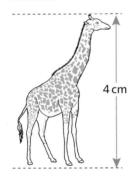
4 cm

Enlargement
factor 150

←—— 5 cm ——→

Enlargement
factor 52

←——— 5·5 cm ———→

Enlargement
factor 60

4 The Empire State Building is 450 m high.
A scale model is made using the reduction scale factor of $\frac{1}{50}$.
How tall will the model be?

5 The highest waterfall in the world is called Angel Falls.
Its total drop is 976 metres.
The reduction scale factor of a photograph is $\frac{1}{1220}$.
How high, in centimetres, is the image of the waterfall?

6 A photograph of Ben Nevis is $\frac{1}{33500}$ real-life size.

   a The height of the image of the mountain in the photo is 4 cm.
What is the actual height of Ben Nevis?

   b The mountain beside Ben Nevis is called Carn Mor Dearg. It is 1220 metres high.
Using the same reduction scale factor, what would be the height of the image of
this mountain in the same photo? (Give your answer to the nearest millimetre.)

7 A rectangular garden measures 27 m by 18 m.
Kirsty is designing her garden using a computer program.
The reduction scale factor of the plan on the screen is $\frac{1}{60}$.

   a What are the dimensions of the garden on the screen?

   b She draws a circular area on the screen to represent grass.
The radius of the circle is 5·5 cm.
What is the actual area of the circle of grass?

7 Similar shapes

Two shapes are mathematically *similar* if one shape is an enlargement of the other.

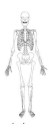 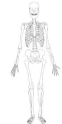

  A shape   Similar but smaller   Similar but larger   Not similar

Each corresponding measurement must be scaled by the same factor.

We can work out if shapes are similar by using this fact, that is by checking that the
ratios of corresponding sides are equal.

Example
An art gallery sells posters and
postcards of works of art.

Are the images similar?

36 cm

42 cm

6 cm

7 cm

Check corresponding sides:

$$\frac{\text{length of poster}}{\text{length of postcard}} = \frac{42}{7} = 6; \quad \frac{\text{height of poster}}{\text{height of postcard}} = \frac{32}{6} = 6$$

The ratios are the same, so the shapes are similar … with an enlargement factor of 6.

Exercise 7.1

1 Souvenir statues of different sizes are on sale.

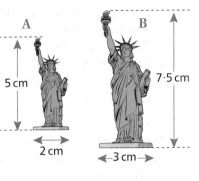

  a Calculate height of $\dfrac{\text{statue B}}{\text{height of statue A}}$.

  b Calculate $\dfrac{\text{base of statue B}}{\text{base of statue A}}$.

  c Are the statues similar?

2 For each pair of rectangles:
  i work out if they are similar
  ii state the enlargement factor of those pairs that are.

a
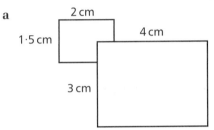

b
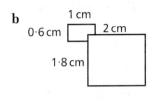

c
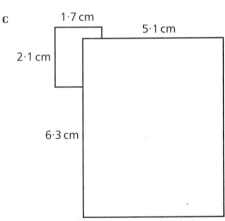

d

3 These diagrams of football pitches are similar.
  a Write down the reduction scale factor.
  b Calculate x, the breadth of the smaller pitch.

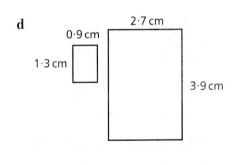

4 These television screens are similar.

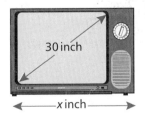

  a Write down the enlargement scale factor.
  b Calculate the length of the larger television screen.

5 Samantha has two rectangular photographs.
One measures 8 cm by 12 cm and the other 6 cm by 9 cm.
Are the photographs similar?
Give a reason for your answer.

6 Two different posters advertising a local disco are similar.

60 cm

75 cm

h cm

30 cm

a Calculate the reduction scale factor.
b What is the height of the smaller poster?

7 A manufacturer produces two different sizes of kitchen cabinet doors.

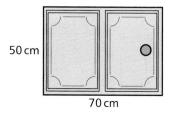

50 cm

70 cm

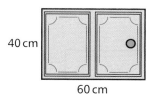

40 cm

60 cm

Are the doors similar?
Give a reason for your answer.

8 An artist has used mathematical shapes to create this design.

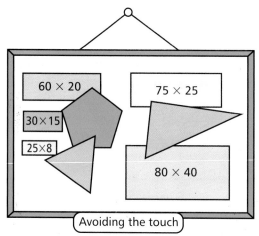

60 × 20

75 × 25

30×15

25×8

80 × 40

Avoiding the touch

Which of the rectangles are similar?

8 Similar right-angled triangles

As with other shapes, when triangles are similar **the ratios of corresponding sides are equal**. The pairs of corresponding sides are easy to spot as they will be opposite the equal angles.

Example   The following pair of triangles are similar.

a Name the pairs of corresponding sides.
b State the equal ratios.

a Opposite the right angle: AB corresponds to FE
Opposite the 30° angle: AC corresponds to DE
Opposite the 60° angle: BC corresponds to DF

b $\dfrac{AB}{FE} = \dfrac{AC}{DE} = \dfrac{BC}{DF}$

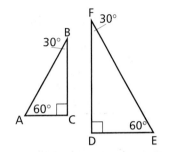

Exercise 8.1

1 The following pairs of triangles are similar.

a 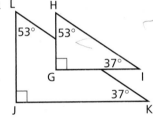   **b** 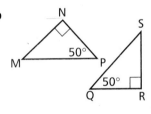   **c**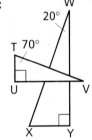

i Name the pairs of corresponding sides.
ii State the equal ratios.

2 The roof of a house has three dormer windows in the shape of similar right-angled triangles. Equal angles have been marked.

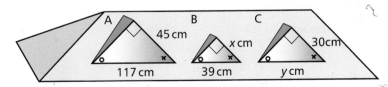

a Calculate the reduction scale factor from window A to window B.
b Calculate x, one of the sides of window B.
c Calculate the reduction scale factor from window A to window C.
d Find the length of y.

3 Rachael has designed tablemats which are similar.

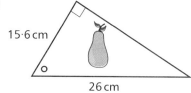

a What is the reduction scale factor?

b Calculate the length of x.

c Find the missing sides of both triangles.

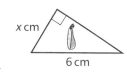

4 Greg uses garden canes to support his young plants.
He has two different sizes of supports. The triangles are similar.
Equal angles are marked.

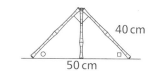

a What is the reduction scale factor?

b Work out the length, x cm, of the smaller cane.

5 Tam is putting a roof on a house.
The roof trusses he is using are similar right-angled triangles.

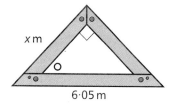

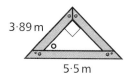

a Find the enlargement scale factor.

b Work out the length of x to the nearest centimetre.

6 The diagram shows a clothes drier viewed from above.
In each part, the right-angled triangles are similar.

The reduction scale factor from the outer line to the middle line is 0·8 and for the inner line is 0·5.

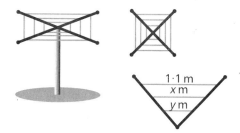

a Work out the length of x and y.

b What is the total length of line needed for the clothes drier?

7 These two triangles are similar.
The side that measures 7·4 cm corresponds to side d.

a Work out the length of d.

b Calculate the lengths of b and c.

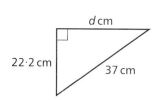

9 Areas of similar shapes

These rectangles are similar. The enlargement factor is 3.

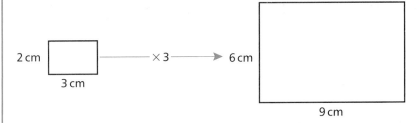

2 cm
3 cm
×3
6 cm
9 cm

Area $= 2 \times 3 = 6$ cm^2 Area $= 6 \times 9 = 54$ cm^2

Note that the ratio of their areas $= \frac{54}{6} = 9$ and that this is the square of the scale factor!

(Why? Larger area $= 6 \times 9 = 2 \times 3 \times 3 \times 3 = 2 \times 3 \times 3 \times 3 = $ smaller area $\times 3^2$)

> The ratios of the areas of similar shapes = the square of the scale factor.

Example
These are similar triangles.
Their bases are given.
The area of the smaller triangle is 6 cm^2.
What is the area of the larger triangle?

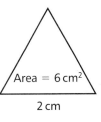

Area $= 6$ cm^2
2 cm
Area $= ?$ cm^2
8 cm

Scale factor $= \frac{8}{2} = 4$
Thus area is enlarged by a factor of $4^2 = 16$.
Thus larger area $= 16 \times 6 = 96$ cm^2.

Exercise 9.1

1 These rectangles are similar.

   a Write down the enlargement scale factor.
   b Calculate the areas of both rectangles.

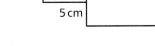

1 cm
4 cm
20 cm
5 cm

   c Copy and complete: $\dfrac{\text{area of larger rectangle}}{\text{area of smaller rectangle}} = -$

   d Check that the ratio of the areas = the square of the enlargement factor.

2 These rectangles are also similar.

   a Write down the reduction scale factor.
   b Calculate the areas of both rectangles.

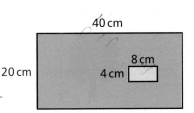

40 cm
8 cm
20 cm
4 cm

   c Copy and complete: $\dfrac{\text{area of smaller rectangle}}{\text{area of larger rectangle}} = -$

   d Check that the ratio of the areas = the square of the reduction factor.

5 Formulae

Formulae are everywhere

There are 60 seconds in a minute:

$S = 60M$

There are 90 degrees in a right angle:

$D = 90R$

Speed measures the distance travelled in a fixed time:

$S = \dfrac{D}{T}$

The area of a circle is just over 3 times the radius squared:

$A = \pi r^2$

Your profit is the difference between your selling price and your buying price:

$P = S - B$

1 Review

Reminders

1 There is an order of doing calculations:
   Brackets – Of – Division and Multiplication – Addition and Subtraction.
   Remember BODMAS.

Examples   **a** $(12 - 8) \times 2 = 4 \times 2 = 8$ Brackets calculated before multiplication.

  b $\frac{1}{3}$ of $6 + 3 = 2 + 3 = 5$ 'Of' calculated before addition.

  c $8 + 2 \times 3 = 8 + 6 = 14$ Multiplication calculated before addition.

  d $\frac{6}{3} - 1 = 2 - 1 = 1$ Division calculated before subtraction.

2 Squares and square roots:

Examples   **a** If $x = 3$ then $x^2 = 3^2 = 3 \times 3 = 9$

  b If $x = 9$ then $\sqrt{x} = 3$ (since $3^2 = 9$)

  c If $x = 16$ then $x^2 + \sqrt{x} = 16^2 + \sqrt{16} = 256 + 4 = 260$

◀◀ **Exercise 1.1**

1 Calculate:

   a $3 + 2 \times 4$ **b** $14 - 2 \times 6$ **c** $10 + \frac{1}{2}$ of 8 **d** $\frac{1}{3}$ of $6 + 9$

   e $4 \times 5 - 7$ **f** $6 + 4 - 2$ **g** $6 - 4 + 2$ **h** $6 - (4 + 2)$

   i $\dfrac{2 + 6}{4}$ **j** $\dfrac{9}{2 + 1}$ **k** $\frac{1}{2}$ of $\frac{4}{2}$ **l** $\frac{15}{5} - 2$

   m 5^2 **n** $30 - 4^2$ **o** $\frac{1}{2}$ of 6^2 **p** $9 + 2^2$

   q $\sqrt{49}$ **r** $\sqrt{81}$ **s** $\frac{1}{10}$ of $\sqrt{100}$ **t** $\sqrt{3 + 22}$

   u $\sqrt{6^2 + 8^2}$ **v** $9^2 + \sqrt{9}$ **w** $\dfrac{5 - \sqrt{4}}{6}$ **x** $\dfrac{5 + 4}{5 - 2}$

2 If $x = 3$ and $y = 16$ find the value of:

   a $5x$ **b** $3y$ **c** $x + 5$ **d** $y - 14$

   e $15 - x$ **f** $2x + y$ **g** $2y - x$ **h** $20 - 4x$

   i xy **j** $x^2 + y$ **k** $y - x^2$ **l** $(y - x)^2$

   m $(10 - x)^2$ **n** $(y - 2x)^2$ **o** $(y - 5x)^2$ **p** $x^2 + y^2$

3 Simplify:

   a $3n + 2m - n$ **b** $4x + y + 3x - y$ **c** $x + 3 + 4x - 2$

   d $4k + 1 - k + 3$ **e** $5 + 6a + b - 3a - b$ **f** $1 + x - 1 + 4x - y$

   g $2a - 3 + 3b - a - 2b$ **h** $m + 5n - 5 - m - 2n$ **i** $12 + h + 2g - 7 + 5h - g$

4 Remove the brackets:

   a $3(x + 2)$ **b** $5(y - 2)$ **c** $6(x + y)$ **d** $8(a - b)$

   e $3(5 - y)$ **f** $2(2x + 1)$ **g** $3(8 - 3y)$ **h** $7(2x + 3y)$

   i $6(4m - 5)$ **j** $3(12 - 4y)$ **k** $6(2x + 4y)$ **l** $9(10 - 8k)$

5 Solve these equations.

   (Remember to check your solution by substituting the value back into the equation.)

   a $y + 2 = 13$ **b** $14 - a = 8$ **c** $23 - k = 15$ **d** $12 = 2 + x$

   e $15 = 18 - t$ **f** $20 = 32 - h$ **g** $8n = 24$

   h $5y = 35$ **i** $16 = 4d$ **j** $32 = 4x$

   k $2w = 3$ **l** $2x = 7$ **m** $3y = 1$

   n $3z = 4$ **o** $5v = 1$ **p** $3t = 4$

   q $2x - 3 = 13$ **r** $3 + 5g = 8$ **s** $7 + 3m = 13$ **t** $5k + 8 = 58$

   u $3y + 5 = 29$ **v** $12 - 8x = 4$ **w** $2 = 20 - 3m$ **x** $50 - 5h = 15$

6 Remove the brackets and simplify:

   a $2(a + 4) + 6$ **b** $3(2 + n) + n$ **c** $2m + 6(n + m) + n$

   d $7 + 3(x - 2)$ **e** $12 + 8(r - 1)$ **f** $12y + 4(x - y) + 2x$

7 These formulae should be familiar.

a If the selling price is £23·40 and the cost price is £17·20, use the formula:

$$\text{profit} = \text{selling price} - \text{cost price}$$

to calculate the profit.

b If you made a profit of £6 and your cost price was £10, use the formula:

$$\text{percentage profit} = \frac{\text{profit}}{\text{cost price}} \times 100\%$$

to find your percentage profit.

c Pythagoras' theorem states: $c^2 = a^2 + b^2$
Calculate c^2 if $a = 5$ and $b = 13$.

d The area, A cm^2, of a circle with radius
r cm is given by the formula $A = \pi r^2$.
Calculate, to 1 decimal place, the area of a circle with radius:

    i 2 cm   **ii** 2·3 cm   **iii** 0·7 cm   **iv** 1·3 cm

8 Write down the next three terms in these sequences:

  a 7, 9, 11, 13, ...   **b** 7, 14, 21, 28, 35, ...   **c** 1, 4, 9, 16, 25, ...
  d 1, 3, 6, 10, 15, ...   **e** 45, 40, 35, 30, ...   **f** 100, 91, 82, 73, ...

9 Write down an expression for the perimeter of each rectangle.

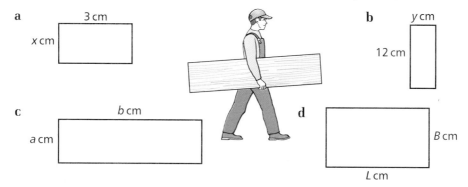

10 a If you know x how do you calculate y?

$$y = \ldots$$

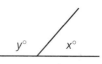

   b If you know n how do you calculate m?

$$m = \ldots$$

2 Substitution and evaluation

Example   Evaluate $3ab - 2$ when $a = 5$ and $b = 1$.

             Substituting gives $3ab - 2 = 3 \times 5 \times 1 - 2 = 15 - 2 = 13$.

Exercise 2.1

1 If $a = 2$ and $b = 3$ calculate:

a $3a$	**b** $4b$	**c** $5a$	**d** $a + 6$	**e** $a - 1$
f $b + 4$	**g** $b - 2$	**h** $2a + 3$	**i** $3b - 5$	**j** $b - a$
k $2b + a$	**l** $3a + b$	**m** $4a - b$	**n** $b + 3a$	**o** $12 - 2a$
p $3b - 4a$	**q** ab	**r** $5 + ab$	**s** $2ab$	**t** $2a + b$
u $5a - 2b$	**v** $b + ab$	**w** $ab - a$	**x** $3ab$	**y** $4b - ab$

2 a $A = 5x$; find A if $x = 4$.
   b $Q = 8r$; find Q if $r = 0\cdot5$.
   c $C = T - 5$; find C if $T = 14$.
   d $W = x - 2$; find W if $x = 6$.
   e $P = 3y + 4$; find P if $y = 5$.
   f $M = 2K - 3$; find M if $K = 12$.
   g $A = DL$; find A if $D = 4\cdot5$ and $L = 2$.
   h $W = am$; find W if $a = 8$ and $m = 12$.
   i $M = 12 - BK$; find M if $B = 2$ and $K = 3$.
   j $Q = LM + 4$; find Q if $L = 6$ and $M = 9$.
   k $A = \sqrt{k}$; find A if $k = 49$.
   l $W = \sqrt{a}$; find W if $a = 81$.
   m $P = \sqrt{Q} + a$; find P if $Q = 16$ and $a = 5$.
   n $x = \sqrt{y} - 5$; find x if $y = 25$.
   o $C = \dfrac{D}{E}$; find C if $D = 16$ and $E = 2$.
   p $r = \dfrac{s}{t}$; find r if $s = 24$ and $t = 6$.
   q $x = \dfrac{2y}{3}$; find x if $y = 18$.
   r $L = \dfrac{5k}{2}$; find L if $k = 10$.
   s $M = abt$; find M if $a = 4$, $b = 2$ and $t = 0\cdot5$.
   t $A = B^2$; find A if $B = 7$.
   u $Y = Q^2 - 4$; find Y if $Q = 3$.
   v $N = a + pt$; find N if $a = 4\cdot5$, $p = 6$ and $t = 0\cdot5$.
   w $B = t - uv$; find B if $t = 50$, $u = 8$ and $v = 3$.
   x $R = \sqrt{E} + F^2$; find R if $E = 64$ and $F = 3$.

Challenge

Formulae unscramble

Looking at set 1 and the formula $A = 2 + \sqrt{B}$, when $B = 4$ then A is 4. However, that option for A is not on offer. Now when $B = 16$, $A = 2 + \sqrt{16} = 6$, which *is* there. So $A = 6$, $B = 16$ and $A = 2 + \sqrt{B}$ go together.

Find all the other things which go together.

Set 1

$$A = \tfrac{1}{2}B^2$$

$$A = \frac{2B}{3} - 5$$

$B = 16$

$A = 7$

$$A = \frac{2B}{3} + 1$$

$B = 15$

$B = 4$

$A = 8$

$$A = 2 + \sqrt{B}$$

$B = 9$

$A = 6$

$A = 5$

Set 2

$$C = \frac{14 - D}{E}$$

$C = 2$

$$C = \frac{16}{2D + E}$$

$D = 3$ and $E = 2$

$D = 2$ and $E = 4$

$C = 4$

$C = 1$

$C = 3$

$$C = \frac{40}{D - E}$$

$D = 5$ and $E = 3$

$$C = \frac{D - E}{2}$$

$D = 12$ and $E = 2$

3 Formulae

Exercise 3.1

1 The circumference, C cm, of a circle with diameter D cm, is given by the formula:

$$C = \pi \times D$$

Find C (to 1 d.p.) for:

use the π button.

a $D = 12$	**b** $D = 2\cdot6$	**c** $D = 8\cdot4$
d $D = 0\cdot1$	**e** $D = 23$	**f** $D = 125$

2 The area, A cm², of a circle with radius r cm is given by the formula:

$$A = \pi r^2$$

Find A (to 1 d.p.) for:

a $r = 2$	**b** $r = 5\cdot1$	**c** $r = 0\cdot8$
d $r = 12\cdot5$	**e** $r = 1\cdot9$	**f** $r = 0\cdot3$

3 The curved surface area, A cm², of a cylinder is given by the formula:

$$A = 2\pi r h$$

where r cm is the radius and h cm is the height.
Find A (to 1 d. p.) for:

a $r = 3$ and $h = 4$	**b** $r = 5\cdot1$ and $h = 2\cdot6$
c $r = 10\cdot2$ and $h = 3\cdot1$	**d** $r = 8\cdot2$ and $h = 4\cdot3$
e $r = 0\cdot8$ and $h = 1\cdot4$	**f** $r = 9\cdot6$ and $h = 2\cdot9$

4 The volume, V cm³, of a cylinder is given by the formula:

$$V = \pi r^2 h$$

where r cm is the radius and h cm is the height.
Find V (to 1 d.p.) for:

a $r = 5$ and $h = 12$	**b** $r = 8\cdot9$ and $h = 12\cdot6$
c $r = 0\cdot9$ and $h = 2\cdot8$	**d** $r = 12\cdot4$ and $h = 23\cdot6$
e $r = 1\cdot1$ and $h = 4\cdot7$	**f** $r = 82\cdot3$ and $h = 147\cdot9$

5 You will find a variety of practical formulae in this question.
  a Speed (S), distance (D) and time (T) are connected by the formula $D = ST$.
   i Calculate D if $S = 25$ and $T = 5$.
   ii A bus travels at a steady 35 mph (S) for $3\frac{1}{2}$ hours (T).
       How many miles, D, did it travel?
   iii How far does a plane travel if it flies at 220 mph for $1\frac{1}{4}$ hours?
  b The mean weight, W, of three weights, a, b and c, is calculated using the formula:

$$W = \frac{a + b + c}{3}$$

   i Calculate W if $a = 23$, $b = 35$ and $c = 26$.
   ii Three brothers weigh 60·4 kg (a), 65·2 kg (b) and
       63·7 kg (c). What is their mean weight (W)?
   iii What is the mean weight of three elephants weighing
       4500 kg, 5200 kg and 4100 kg?

c In a circuit, the total resistance R of three resistors can be calculated by
$R = R_1 + R_2 + R_3$ where R_1, R_2 and R_3 are the individual resistances.

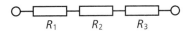

R_1 R_2 R_3

    i Calculate R if $R_1 = 5$, $R_2 = 8$ and $R_3 = 10$.

    ii Three resistors, in series as in the diagram, have resistances 2·5 ohms (R_1),
3·5 ohms (R_2) and 7·6 ohms (R_3). Find their total resistance (R) in ohms.

d The distance to the horizon (D miles) depends on how high up you are (h feet):

$$D = 1·4 \times \sqrt{h}$$

    i Calculate D if $h = 25$.

    ii Iain is looking out of his bedroom window which is 36 feet above sea level (h).
How far is his horizon (D)?

    iii Looking out from 200 feet up a crane, how far is the horizon?

e The aspect ratio of a kite, R, is worked out using the formula:

$$R = \frac{S^2}{A}$$ where S is the span of the kite in centimetres and A is its

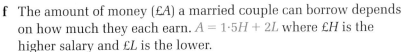

surface area in cm².

    i Calculate R if $S = 50$ and $A = 10\,000$.

    ii Work out the aspect ratio of a kite with span 80 cm (S) and
surface area 20 000 cm² (A).

    iii Does a toy kite with span 10 cm and surface area 100 cm²
have a greater or lesser aspect ratio than a toy kite with span
15 cm and surface area 200 cm²?

f The amount of money ($£A$) a married couple can borrow depends
on how much they each earn. $A = 1·5H + 2L$ where $£H$ is the
higher salary and $£L$ is the lower.

    i Calculate A if $H = 18\,000$ and $L = 10\,000$.

    ii Teresa earns £25 000 (H) and Martin earns £15 000 (L).
What size of loan (A) can they get to buy a house?

    iii Bob and Hannah earn £24 000 and £28 000.
They borrow money for their new house.
How much can they borrow?

6 The length, c cm, of the longest side of a right-angled triangle can
be worked out using the formula:

$$c = \sqrt{(a^2 + b^2)}$$

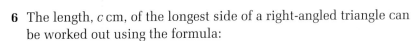

where a cm and b cm are the lengths of the two shorter sides.
Find c (to 1 d.p.) for:

a $a = 4·2$ and $b = 3·9$ **b** $a = 13·2$ and $b = 8·5$

c $a = 6·6$ and $b = 7·2$ **d** $a = 5$ and $b = 5$

e $a = 0·92$ and $b = 1·43$ **f** $a = 13$ and $b = 46$

Challenge

Heart rate and life span

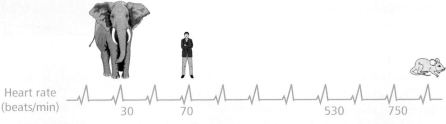

Heart rate
(beats/min)   30   70   530   750

Animal	Heart rate (beats/min)	Life span (years)
Elephant	around 30	55–60 years
Mouse	around 670	2–3 years
Shrew	600–1000	up to 23 months
Rabbit	around 200	up to 9 years

Try creating a graph to show all these facts

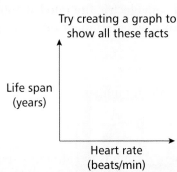

Life span
(years)

Heart rate
(beats/min)

Dr Animaux is trying to develop a formula that calculates the life span, L years, of a mammal in the wild. His latest version is:

$L = 1800 \div h$ where h is the animal's heart rate in beats per minute.

a Check if the formula gives a reasonable result for each of the mammals listed in the table.

b Humans in our country have a life span of 55–75 years.
Our heart rate is 75–85 beats per minute.
Does the formula give a reasonable result?
Why do you think this is?

c The Bowhead Whale has a heart rate of 7 beats per minute.
Its average life span is not known.
In recent years Eskimo hunters have discovered 19th century harpoon heads in some of the whales that they have hunted.
According to the formula is this possible?

---

4 Constructing formulae

Example 1   Make a formula for the total weight, W, on the scales.
The total weight, W kg, is given by the weight of the three weights plus the pan in which they sit:

$W = 3x + p$

Example 2   Write down an expression for the total length of the bookends and books.

The total length, L cm, of the books and bookends is given by:

$$L = 30 + n \times 2$$
or $$L = 30 + 2n$$

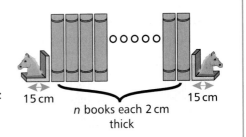

15 cm   15 cm

n books each 2 cm thick

Example 3   Construct a formula for P, the perimeter of the frame.

The perimeter, P m, of this picture is given by:

$$P = 2l + 2b$$
or $$P = 2(l + b)$$

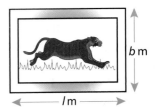

b m

l m

Exercise 4.1

1 Write down a formula for the perimeter, P cm, of each shape.
   (All measurements are in centimetres.)

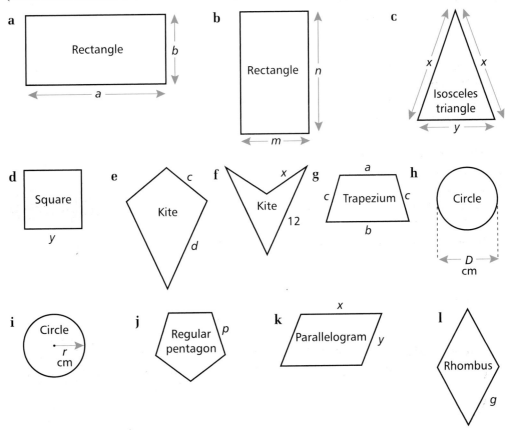

a Rectangle b a

b Rectangle n m

c Isosceles triangle x x y

d Square y

e Kite c d

f Kite x 12

g Trapezium a c c b

h Circle D cm

i Circle r cm

j Regular pentagon p

k Parallelogram x y

l Rhombus g

Exercise 5.1

1 A blank DVD disk costs 25 pence.

a Complete this table:

Cost of DVDs

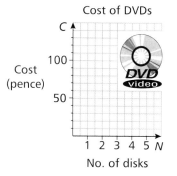

No. of disks (N)	1	2	3	4	5
Cost in pence (C)	25				

Cost (pence)

100

50

b Draw a graph showing the information in the table.

c Complete this formula: $C = \ldots \times N$
where C is the total cost in pence of N disks.

1 2 3 4 5 N

No. of disks

2 Zoe travels on the motorway at a steady 75 km/h.

a Complete this table.

Distance travelled

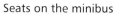

Time in hours (T)	1	2	3	4	5	6
Distance in km (D)	75					

Distance (km)

400

200

b Draw a distance/time graph showing this information.

c Complete this formula: $D = \ldots \times T$
where D is the distance travelled in kilometres in T hours.

1 2 3 4 5 6 T

Time (h)

3 A travel hire company owns a nine-seater minibus.

a Complete this table:

Seats on the minibus

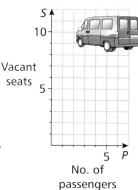

No. of passengers (P)	1	2	3	4	5	6
Vacant seats (S)	8					

Vacant seats

10

5

b Draw a graph showing the information in the table.

c Complete this formula: $S = \ldots - P$
where S is the number of seats left when P are occupied.

5 P

No. of passengers

4 Tickets for the Motocross event cost £1.
A Youth Club has £15 of funds to buy tickets for club members.

a Complete this table:

No. of tickets bought (T)	1	2	3	4	5	6
Money left in fund (£M)	14					

b Draw a graph showing the information in the table, choosing suitable scales.

c Complete this formula: $M = \ldots - T$
where £M is the money left in the funds after T tickets have been bought.

5 There are 10 mm in 1 cm.
   a Complete this table:
   b Draw a 'conversion graph' showing the information in the table.

No. of mm (*M*)	10	20	30	40	50
No. of cm (*C*)					

   c Complete this formula: $C =$
   where *C* is the number of centimetres equal to *M* millimetres.

6 The area of a stone slab is 1·5 m².
   a Complete the table.
   b Draw a graph showing the information in the table.

No. of slabs (*S*)	1	2	3	4	5	6
Total area (*A* m²)						

   c Complete this formula: $A = ... \times S$
   where *A* m² is the total area of *S* slabs.

Exercise 5.2

1 Alex was given an exchange rate of 1 euro = 70 pence.
   a Make a table of values showing number of euro (*E*) and number of pence (*P*) with *E* = 1, 2, 3, 4 and 5.
   b Make a formula to find *P* if you know *E*.
   c Draw a graph showing all this information.

2 Corrie needs three packets of food each week.
   a Make a table showing the number of weeks (*W*) and the number of packets (*P*) for *W* = 1, 2, 3, 4, 5 and 6.
   b Make a formula to find *P* if you know *W*.
   c Construct a graph to show this information.

3 There are 100 cm in 1 metre.
   a Make a table of values for the number of centimetres (*C*) and the corresponding number of metres (*M*). Use *C* = 100, 200, 300, 400 and 500.
   b Make a formula for *M* if you are given *C*.
   c Draw a graph for this situation.

4 Here are the graphs of three situations. In each case:
   i use the five highlighted points on the graph to make a table of values
   ii write down a formula connecting the two quantities.

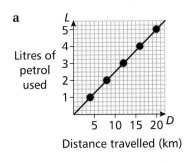

a Litres of petrol used / Distance travelled (km)

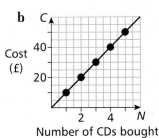

b Cost (£) / Number of CDs bought

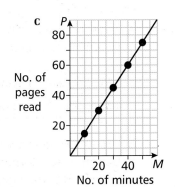

c No. of pages read / No. of minutes

5 A factory makes plastic discs of various sizes. The volume, V cm³, of plastic needed for a disc is given by the formula: $V = 0.6 \times r^2$ where r is the radius of the disc in centimetres.

Radius (r cm)	1	2	3	4	5
Volume (V cm³)					

a Complete the table.

b Draw a graph showing this information.

c Is this graph different from the other graphs that you have drawn so far?
What is different in the formula?

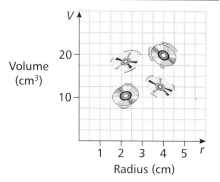

Volume (cm³) — Radius (cm)

Challenge

A triangular prism has:
6 vertices or corners ($V = 6$)
5 faces or surfaces ($F = 5$)
9 edges ($E = 9$).

Solid	V	F	E
Triangular prism	6	5	9

a Use the solids shown below, or other solids in your classroom, to complete more rows of the table.

b Discover a formula that calculates E if you are given the values of V and F.

    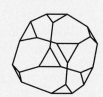

Tetrahedron   Octahedron   Cube   Truncated tetrahedron   Truncated cube

---

6　Formulae and sequences

A formula can be used to describe a sequence of numbers.

Example

Write down the first four terms of the sequence for which the nth term $= 4n - 3$.

$n = 1$　1st term $= 4 \times 1 - 3 = 1$　　$n = 2$　2nd term $= 4 \times 2 - 3 = 5$

$n = 3$　3rd term $= 4 \times 3 - 3 = 9$　　$n = 4$　4th term $= 4 \times 4 - 3 = 13$

Note 1:　Here is the same information in a table.
See how the terms of the sequence go up in *fours* – like the multiples of 4.

n	1	2	3	4
$4n - 3$	1	5	9	13

Note 2:　The nth term formula can be used to find other terms in the sequence.
Using $n = 34$:　　34th term $= 4 \times 34 - 3 = 133$
Using $n = 100$:　　100th term $= 4 \times 100 - 3 = 397$

Exercise 6.1

1 Copy and complete these tables. In each case look at the step between one term and the next and say which multiples this reminds you of.

a

n	1	2	3	4		12
$3n - 1$						

b

n	1	2	3	4		15
$5n - 2$						

c

n	1	2	3	4		13
$2n + 4$						

d

n	1	2	3	4		23
$4n + 1$						

e

n	1	2	3	4		18
$6n - 5$						

f

n	1	2	3	4		31
$5n - 1$						

g

n	1	2	3	4		27
$3n + 2$						

h

n	1	2	3	4		19
$7n - 1$						

2 For each nth term formula:

    i   list the first five terms of the sequence

    ii calculate the 15th and 27th terms

    iii say which multiples the sequence behaves like.

a nth term $= 7n + 5$ **b** nth term $= 6n + 9$ **c** nth term $= 7n - 2$

d nth term $= 2n - 1$ **e** nth term $= 3n + 7$ **f** nth term $= 4n - 1$

g nth term $= 8n + 2$ **h** nth term $= 9n - 5$ **i** nth term $= 11n - 2$

j nth term $= 5n + 1$ **k** nth term $= 12n - 5$ **l** nth term $= 6n - 1$

3 Complete the missing entries in these tables.

a

n	1	2	3	4	5
(Multiples of 5) $5n$					
$5n - 3$					
$5n + 2$					

b

n	1	2	3	4	5
(Multiples of 6) $6n$					
$6n + 1$					
$6n - 2$					

c

n	1	2	3	4	5
(Multiples of 7) $7n$					
$7n + 3$					
$7n - 4$					

d

n	1	2	3	4	5
(Multiples of 4) $4n$					
$4n - 2$					
$4n + 3$					

4 Complete the missing nth term expression.

a

n	1	2	3	4
$8n$	8	16	24	32
?	9	17	25	33

b

n	1	2	3	4
$6n$	6	12	18	24
?	2	8	14	20

c

n	1	2	3	4
$10n$	10	20	30	40
?	7	17	27	37

d

n	1	2	3	4
$5n$	5	10	15	20
?	8	13	18	23

e

n	1	2	3	4
$11n$	11	22	33	44
?	6	17	28	39

f

n	1	2	3	4
$7n$	7	14	21	28
?	4	11	18	25

5 Find the nth term formula for these sequences:

a 7, 14, 21, 28, ...

b 5, 10, 15, 20, ...

c 8, 16, 24, 32, ...

d 12, 24, 36, 48, ...

e 2, 4, 6, 8, 10, ...

f 9, 18, 27, 36, ...

g 17, 34, 51, 68, ...

h 1, 2, 3, 4, ...

i 20, 40, 60, 80, ...

Challenge

Find the formula for the number of coins (C) in Pattern n.

Pattern 1   Pattern 2   Pattern 3   Pattern 4

7 Finding the nth term formula

Example　**a** Find the formula for the nth term of the sequence 1, 6, 11, 16, ...
　　　　　b Use your formula to find the 50th term.

a *Step 1*　Look at the step between one term and the next.
　　　　　It is a constant step of 5.

　Step 2　Compare your sequence with an appropriate set of multiples.
　　　　　In this case the multiples of 5.

　Step 3　Find the 'adjustment' that changes the multiples into the sequence.
　　　　　In this case 'subtract 4'.

　Step 4　nth term = (*step size*) $\times n$ + *adjustment*
　　　　　nth term $= 5n - 4$

b 50th term $= 5 \times 50 - 4 = 246$

Exercise 7.1

1 Find the *n*th term formula for each of the following sequences.

a 3, 5, 7, 9, ...
b 7, 10, 13, 16, ...
c 3, 9, 15, 21, ...
d 7, 15, 23, 31, ...
e 1, 8, 15, 22, ...
f 7, 9, 11, 13, ...
g 6, 10, 14, 18, ...
h 5, 13, 21, 29, ...
i 3, 13, 23, 33, ...
j 11, 17, 23, 29, ...
k 5, 7, 9, 11, ...
l 1, 12, 23, 34, ...
m 14, 17, 20, 23, ...
n 2, 9, 16, 23, ...
o 8, 17, 26, 35, ...
p 11, 18, 25, 32, ...
q 2, 17, 32, 47, ...
r 5, 16, 27, 38, ...

2 For these sequences: **i** find the *n*th term formula
ii use this formula to find the indicated term.

a 4, 6, 8, 10, ... the 14th term
b 8, 11, 14, 17, ... the 21st term
c 1, 4, 7, 10, ... the 19th term
d 8, 14, 20, 26, ... the 25th term
e 7, 16, 25, 34, ... the 20th term
f 8, 15, 22, 29, ... the 40th term
g 0, 2, 4, 6, ... the 33rd term
h 11, 21, 31, 41, ... the 51st term
i 3, 11, 19, 27, ... the 58th term
j 13, 24, 35, 46, ... the 17th term
k 11, 20, 29, 38, ... the 100th term
l 12, 25, 38, 51, ... the 13th term

Challenge

There are four sequences and four terms. Which term can be found in which sequence?

Sequence A: 2, 7, 12, 17, ...   Term e: 1000
Sequence B: 9, 17, 25, 33, ...   Term f: 1001
Sequence C: 13, 24, 35, 46, ...   Term g: 1002
Sequence D: 12, 25, 38, 51, ...   Term h: 1003

8 Problem solving

Example   Below is a sequence of matchstick designs.
The designs continue to build up in the same way.
How many matchsticks are needed for Design 47?

  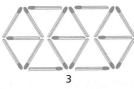 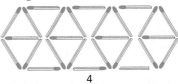

| 1 | 2 | 3 | 4 |

Step 1   Make a table.

Design number (*n*)	1	2	3	4
No. of matches (*M*)	5	12	19	26

Step 2   Find a formula for the *n*th term ... step size 7, adjustment –2
... *n*th term = $7n - 2$

Step 3   Check the formula 'works' for the 5th term, i.e. 33.
5th term = $7 \times 5 - 2 = 33$ ✓

Step 4   Use the formula to help you answer the question.
Design 47: 47th term = $7 \times 47 - 2 = 327$.   327 matches are needed.

Exercise 8.1

1 Here is another pattern building up.

1 square   2 squares   3 squares

a Copy and complete the table.
b Write down a formula for calculating M
    when you know n.
c Check the formula for $n = 4$.
d Use the formula to help you find the number of matches needed to make
    45 squares.

No. of squares (n)	1	2	3	4
No. of matches (M)	4			

2 Look at this matchstick pattern.

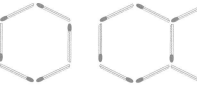

1 hexagon   2 hexagons   3 hexagons

a Copy and complete the table.
b Write down a formula for calculating M
    when you know n.
c Check the formula for $n = 4$.
d Use the formula to help you find the number of matches needed to make
    33 hexagons.

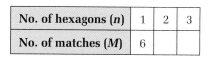

No. of hexagons (n)	1	2	3
No. of matches (M)	6		

3 Here is a coin pattern.

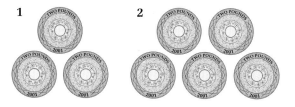
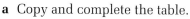

a Copy and complete the table.
b Write down the formula for calculating C
    when you know n.
c Check the formula for $n = 4$.
d Use the formula to find the number of coins needed to make the 17th design.

Design number (n)	1	2	3
No. of coins (C)			

4 Each model below is made from construction strips like this:

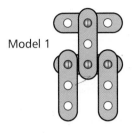

Model 1

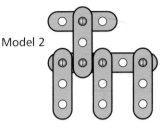

Model 2

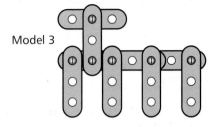

Model 3

    a Copy and complete the table.
    b Write down the formula for calculating S
       when you know m.
    c Check the formula for $m = 4$.
    d Iain is building Model 56. How many strips does he need?
    e Jill is building Model 8 and Model 16. How many strips does she need in total?

Model number (m)	1	2	3
No. of strips (S)			

Challenge

Model 1 in question **4** has 11 holes ($H = 11$).
Can you find a formula for calculating H if you know the Model number m?
How many holes are there in Model 100?

Exercise 8.2

1 Scaffolding frames come in various lengths.
They are built from tubes bolted together by couplers.
Here are two tubes bolted together by one coupler.

1 section
8 couplers
12 tubes

2 section
12 couplers
20 tubes

    a Copy and complete the table.
    b Find a formula for calculating:
       i C if you know n
       ii T if you know n.
    c A building site requires three frames each
       with 21 sections.
       How many tubes and couplers are required?

No. of sections (n)	1	2	3	4
No. of couplers (C)	8			
No. of tubes (T)	12			

2 Building bridges.

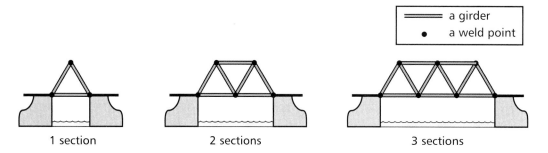

1 section　　　　　　　2 sections　　　　　　　3 sections

a Complete this table for *one side* of the bridge shown.

No. of sections (*n*)	1	2	3	4	5
No. of weld points (*W*)	3				
No. of girders (*G*)	3				

b Find formulae for calculating:

　i *W* if you know *n*

　ii *G* if you know *n*.

c Find the number of weld points and girders required for one side of a 12-section bridge of this type.

3 a Complete a table for *one side* of this type of bridge showing the number of weld points (*W*) and girders (*G*) required.

The number of sections (*n*) shown in your table should be from 1 to 5.

Note: a 1-section bridge still needs two end supports.

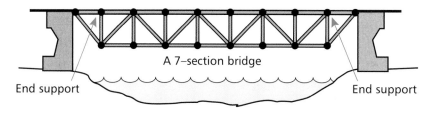

A 7–section bridge

End support　　　　　　　　　　　　　　　　　End support

b Find formulae for calculating *W* and *G* from *n*.

c Find *W* and *G* in the case of a 20-section bridge of this type.

◄◄ **RECAP**

A **formula** allows you to calculate the value of one quantity if you know the values of the other quantities on which it depends.

For example: $A = b^2 - c$ is a formula for A. It expresses A in terms of b and c.
If $b = 5$ and $c = 3$, then $A = 5^2 - 3 = 25 - 3 = 22$.

Here are some formulae you should know.

The circle: $C = \pi D$ $C = 2\pi r$ $A = \pi r^2$
    where C = circumference; D = diameter; r = radius; A = area; $\pi \approx 3\cdot14$.

The cylinder: $A = 2\pi rh$ $V = 2\pi r^2 h$
    where A = area of the curved surface; r = radius; h = height; V = volume.

The right-angled triangle: $A = \frac{1}{2}ab$ $c^2 = a^2 + b^2$
    where A = area; c = hypotenuse; a and b are the shorter sides.

The triangular prism: $V = Ah$
    where A = area of the triangular end; h = distance between the ends.

Values calculated using a formula can be displayed in a **table** or shown on a **graph**.

Example

$C = 6N$

N	1	2	3	4
C	6	12	18	24

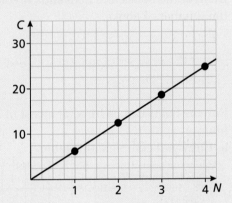

A formula can be used to describe a **sequence** of numbers.
For example the formula nth term $= 4n - 3$ gives:
    1st term = 1 (use $n = 1$), 2nd term = 5, 3rd term = 9, etc.

To find the **nth term formula** of a sequence, compare the terms of the sequence with a suitable set of multiples, e.g. the multiples of the step size between the terms.

1 If $x = 5$ and $y = 7$ calculate:

   a $5x$ **b** $y - 4$ **c** $3x + 5$ **d** $y - x$ **e** $20 - 2y$ **f** $6x - 4y$

   g xy **h** x^2 **i** $3xy$ **j** $2y^2$ **k** $xy - y$ **l** $10y - xy$

2 **a** $R = \sqrt{M} + n$; find R if $M = 36$ and $n = 2$.

   b $A = \dfrac{5B}{2}$; find A if $B = 6$.

   c $L = S^2 - 4$; find L if $S = 9$.

   d $W = a - bc$; find W if $a = 35$, $b = 3$ and $c = 9$.

3 The amount a couple may borrow from a building society to buy a house depends on their income. The building society uses the formula:

$$A = 2 \cdot 5H + 1 \cdot 5L$$

where £H is the higher income and £L is the lower income.
Kevin earns £16 500 and his wife Katie earns £18 500.
Calculate the amount they, as a couple, can borrow.

4 Find a formula that calculates the total length, L cm, of the books and bookends if you know m, the number of books.

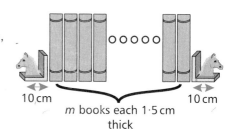

10 cm m books each 1·5 cm thick   10 cm

5 Rowing boats can be hired at a cost of £6 per hour.

   a Copy and complete this table.

No. of hours (H)	1	2	3	4	5	6
Cost (£C)						

   b Write down the formula for calculating C if you know H.

   c Draw a graph using the information in the table. Choose suitable scales.

6 The terms of a sequence are given by nth term $= 7n + 3$.

   a List the first five terms of the sequence.   **b** Calculate the 46th term.

7 **a** Make a table of values for the first four designs.

    1    2    3

   b Write down the formula for calculating M when you know n.

   c Check the formula for $n = 5$.

   d Use the formula to find the number of matches needed to make design number 80.

6 Equations and inequations

Equations
Parking ticket
£50 fine

$F = 50$

Inequations
Speed limit
30 mph

$S \leqslant 30$

1 Review

Reminder When multiplying out brackets, each term inside the bracket is multiplied by the term outside.

Example $4(x - 5)$ ... 4 lots of $x - 5$ ... $x - 5 + x - 5 + x - 5 + x - 5$
$= 4x - 20$ ... 4 lots of x subtract 4 lots of 5

◀◀ **Exercise 1.1**

1 If $a = 5$ and $b = 2$ find the value of:
  a $a + b$ **b** $3a$ **c** $5b$ **d** $a - b$
  e $a + 2b$ **f** $a - 2b$ **g** $4a + 3b$ **h** $5a - 7b$

2 If $m = 3$ and $n = 4$ find the value of:
  a $2(m + 1)$ **b** $3(n - 2)$ **c** $5(m + n)$ **d** $4(n - m)$
  e $3(6 - m)$ **f** $7(6 - n)$ **g** $m(m + 2)$ **h** $n(n - 1)$

3 Multiply out the brackets:
  a $2(x + 1)$ **b** $5(y - 2)$ **c** $8(2 - x)$ **d** $3(10 - y)$
  e $7(2k + 3)$ **f** $10(5 + 3a)$ **g** $6(4 - 3b)$ **h** $9(2m - 3n)$

4 Multiply out the brackets and simplify:
  a $2(y + 3) + 7$ **b** $8 + 2(x - 3)$ **c** $3(m + 2) + 2m$
  d $4(n - 2) + n$ **e** $3k + 2(8 - k)$ **f** $5c + 3(2 + c)$

5 Find simplified expressions for   **i** the perimeter   **ii** the area
of each rectangle. All lengths are in centimetres.

a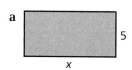
5

x

b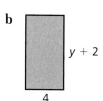
$y + 2$

4

c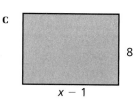
8

$x - 1$

d
x

$3x$

e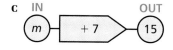
n

$n + 1$

6 Solve these equations.
Check your solutions by substituting the value back into the equation.

a $m + 3 = 15$ **b** $n - 3 = 8$ **c** $12 - x = 2$ **d** $8 - k = 5$
e $14 + y = 25$ **f** $7 = 10 - x$ **g** $20 = y + 7$ **h** $4x = 8$
i $16 = 2y$ **j** $3x = 6$ **k** $2x = 1$ **l** $2x = 3$

7 Make an equation and solve it for each of these.

a    **b** IN   OUT   **c** IN   OUT

8 Solve these equations. Remember to check your solutions.

a $6x - 3 = 27$ **b** $5n + 4 = 19$ **c** $31 = 5y + 1$ **d** $23 = 7 + 4k$
e $14 = 9y - 4$ **f** $3 + 6m = 33$ **g** $8f - 10 = 6$ **h** $14 + 3x = 20$

9 Make and solve an equation for each of these.

a 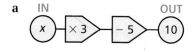   **b**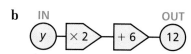

10 i Remove the brackets.   **ii** Solve the equation.

a $3(x - 2) = 21$ **b** $4(y + 3) = 36$ **c** $8(2 + m) = 64$
d $2(4 + n) = 18$ **e** $7(k - 9) = 42$ **f** $9(x + 3) = 45$

11 Say whether each inequation is true or false.

a $5 > 2$ **b** $3 \leqslant 3$ **c** $2 < 1$ **d** $2 > 0$
e $7 \geqslant 3$ **f** $-3 < 2$ **g** $3 > -4$ **h** $-2 < -1$

12 Solve each inequation, choosing from the numbers $\{1, 2, 3, 4, 5, 6\}$.

a $x < 3$ **b** $x \geqslant 4$ **c** $x \leqslant 2$ **d** $x > 5$

13 Describe each situation using an inequation.

a

b

c

d

e

f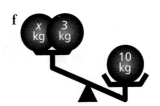

---

2 The cover-up

Reminder If the letter appears in one place only, then you can cover up the term containing it.

Example 1 Solve $3x - 6 = 9$.

$3x - 6 = 9$

$\Rightarrow \qquad 3x = 15$

$\Rightarrow \qquad x = 5$

(Check: $3x - 6 = 3 \times 5 - 6 = 15 - 6 = 9$)

> ▭ $- 6 = 9$
> **3x must be 15**

> 3▭ $= 15$
> **x must be 5**

Example 2 Solve $26 - 4x = 18$.

$26 - 4x = 18$

$\Rightarrow \qquad 4x = 8$

$\Rightarrow \qquad x = 2$

(Check: $26 - 4x = 26 - 4 \times 2 = 26 - 8 = 18$)

> $26 -$ ▭ $= 18$
> **4x must be 8**

> 4▭ $= 8$
> **x must be 2**

Example 3 Solve $3(x + 2) = 18$.

$3(x + 2) = 18$

$\Rightarrow \qquad x + 2 = 6$

$\Rightarrow \qquad x = 4$

(Check: $3(x + 2) = 3 \times (4 + 2) = 3 \times 6 = 18$)

... 3 lots of something make 18

> $3($▭$) = 18$
> **x + 2 must be 6**

Exercise 2.2

1 Solve each equation. (First simplify the left-hand side of the equation.)

    a $4x + x + 12 = 22$ **b** $2y + 18 + 3y = 38$

    c $5m - m - 8 = 12$ **d** $6a - 5 - 4a = 9$

    e $6 + 5x + 3x = 22$ **f** $2t - 12 + 6t = 28$

    g $9w - 2w + 5 = 61$ **h** $20 + 3k - k = 120$

    i $40 + 9x + x = 180$ **j** $5x + 20 + 3x = 180$

    k $35 + 2x + 15 = 180$ **l** $x + 60 + 2x - 30 = 180$

2 For each triangle:

    i write an equation (remember the sum of the angles of a triangle is $180°$)

    ii solve the equation

    iii find the sizes of the unknown angles.

a
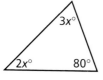

b
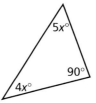

c
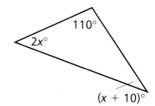

d
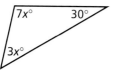

e
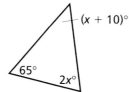

f
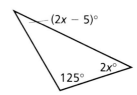

g
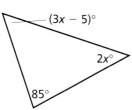

h

i
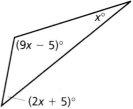

3 Solve these equations. Always check your solutions.

    a $2(2x + 3) = 10$ **b** $3(3x - 2) = 12$

    c $16 = 8(4x - 6)$ **d** $10 = 5(3x - 1)$

    e $4(3x + 3) = 36$ **f** $7(2x - 1) = 63$

    g $30 = 3(1 + 3x)$ **h** $7(4x - 12) = 56$

    i $28 = 4(5x - 3)$ **j** $6(2x - 13) = 30$

    k $27 = 3(6x - 21)$ **l** $6(3x - 8) = 6$

4 The picture shows three display screens.
They all meet in the middle.
Each diagram below shows a different arrangement of the
screens.
In each case:
  i form an equation (remember the angles round a point
     add up to 360°)
  ii solve it to find the three angles.

a

$3x°$ $(x + 20)°$

$(5x - 20)°$

b $(5x - 30)°$

$4x°$ $4x°$

c $(x + 5)°$ $2x°$

$(5x - 5)°$

d

$2x°$

$x°$

$(10x - 30)°$

e $(x + 10)°$ $9x°$

$4x°$

f $10x°$

$(5x - 5)°$

$(5x + 25)°$

5 For each framed picture:
  i write an equation   **ii** solve it   **iii** give the dimensions of the picture.
  (All sizes are in centimetres.)

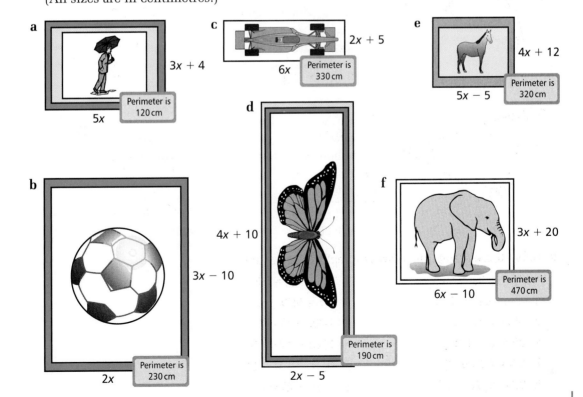

a

$3x + 4$

Perimeter is
120 cm

$5x$

c

$2x + 5$

$6x$ Perimeter is
330 cm

e

$4x + 12$

Perimeter is
320 cm

$5x - 5$

b

$4x + 10$

$3x - 10$

Perimeter is
230 cm

$2x$

d

Perimeter is
190 cm

$2x - 5$

f

$3x + 20$

Perimeter is
470 cm

$6x - 10$

Challenge

Copy and complete this cross-number puzzle.

Across

1 $2(3x - 6) = 60$

3 $171 = 3(2x + 7)$

4 $2x - 10 + x + 15 = 74$

6 $32 = 100 - 2x$

7 $6(5x - 15) = 330$

9 $224 = x + 20 + 3x$

11 $2(40 - x) = 16$

12 $2x + 8x - 40 = 600$

14 $152 = 2(8x - 4)$

15 $10 = 5(35 - x)$

Down

1 $5(4x + 8) = 340$

2 $x - 5 + 2x + 35 = 96$

3 $160 = 2(8 + 3x)$

5 $45 = 5(40 - x)$

6 $117 = 4x - x + 12$

8 $3(85 - 2x) = 3$

10 $2(9x - 100) = 88$

11 $5x + 12 - 3x + 8 = 80$

13 $0 = 10(43 - x)$

14 $2(15 - x) = 4$

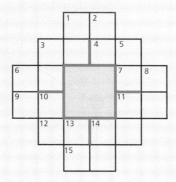

3 Balancing again

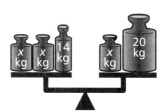

You can add, subtract, multiply or divide both sides of an equation by any amount and the two sides will remain equal.

The same action must be done to both sides to maintain the balance.

Example 1 Solve $2x + 14 = x + 20$.

$$2x + 14 = x + 20$$

$\Rightarrow \quad 2x + 14 - x = x + 20 - x$ (Action: subtract x from both sides)

$\Rightarrow \quad\quad\quad x + 14 = 20$

$\Rightarrow \quad x + 14 - 14 = 20 - 14$ (Action: subtract 14 from both sides)

$\Rightarrow \quad\quad\quad\quad x = 6$

Check

Left-hand side: $2x + 14 = 2 \times 6 + 14 = 12 + 14 = 26$

Right-hand side: $x + 20 = 6 + 20 = 26$

The two sides are equal.

Example 2   Solve $5x - 2 = 2x + 13$.

$$5x - 2 = 2x + 13$$

$\Rightarrow \quad 5x - 2 + 2 = 2x + 13 + 2$ (Action: add 2 to both sides)

$\Rightarrow \quad\quad\quad 5x = 2x + 15$

$\Rightarrow \quad\quad 5x - 2x = 2x + 15 - 2x$ (Action: subtract 2x from both sides)

$\Rightarrow \quad\quad\quad 3x = 15$

$\Rightarrow \quad\quad 3x \div 3 = 15 \div 3$ (Action: divide both sides by 3)

$\Rightarrow \quad\quad\quad x = 5$

Check

Left-hand side: $5x - 2 = 5 \times 5 - 2 = 25 - 2 = 23$

Right-hand side: $2x + 13 = 2 \times 5 + 13 = 10 + 13 = 23$

The two sides are equal.

Exercise 3.1

1 Solve these equations by first performing the suggested action on both sides.

   a $3y = y + 8$ (subtract y from both sides)

   b $7x = 3x + 4$ (subtract $3x$ from both sides)

   c $5m = 2m + 12$ (remove $2m$ from both sides)

   d $6y = 14 - y$ (add y to both sides)

   e $5k = 16 - 3k$ (add $3k$ to both sides)

   f $8x = 15 - 2x$ (add $2x$ to both sides)

2 Solve these equations.

   a $6x = 5x + 8$ **b** $4k = 2k + 10$ **c** $7m = m + 6$

   d $3y = 2y + 1$ **e** $6w = w + 15$ **f** $9n = 3n + 24$

   g $5a = 18 - a$ **h** $8x = 30 - 2x$ **i** $5y = y + 16$

   j $n = 3 - n$ **k** $6y = 2y + 36$ **l** $7c = 32 - c$

   m $8x = 27 - x$ **n** $4h = 42 - 2h$ **o** $9y = 50 - y$

   p $12y = 33 + y$ **q** $11x = 30 - 4x$ **r** $12w = 100 + 2w$

3 The straws in each pair are equal in length. All measurements are in centimetres.

   For each pair:

   i write an equation   **ii** solve the equation   **iii** find the length of a straw.

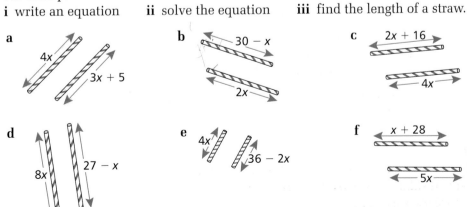

4 Solve these equations by performing the two actions.

	Equation	Action 1	Action 2
a	$3x - 4 = x + 6$	add 4 to both sides	take x from both sides
b	$5y + 4 = 2y + 10$	take 4 from both sides	take $2y$ from both sides
c	$3m - 1 = 11 - m$	add 1 to both sides	add m to both sides
d	$2 + 6n = 23 - n$	take 2 from both sides	add n to both sides
e	$9x - 3 = 4x + 27$	add 3 to both sides	take $4x$ from both sides
f	$y + 1 = 7 - y$	take 1 from both sides	add y to both sides

5 Solve these equations:

a $9a + 3 = 2a + 17$
b $4 + 5k = 3k + 14$
c $5 + 2y = 35 - 3y$
d $13w - 12 = 7w + 30$
e $8x + 4 = 5x + 28$
f $6 + 6x = 2x + 42$
g $7 + 9m = 39 + m$
h $15c - 15 = 6c + 12$
i $10w + 7 = 5w + 27$
j $13 + 20r = 11r + 76$
k $24f - 14 = 20f - 2$
l $15n + 9 = 13n + 25$
m $11h - 12 = 5h + 18$
n $21 + 13x = 27 + 10x$
o $37 + 2c = 100 - 5c$

Challenge

Copy and complete this cross-number puzzle.

Across

1 $3x - 1 = x + 49$
3 $2x + 7 = 70 - x$
5 $48 + 7x = x + 150$
6 $8x - 32 = 32 + 4x$
7 $2x - 12 = 24 - x$
9 $19 + x = 181 - x$
11 $7x + 8 = 200 + x$
13 $51 + 6x = 351 - 4x$
14 $4x - 19 = 21 + 3x$
15 $10x - 89 = x + 100$

Down

1 $4x + 5 = 140 - x$
2 $6x - 57 = 4x + 45$
3 $22 + 5x = 2x + 100$
4 $4x - 33 = 66 - 5x$
5 $6 + 3x = 2x + 24$
8 $3x - 17 = 103 - 3x$
10 $15 + 8x = 3x + 85$
11 $11x - 65 = 9x - 5$
12 $6 + 12x = 72 + 9x$
13 $5x - 70 = 3x - 8$

Example 3 Solve $3x = 4$.

$$3x = 4$$

$$\Rightarrow \quad \frac{3x}{3} = \frac{4}{3}$$

(dividing both sides by 3)

$$\Rightarrow \quad x = \frac{4}{3} = 1\tfrac{1}{3}$$

Example 4 Solve $5 = 2m$.

$$5 = 2m$$

$$\Rightarrow \quad \frac{5}{2} = \frac{2m}{2}$$

(dividing both sides by 2)

$$\Rightarrow \quad \frac{5}{2} = m$$

$$\Rightarrow \quad m = \frac{5}{2} = 2\tfrac{1}{2}$$

Exercise 3.2

1 Solve these equations by dividing both sides by a suitable number.

a $2y = 3$ **b** $3n = 5$

c $7 = 2x$ **d** $2 = 3x$

e $2k = 1$ **f** $3w = 7$

g $5x = 2$ **h** $7a = 1$

i $2 = 6n$ **j** $4y = 2$

k $6c = 3$ **l** $10x = 5$

m $14y = 7$ **n** $2x = 11$

o $8y = 2$ **p** $9m = 6$

2 Solve these equations. (Multiply out the brackets first.)

a $4(x - 2) = 2(x + 4)$ **b** $2(2x - 1) = 3(x + 1)$

c $2(3x + 1) = 5(x + 1)$ **d** $8(x - 3) = 4(x - 1)$

e $3(2x + 1) = 5(x + 1)$ **f** $3(2x + 1) = 7(2x - 3)$

g $4(2x - 3) = 2(3x - 1)$ **h** $10(x - 4) = 5(x - 1)$

i $8(x - 2) = 2(2x + 4)$ **j** $4(5x + 2) = 6(5x - 2)$

k $6(12 - x) = 3(3x + 4)$ **l** $5(17 - x) = 2(3x + 4)$

3 Each pair of rectangles are of equal area. All lengths are in centimetres.

i   Form an equation.

ii Solve it.

iii Find the dimensions of each rectangle.

a

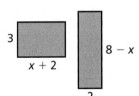

b

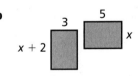

c

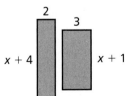

d

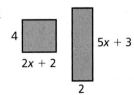

e

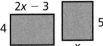

f

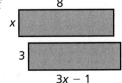

4 In each diagram there are two branches. Both branches give the same result. Find the unknown letter.

a

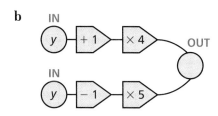

(Hint: $2(x + 3) = 4(x - 2)$)

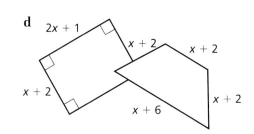

b

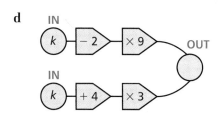

c

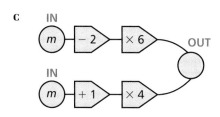

d

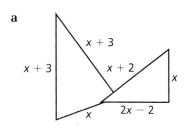

e

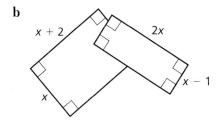

5 The shapes in each pair have the same perimeter. In each case:
  i form an equation
  ii solve it
  iii find the length of each side.

All measurements are in centimetres.

a

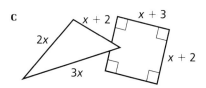

b

c

d

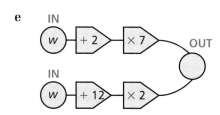

Challenge

For each clue: **i** solve the equation
ii use the solution to find the value of the expression in green.

Across

1 $3(x + 5) = 5x + 19 - 4x$
$25(11 - 4x)$

3 $8(5 - x) = 3x - 4$
$5(3x - 8)$

4 $8 + 3(x + 4) = 32 - x$
$18x + 2$

6 $5(9 + 2x) = 3(4x + 3)$
$15(21 - x)$

8 $2 + 3(12 - x) = 2(x - 6)$
$8(x + 1) + 1$

9 $13x + 1 = 5(3 + 2x) + x$
$9(24 - 2x)$

10 $6(10 - x) = 3(3x - 5)$
$9(2x - 1)$

12 $8 + 2(x - 3) = 4(x - 5)$
$3(20 - x)$

14 $3(2x + 1) = 11(8 - x)$
$2(7x - 4)$

15 $15 + 3(x + 2) = 7(x - 1)$
$x(2x - 7)$

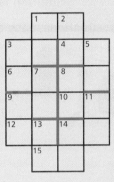

Down

1 $5x + 8 - 3x = 8(6 - x)$
$2(9x - 1)$

2 $3(32 - 2x) = x - 3 + 2x$
$x(16 - x)$

3 $3(2x + 5) = 5(x + 4) + 1$
$8(x - 3)$

5 $8 + 2(12 - x) = 6(x - 4)$
$3(2 + 3x)$

7 $4(2x - 3) = 5(x + 3)$
$25(11 - x)$

8 $3(x + 2) = 11(26 - x)$
$8(x - 9)$

9 $7x + 2 - 3x = 7(x - 1)$
$23(x + 1)$

11 $9(12 - 2x) = 6(x + 2)$
$2(x + 2)$

13 $3(15 - x) = 2(x - 10)$
$2(3x - 2)$

14 $12 + 5(x - 3) = 8(x - 3)$
$3(4x - 5)$

4 Inequations

Reminder   Here are some signs and their meaning.
Note that the arrow always points to the smaller side.

Statement	Meaning	Solution: choosing from {0, 1, 2, 3, 4, 5, 6}
$x < 3$	x is less than 3	0, 1, 2
$x \leqslant 3$	x is less than or equal to 3	0, 1, 2, 3
$x = 3$	x equals 3	3
$x \geqslant 3$	x is greater than or equal to 3	3, 4, 5, 6
$x > 3$	x is greater than 3	4, 5, 6

Example 1 Choosing from {3, 4, 5, 6, 7}, solve:

a $x + 3 \leqslant 8$ **b** $9 > 20 - 2x$

Try $x = 3$	$3 + 3 \leqslant 8$ is true	✓	Try $x = 3$	$9 > 20 - 6$ is false	✗
Try $x = 4$	$4 + 3 \leqslant 8$ is true	✓	Try $x = 4$	$9 > 20 - 8$ is false	✗
Try $x = 5$	$5 + 3 \leqslant 8$ is true	✓	Try $x = 5$	$9 > 20 - 10$ is false	✗
Try $x = 6$	$6 + 3 \leqslant 8$ is false	✗	Try $x = 6$	$9 > 20 - 12$ is true	✓
Try $x = 7$	$7 + 3 \leqslant 8$ is false	✗	Try $x = 7$	$9 > 20 - 14$ is true	✓

Solution is $x = 3$, 4 or 5. Solution is $x = 6$ or 7.

Example 2 Describe each of these situations using an inequation.

a

b

c

'I've got £y.
I don't have
enough.'

Inequation: $S \leqslant 30$ Inequation: $x + 6 > 15$ Inequation: $y < 2 \cdot 5$

Exercise 4.1

1 Solve these inequations, choosing solutions from {1, 2, 3, 4, 5}.

a $x > 2$ **b** $x \geqslant 4$ **c** $x \leqslant 2$ **d** $2 < x$
e $5 > x$ **f** $3 \geqslant x$ **g** $x < 5$ **h** $2 \leqslant x$

2 For each picture:
   i write an inequation to describe the situation
   ii find all the possible values for the weight, choosing from {2, 4, 6, 8, 10}

a

b

c

d

e

f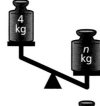

g

h

i

3 Solve these inequations, choosing solutions from {5, 6, 7, 8, 9, 10}.

a $x + 2 > 10$ **b** $x - 6 \geqslant 2$ **c** $x - 1 < 8$ **d** $x + 3 \leqslant 12$

e $13 < x + 4$ **f** $10 - x < 2$ **g** $4 > x - 3$ **h** $10 \geqslant x + 4$

i $1 > 8 - x$ **j** $6 \leqslant x - 1$ **k** $2x \geqslant 15$ **l** $3x \leqslant 24$

4 Describe each situation using an inequation.

a

The maximum crowd capacity, C, is 8500.

b

I parked for P hours and received a parking ticket.

c

I only have £Y and cannot afford this monitor.

d

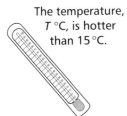

The temperature, T °C, is hotter than 15 °C.

e

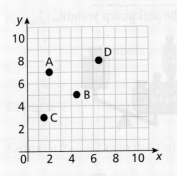

Robert's score, S, beat his previous best score of 75.

(Lower scores are better.)

f All sale goods are under £5.

This book costs £C in the sale.

Challenge

A positive point sort

Here are eight inequations: $x \leqslant 2$; $x < 2$; $x > 4$; $x > 5$; $y \leqslant 5$; $y > 7$; $y < 5$; $y > 5$.

There is only one way of placing these inequations in the eight boxes below so that each inequation correctly describes the x and y coordinates of the point. Can you find it? Each point should have one inequation involving x and one involving y.

Point A

Point B

Point C

Point D

Exercise 5.1

1 Use the signs $<$ and $>$ to write two true inequations for each pair of numbers:

    a -1 and 3   **b** -2 and 4

    c -6 and 2   **d** -3 and 1

    e -3 and -1 **f** -2 and -6

    g 5 and -7 **h** 0 and -3

2 True or false?

    a $-1 < -6$ **b** $-1 < 0$

    c $-2 > 1$ **d** $-3 > -4$

    e $-3 \leqslant 3$ **f** $-3 \geqslant -3$

    g $-5 > -3$ **h** $-2 < 0$

3 Solve these inequations, choosing solutions from $\{-3, -2, -1, 0, 1, 2, 3\}$.

    a $x \geqslant -1$ **b** $x \leqslant -1$

    c $x < -2$ **d** $x > -2$

    e $x \geqslant -4$

4 Solve these inequations, choosing solutions from $\{-5, -4, -3, -2\}$.

    a $x \leqslant -2$ **b** $x > -4$

    c $x \geqslant -5$ **d** $x < -3$

    e $x \leqslant -5$

5 Write an inequation to describe each situation.

    a It's warmer in Glasgow than in Edinburgh.

Edinburgh $-2\ °C$

Glasgow $x\ °C$

    b It's colder in Inverness than in London.

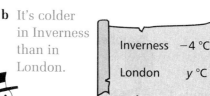

Inverness $-4\ °C$

London $y\ °C$

    c Aberdeen is colder than St Andrews.

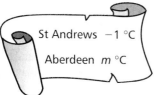

St Andrews $-1\ °C$

Aberdeen $m\ °C$

    d Oban is warmer than Glencoe.

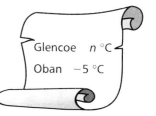

Glencoe $n\ °C$

Oban $-5\ °C$

6 In each diagram compare the positions of the points A and B.
   In each case write a true inequation:
   i using the two *x* coordinates   **ii** using the two *y* coordinates.

a
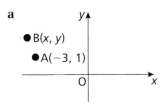

b
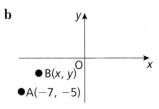

c
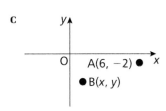

d
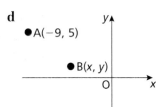

e
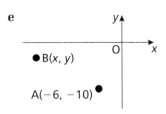

f
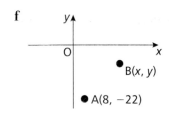

Challenge

Describe each situation using an inequation, then solve it.
Use your solution to make a true statement about the unknown temperature.

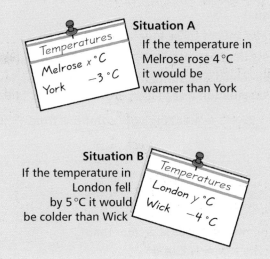

Situation A

If the temperature in
Melrose rose 4 °C
it would be
warmer than York

Temperatures
Melrose x °C
York   −3 °C

Situation B

If the temperature in
London fell
by 5 °C it would
be colder than Wick

Temperatures
London y °C
Wick   −4 °C

◄◄ RECAP

An equation is a statement which contains an equals sign (=) and a letter representing a number.
The value of the letter that makes the statement true is called the solution of the equation.
An equation is solved by finding the solution.
The solution of an equation, once found, should be *checked* by substitution.

The cover-up method
This is only useful for equations where the letter occurs in one place.

Example 1 $15 - 4x = 3$

$\Rightarrow \quad 4x = 12$

$\Rightarrow \quad x = 3$

Check $15 - 4x = 15 - 4 \times 3 = 15 - 12 = 3$

$15 - \boxed{?} = 3$
$4x$ must be 12

$4\boxed{?} = 12$
x must be 3

The balance method
This method involves simplifying the equation by performing the same action to both sides of the equation.

Example 2   Solve $6x - 5 = 2x + 9$.

$$6x - 5 = 2x + 9$$

$\Rightarrow \quad 6x - 5 + 5 = 2x + 9 + 5$ (Action: add 5 to both sides)

$\Rightarrow \quad 6x = 2x + 14$

$\Rightarrow \quad 6x - 2x = 2x + 14 - 2x$ (Action: take $2x$ from both sides)

$\Rightarrow \quad 4x = 14$

$\Rightarrow \quad 4x \div 4 = 14 \div 4$ (Action: divide both sides by 4)

$\Rightarrow \quad x = \frac{14}{4} = \frac{7}{2} = 3\frac{1}{2}$

Check
Left-hand side: $6x - 5 = 6 \times \frac{7}{2} - 5 = 21 - 5 = 16$
Right-hand side: $2x + 9 = 2 \times \frac{7}{2} + 9 = 7 + 9 = 16$
The two sides are equal.

An inequation contains one of these four signs:

$<$ less than $\leqslant$ less than or equal to $>$ greater than $\geqslant$ greater than or equal to.

An inequation can be solved in a similar way to an equation. Several values of a letter may make the inequation true. These are all solutions to the inequation.

Example 3   Solve $2x + 3 > 4$, taking your solutions from $\{-2, -1, 0, 1, 2, 3\}$.

$$2x + 3 > 4$$

$\Rightarrow \quad 2x + 3 - 3 > 4 - 3$ (Action: take 3 from both sides)

$\Rightarrow \quad 2x > 1$

$\Rightarrow \quad 2x \div 2 > 1 \div 2$ (Action: divide both sides by 2)

$\Rightarrow \quad x > \frac{1}{2}$

The unknown number is greater than $\frac{1}{2}$.

$\Rightarrow \quad x = 1, 2 \text{ or } 3$

1 Solve each equation. Remember to check your solutions.

  a $5x + 2 = 17$ **b** $11 = 5 + 3k$ **c** $23 - 7y = 2$

2 Make an equation for each of these then solve the equation. You will need to use brackets.

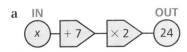

  a

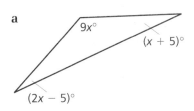

  b

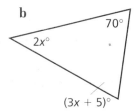

3 For each situation:

  i write an equation   **ii** solve it   **iii** find the size of the unknown angles.

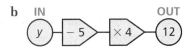

  a   **b**   **c**

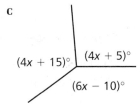

4 Solve these equations, checking your solutions.

  a $5m = 2m + 9$ **b** $6x = 35 - x$ **c** $12y + 2 = 3y + 20$

  d $28 - n = 7n + 4$ **e** $4(x + 1) = 5x - 1$ **f** $7(x - 1) = 3x - 1$

5 Each pair of rectangles have equal area. All lengths are in centimetres.

  i Form an equation.   **ii** Solve it.

  iii Find the dimensions of each rectangle.

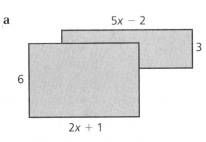

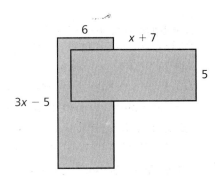

6 Solve these inequations, choosing from $\{7, 8, 9, 10, 11\}$.

  a $x \geqslant 9$ **b** $x < 8$ **c** $x - 2 > 7$ **d** $x + 5 \leqslant 13$

  e $14 > x + 4$ **f** $2x \geqslant 20$ **g** $2x < 19$ **h** $20 - x \leqslant 9$

7 Solve these inequations, giving your answers in the form $x > 5$, $x \leqslant \frac{1}{2}$, etc.

  a $x - 5 \geqslant 9$ **b** $3x + 2 < 17$ **c** $x \leqslant 9 - x$

  d $4x + 2 > x + 8$ **e** $3(3x - 1) \geqslant 2(2x + 1)$ **f** $7 - x < 2(x - 1)$

REVISE

8 Use > and < to write two true inequations connecting the numbers in each pair.

   a -2 and 3   **b** -5 and 1   **c** -4 and -2 **d** -1 and -7

9 Even if the temperature in Newcastle rose 4 °C it would still be colder than in Kirkwall.

   a Write an inequation to describe this situation.

   b Solve the inequation and use it to make a statement about the temperature in Newcastle.

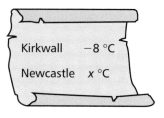

Kirkwall -8 °C

Newcastle x °C

7 Fractions and percentages

Approximately $\frac{3}{4}$ of the planet Earth is covered by water.

Oxygen forms 21% of the atmosphere.

1 Review

◀◀ Exercise 1.1

1 What is the value of:
   a the numerator **b** the denominator in the fraction $\frac{3}{4}$?

2 At a driving test centre 46% of the candidates passed their test first time.
   What percentage failed their first test?

3 There are nine eggs in a bird's nest. Seven of the eggs hatch.
   What fraction: **a** hatch **b** fail to hatch?

4 Which of the following fractions are equal to $\frac{1}{3}$?
   a $\frac{3}{6}$ **b** $\frac{2}{6}$ **c** $\frac{5}{15}$ **d** $\frac{3}{12}$

5 Find:
   a $\frac{1}{2}$ of £10 **b** $\frac{1}{4}$ of £8 **c** $\frac{1}{5}$ of £15 **d** $\frac{1}{10}$ of £40
   e $\frac{2}{3}$ of £12 **f** $\frac{3}{4}$ of £20 **g** $\frac{2}{5}$ of £10 **h** $\frac{7}{10}$ of £20

6 Calculate:
   a 10% of £60 **b** 1% of £2 **c** 50% of £5 **d** 25% of £12

7 Write each of these fractions in its simplest terms:
   a $\frac{2}{4}$ **b** $\frac{6}{8}$ **c** $\frac{10}{15}$ **d** $\frac{8}{10}$

8 Change each of the following to decimal form:
   a $\frac{7}{10}$ **b** $\frac{7}{100}$ **c** $\frac{77}{100}$ **d** $\frac{7}{1000}$
   e $2\frac{1}{2}$ **f** $4\frac{1}{4}$ **g** $7\frac{3}{4}$

9 Write these as common fractions:

   a 0·3   **b** 0·33   **c** 0·03   **d** 0·003   **e** 0·033

10 Change these decimals to percentages:

   a 0·5   **b** 0·05   **c** 0·25

11 Change these percentages to decimals:

   a 20%   **b** 2%   **c** 75%

12 Write these improper fractions as mixed numbers:

   a $\frac{3}{2}$ **b** $\frac{5}{4}$ **c** $\frac{8}{3}$ **d** $\frac{23}{10}$

---

2 Calculating a fraction of an amount

Example 1   Find $\frac{3}{5}$ of 35.

$\frac{1}{5}$ of $35 = 35 \div 5 = 7$ so $\frac{3}{5}$ of $35 = 7 \times 3 = 21$

Exercise 2.1

1 Calculate:

   a $\frac{1}{2}$ of 10   **b** $\frac{1}{2}$ of 26   **c** $\frac{1}{4}$ of 8   **d** $\frac{1}{4}$ of 28   **e** $\frac{1}{3}$ of 12   **f** $\frac{1}{3}$ of 21

   g $\frac{1}{5}$ of 45   **h** $\frac{1}{10}$ of 80   **i** $\frac{1}{6}$ of 42   **j** $\frac{1}{8}$ of 40   **k** $\frac{1}{7}$ of 56   **l** $\frac{1}{9}$ of 27

2 Calculate:

   a i $\frac{1}{3}$ of 15   **ii** $\frac{2}{3}$ of 15   **b i** $\frac{1}{4}$ of 20   **ii** $\frac{3}{4}$ of 20

   c i $\frac{1}{5}$ of 30   **ii** $\frac{2}{5}$ of 30   **d i** $\frac{1}{6}$ of 24   **ii** $\frac{5}{6}$ of 24

   e i $\frac{1}{7}$ of 21   **ii** $\frac{4}{7}$ of 21   **f i** $\frac{1}{8}$ of 16   **ii** $\frac{7}{8}$ of 16

3 Calculate:

   a $\frac{2}{3}$ of 6   **b** $\frac{3}{4}$ of 16   **c** $\frac{2}{5}$ of 25   **d** $\frac{4}{5}$ of 40   **e** $\frac{3}{10}$ of 40   **f** $\frac{5}{8}$ of 24

   g $\frac{5}{6}$ of 18   **h** $\frac{2}{7}$ of 21   **i** $\frac{7}{8}$ of 48   **j** $\frac{4}{9}$ of 45   **k** $\frac{3}{5}$ of 55   **l** $\frac{9}{10}$ of 100

4 Calculate:

   a $\frac{1}{2}$ of £9   **b** $\frac{1}{3}$ of 600 g   **c** $\frac{1}{4}$ of 200 km   **d** $\frac{1}{5}$ of 350 litres   **e** $\frac{3}{4}$ of 80 m

   f $\frac{2}{3}$ of 360°   **g** $\frac{5}{6}$ of 240 kg   **h** $\frac{5}{8}$ of 320 ml   **i** $\frac{7}{10}$ of 900 mm   **j** $\frac{3}{100}$ of £6000

5 Michelle allows herself £60 per week for lunch and fares.

   a She spends $\frac{1}{5}$ each weekday. Calculate $\frac{1}{5}$ of £60.

   b Find out how much she is likely to have spent through the week by calculating:

      i $\frac{2}{5}$ **ii** $\frac{3}{5}$ **iii** $\frac{4}{5}$ **iv** $\frac{5}{5}$ of £60.

6 Eric's video tapes will record 180 minutes of programmes.

$\frac{3}{10}$ of a tape has been used for recording.

How many minutes of it are:

a used   **b** unused?

7 Mary pays $\frac{1}{20}$ of her weekly wage into her pension fund.

How much does she save towards her pension in a week when she earns:

a £200   **b** £300   **c** £350?

8 Susan inherits £5600. She invests $\frac{3}{8}$ of the money in shares and the rest in a savings account. How much is invested in:

a shares   **b** a savings account?

9 Brunel designed a ship with an iron hull called the *Great Britain*.

It was 98 metres long. A model of it is made using a scale of $\frac{1}{72}$.

Calculate the length of the model, correct to the nearest centimetre.

10 Mr Simpson's annual pension is $\frac{29}{80}$ of £32 000.

Mrs Simpson receives $\frac{27}{60}$ of £29 000.

a How much pension does each of them receive?

b Who has the greater pension? By how much?

Example 2

The number of customer complaints at Spotlight Stores has dropped by $\frac{1}{4}$.

Last month there were 72 complaints.

How many: **a** fewer complaints

                    b complaints were there this month?

a $\frac{1}{4}$ of 72 = 72 ÷ 4 = 18 fewer complaints

b number of complaints = 72 − 18 = 54

Exercise 2.2

1 This size of jar normally holds 200 g of coffee.

     a How much extra coffee is in the jar?

     b What is the total weight of coffee?

2 Find:

     a the discount

     b the sale price of the shirt.

SHIRT Normal price £27

Sale price $\frac{1}{3}$ off

3 Tempest Tea boxes normally hold 320 bags.
A box on special offer contains an extra quarter.
  a How many extra tea bags are in the box?
  b How many are there in total?

4 Last year there were 90 accidents at Continental Constructions.
This year the number has been cut by $\frac{2}{3}$.
  a How many fewer accidents have there been this year?
  b What is the number of accidents this year?

5 Last week Bert's birdwatching website had 560 'hits'.
This week the number of 'hits' has gone up by $\frac{5}{8}$.
Calculate: **a** the increase   **b** the total number of hits this week.

6 Last month 8400 passengers flew with Astral Airways.
This month the number of passengers has dropped by $\frac{3}{4}$.
  a How many *fewer* passengers flew this month?
  b How many passengers were there this month?

7 Titan Textiles have increased their profits by $\frac{3}{10}$.
They made £72 000 profit last year.
Calculate: **a** the increase in profit   **b** this year's profit.

8 Henry is paid at time and a half for overtime (an increase of $\frac{1}{2}$ on top of his normal rate).
His normal rate of pay is £9 per hour.
How much is he paid for each hour's overtime?

9 What is the cost of a Glasgow to Paris flight which normally costs £240?

Global Airlines

$\frac{1}{10}$ **OFF ALL FLIGHTS**

10 Last week the magazine sold 6000 copies.
How many have been sold this week?

WEEKLY
WHINGE
Sales down by $\frac{5}{12}$

Challenge

When he's hillwalking, Hugh uses this to do a rough conversion of metres to feet:

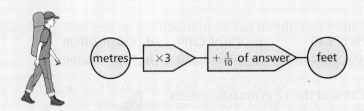

Example   To get a rough approximation for 1000 m:

1000 × 3 = 3000

$3000 + \frac{1}{10}$ of 3000 = 3000 + 300 = 3300

So 1000 m is roughly 3300 feet.

Find the approximate height, in feet, of:

a a hill which is 600 m high
b Ben Nevis at 1344 metres.

3 Calculating a percentage of an amount

Example 1   Find: **a** 10%   **b** 5%   **c** 20%   **d** 15%   **e** 50%   **f** 25% of £12.

a 10% of £12 = £12 ÷ 10 = £1·20   (for 10% divide by 10)
b   5% of £12 = £1·20 ÷ 2 = £0·60   (5% = 10% ÷ 2)
c 20% of £12 = £1·20 × 2 = £2·40   (20% = 10% × 2)
d 15% of £12 = £1·20 + £0·60 = £1·80   (15% = 10% + 5%)
e 50% of £12 = £12 ÷ 2 = £6   (for 50% divide by 2)
f 25% of £12 = £6 ÷ 2 = £3   (25% = 50% ÷ 2)

Example 2   Brass is made from 60% copper and 40% zinc.
Calculate the weight of: **a** copper   **b** zinc in a brass ingot weighing 800 g.

a Weight of copper = 60% of 800 g = 60 ÷ 100 × 800 = 480 g
b Weight of zinc = 40% of 800 g = 40 ÷ 100 × 800 = 320 g

Exercise 3.1

1 Calculate   **i** 10%   **ii** 5%   **iii** 20%   **iv** 15%   **v** 50%   **vi** 25% of:
   a £8   **b** £60   **c** £16   **d** £700   **e** £250

7 Ron is interested in the car.
  a How much would he save with the offer?
  b What would he pay for the car?

Saturn Sports Car
£8500
15% OFF THIS WEEK

8 The packet normally has a volume of 3 kg.
Calculate:
  a the extra weight
  b the total weight of powder in the packet.

SUDSO WASHING POWDER
12·5% EXTRA

SUDSO
Washing powder

9 Since City got promotion their gates have increased by 75%.
Last season their average attendance was 12 600.
Calculate their average attendance this season.

10 Cindy's old washing-machine used 54 litres of water in an average wash.
Her new economy model uses $66\frac{2}{3}\%$ less water.
How much water does her new machine use per wash?

Brainstormer

MOONRIDER £3950
less 17·5% discount
(VAT paid)

MUDSLINGER
£2850
+ VAT at 17·5%

  a Which motorbike is cheaper?   **b** By how much?

4 Expressing an amount as a percentage

Example 1   In a quiz Patrick got 19 out 25 questions correct.
What percentage did he score?

Fraction scored $= \frac{19}{25}$

Percentage scored $= \frac{19}{25}$ of $100 = 19 \div 25 \times 100 = 76\%$

Exercise 4.1

1 Sally reckons that one out of every four e-mails she receives is SPAM.
What percentage of her e-mails is SPAM?

2 Nine out of ten people are right-handed. Write this as a percentage.

3 In a five-day week Walter is late for work twice.
Express the number of late days as a percentage of his working days.

4 Express the child's fare as a percentage
of the adult fare.

Passenger Fares
ADULT £30
CHILD £12

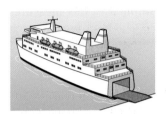

5 Graham makes a new garden gate.
The table shows his costs.
Calculate the percentage of the total cost spent on:
  a wood
  b hinges etc.
  c preservative
  d paint.

Item	Cost
Wood	£25
Hinges etc.	£12
Preservative	£9
Paint	£4
Total	£50

6 22 carat is pure gold. Calculate the percentage of
gold in these rings, correct to 1 decimal place.
  a 11 carat   **b** 18 carat   **c** 20 carat

7 In a season, Dean scores 5 goals from penalties and misses 3 penalties.
  a How many penalties has he taken?
  b What percentage of penalties has he: **i** scored from   **ii** missed?

8 One morning Martin counts the birds feeding in his garden.

Type	Blue tit	Great tit	Sparrow	Blackbird	Chaffinch	Other
Number	20	10	3	2	4	1

Express the number of each type of bird as a percentage of the total.

9 The weight of the actual tuna is 149 g.
Calculate the weight of tuna in the tin as a
percentage of the net weight.
Answer correct to the nearest whole number.

TUNA STEAK in oil

Net weight 198g
Drained weight 149g

10 In 2003 there were 3 million grey squirrels and 160 000 red squirrels in the UK. What percentage (correct to the nearest whole number) of the total squirrel population of the UK are:
    a red   **b** grey?

11 The table gives data from the 2001 census of Scotland. Calculate, correct to 1 decimal place, the percentage of the total population that are:
    a men   **b** women.

	Number
Men	2 432 494
Women	2 629 517

Example 2   Alex measures a sunflower to be 40 cm tall.
A week later it has grown to 50 cm.
Calculate the increase in height as a percentage of its original height.

Increase $= 50 - 40$ cm $= 10$ cm.

Increase as a percentage $= \dfrac{\text{increase}}{\text{original}} \times 100\%$

$$= \tfrac{10}{40} \times 100\% = 25\%$$

Exercise 4.2

1 The entrance charge to Tom's sports club rises from £1 to £2.
    a By how much has the charge risen?
    b Express the increase as a percentage of the original charge.

2 **a** By how much is the tennis racket reduced?
    b Express the reduction as a percentage of the original price.

Tennis Racket
NORMAL PRICE £30
Sale Price £15

3 Last month baby Jane weighed 10 kg. This month she weighs 11 kg.
    a What is her increase in weight?
    b Calculate the increase in weight as a percentage of her weight last month.

4 It used to take Vic 40 minutes to drive to work. A new by-pass means it now takes him 25 minutes.
    a How much less time does the journey take him?
    b Calculate the saving in time as a percentage of the time he used to take.

5 Jean's hourly rate increases from £7·60 to £7·98.
    a By how much has her pay gone up?
    b Calculate her percentage pay rise.

6 Len replaces a 60 watt light bulb with an energy saving 20 watt bulb.
    a By how much has the power been reduced?
    b Express this as a percentage of the original wattage.
      Give your answer correct to the nearest whole number.

7 Cora buys a smaller car. Her old car travelled 12 km on 1 litre of petrol.
Her new car does 15 km per litre.
Calculate the increase in distance travelled on 1 litre as a percentage of her
old car's figure.

8 Last year Wildtrust Woods planted 8000 trees.
This year they have planted 9000 trees.
Calculate the increase as a percentage of the number planted last year.

9 The total first prize money in last week's lottery was £7 750 000.
This week the prize increased to £8 250 000.
Calculate the increase as a percentage, correct to 1 decimal place, of last week's prize.

10 a Calculate the percentage of the marmalade that is sugar.
   b By increasing the fruit content Merlin reduce the amount of
   sugar to 500 g.
   For the new jars calculate the reduction in sugar as a percentage
   of the total contents.
   Give your answers correct to the nearest whole number.

Brainstormer

a How much is saved, per minute,
by using Cheapcall rather than
Phonesave for
   i peak time   **ii** off-peak calls?
b Express the saving for
   i peak time   **ii** off-peak calls as a percentage of the cost of the Phonesave rate.

Company	Peak rate	Off-peak
Phonesave	4p per min	0·8p per min
Cheapcall	2·5p per min	0·75p per min

---

5 Proper fractions and mixed numbers

Example 1   How many quarters are there in: **a** 2   **b** $2\frac{3}{4}$?

   a In 2 there are $2 \times 4 = 8$ quarters
   b In 2 there are $8 + 3 = 11$ quarters

Example 2   Express $2\frac{3}{4}$ as an improper fraction.

   From *Example 1* there are 11 quarters in $2\frac{3}{4}$
   so $2\frac{3}{4} = \frac{11}{4}$

Example 3   Express $\frac{17}{5}$ as a mixed number.

   $17 \div 5 = 3$ remainder 2, that is 3 wholes and 2 fifths
   $\frac{17}{5} = 3\frac{2}{5}$

Exercise 5.1

1 How many halves are there in:

   a 1   **b** $1\frac{1}{2}$ **c** 2   **d** $2\frac{1}{2}$?

2 How many thirds are there in:

   a 1   **b** $1\frac{1}{3}$ **c** $1\frac{2}{3}$ **d** 2?

3 How many fifths are there in:

   a 1   **b** $1\frac{4}{5}$ **c** $2\frac{3}{5}$ **d** $4\frac{1}{5}$?

4 How many eighths are there in:

   a 1   **b** $2\frac{1}{8}$ **c** $3\frac{5}{8}$ **d** $5\frac{7}{8}$?

5 When these mixed numbers are changed to improper fractions what number replaces each *?

   a $4\frac{1}{2} = \frac{*}{2}$ **b** $5\frac{1}{2} = \frac{*}{2}$ **c** $8\frac{1}{2} = \frac{*}{2}$ **d** $12\frac{1}{2} = \frac{*}{2}$

6 When these mixed numbers are changed to improper fractions what number replaces each *?

   a $1\frac{1}{4} = \frac{*}{4}$ **b** $3\frac{1}{4} = \frac{*}{4}$ **c** $5\frac{1}{4} = \frac{*}{4}$ **d** $10\frac{3}{4} = \frac{*}{4}$

7 Write these mixed numbers as improper fractions.

   a $6\frac{1}{2}$ **b** $3\frac{1}{3}$ **c** $4\frac{3}{4}$ **d** $3\frac{2}{5}$ **e** $2\frac{5}{6}$

   f $5\frac{2}{7}$ **g** $4\frac{5}{8}$ **h** $3\frac{7}{9}$ **i** $6\frac{9}{10}$ **j** $3\frac{5}{12}$

8 Change these improper fractions to mixed numbers by replacing each * with a number.

   a $\frac{7}{2} = 3\frac{*}{2}$ **b** $\frac{9}{4} = 2\frac{*}{4}$ **c** $\frac{8}{3} = 2\frac{*}{*}$

   d $\frac{24}{5} = 4\frac{*}{*}$ **e** $\frac{23}{6} = *\frac{5}{*}$ **f** $\frac{35}{8} = *\frac{3}{*}$

9 Change these improper fractions to mixed numbers.

   a $\frac{19}{2}$ **b** $\frac{13}{3}$ **c** $\frac{27}{4}$ **d** $\frac{19}{5}$ **e** $\frac{35}{6}$

   f $\frac{31}{7}$ **g** $\frac{51}{8}$ **h** $\frac{44}{9}$ **i** $\frac{67}{10}$ **j** $\frac{91}{20}$

10 Which of the following are correct?

   a $5\frac{1}{3} = \frac{16}{3}$ **b** $7\frac{1}{4} = \frac{29}{4}$ **c** $2\frac{6}{7} = \frac{22}{7}$ **d** $3\frac{3}{11} = \frac{36}{11}$

   e $\frac{23}{2} = 10\frac{1}{2}$ **f** $\frac{37}{5} = 7\frac{3}{5}$ **g** $\frac{47}{8} = 5\frac{7}{8}$ **h** $\frac{41}{12} = 4\frac{5}{12}$

Challenge

The following mixed numbers may be used as an approximation for π.

1 Write these mixed numbers as improper fractions: **a** $3\frac{1}{7}$ **b** $3\frac{16}{113}$

2 Express these improper fractions as mixed numbers: **a** $\frac{311}{99}$ **b** $\frac{333}{106}$

6 Equivalent fractions

Example 1   Find the value of * in $\frac{2}{3} = \frac{*}{12}$

Look at the denominators: $3 \times 4 = 12$

So the numerator $= 2 \times 4 = 8$

So $\frac{2}{3} = \frac{8}{12}$

Example 2   Find two fractions that are equivalent to $\frac{2}{3}$.

$$\frac{2 \times 2}{3 \times 2} = \frac{4}{6} \quad \frac{2 \times 3}{3 \times 3} = \frac{6}{9}$$

So $\frac{4}{6}$ and $\frac{6}{9}$ are equivalent to $\frac{2}{3}$.

Example 3   Express $\frac{3}{4}$ and $\frac{2}{5}$ as two fractions with a common denominator.

The denominators, 4 and 5, have a common multiple of 20.

$$\frac{3}{4} = \frac{3 \times 5}{4 \times 5} = \frac{15}{20} \quad \frac{2}{5} = \frac{2 \times 4}{5 \times 4} = \frac{8}{20}$$

Exercise 6.1

1 Find the value of * in each of the following:

   a $\frac{1}{2} = \frac{*}{8}$ **b** $\frac{1}{4} = \frac{*}{12}$ **c** $\frac{1}{3} = \frac{*}{9}$ **d** $\frac{3}{4} = \frac{*}{8}$ **e** $\frac{1}{2} = \frac{6}{*}$ **f** $\frac{1}{5} = \frac{4}{*}$ **g** $\frac{3}{4} = \frac{12}{*}$ **h** $\frac{5}{6} = \frac{15}{*}$

2 Find two fractions that are equivalent to:

   a $\frac{1}{8}$ **b** $\frac{5}{6}$

3 Write each fraction in its simplest form.

   a $\frac{2}{10}$ **b** $\frac{8}{16}$ **c** $\frac{6}{15}$ **d** $\frac{8}{14}$ **e** $\frac{10}{12}$ **f** $\frac{12}{16}$ **g** $\frac{6}{18}$ **h** $\frac{14}{24}$

4 Match equal pairs:

   $\frac{1}{2}$ $\frac{1}{3}$ $\frac{2}{5}$ $\frac{5}{6}$

   $\frac{12}{30}$ $\frac{25}{30}$ $\frac{10}{30}$ $\frac{15}{30}$

5 Find equivalent fractions so that each of these has a denominator of 24.

   a $\frac{1}{2}$ **b** $\frac{1}{3}$ **c** $\frac{1}{4}$ **d** $\frac{1}{6}$ **e** $\frac{1}{8}$ **f** $\frac{1}{12}$

6   **a** Express $\frac{1}{3}$ and $\frac{1}{4}$ with a common denominator of 12.

   b Express $\frac{5}{6}$ and $\frac{3}{4}$ with a common denominator of 12.

   c Express $\frac{2}{3}$ and $\frac{4}{5}$ with a common denominator of 15.

   d Express $\frac{3}{8}$ and $\frac{7}{10}$ with a common denominator of 40.

7 For each pair of fractions
  i find the lowest common denominator
  ii express each fraction with the lowest common denominator.
  a $\frac{1}{2}$ and $\frac{1}{3}$ **b** $\frac{1}{4}$ and $\frac{1}{5}$ **c** $\frac{2}{3}$ and $\frac{4}{7}$ **d** $\frac{5}{6}$ and $\frac{2}{5}$

8 Mrs Wilson's pension is $\frac{36}{80}$ times her final salary.
  Write $\frac{36}{80}$ in its simplest form.

Example 4 Write these improper fractions as mixed numbers in their simplest form.
  a $\frac{6}{4}$ **b** $\frac{30}{9}$

  a $\frac{6}{4} = \frac{3}{2} = 1\frac{1}{2}$ **b** $\frac{30}{9} = \frac{10}{3} = 3\frac{1}{3} = 3$

Exercise 6.2

1 Write each fraction in its simplest form.
  a $\frac{30}{36}$ **b** $\frac{50}{60}$ **c** $\frac{35}{40}$ **d** $\frac{33}{36}$ **e** $\frac{24}{36}$ **f** $\frac{21}{28}$ **g** $\frac{20}{32}$ **h** $\frac{36}{60}$

2 Write each improper fraction as a mixed number in its simplest form.
  a $\frac{9}{6}$ **b** $\frac{10}{4}$ **c** $\frac{20}{12}$ **d** $\frac{18}{8}$ **e** $\frac{25}{10}$ **f** $\frac{24}{20}$ **g** $\frac{27}{18}$ **h** $\frac{48}{18}$

3 Find equivalent fractions so that each of these has a denominator of 100.
  a $\frac{1}{2}$ **b** $\frac{3}{4}$ **c** $\frac{4}{5}$ **d** $\frac{7}{10}$ **e** $\frac{11}{20}$ **f** $\frac{39}{50}$

4 Express each pair as fractions with a common denominator.
  a $\frac{1}{6}$ and $\frac{1}{10}$ **b** $\frac{1}{8}$ and $\frac{1}{12}$ **c** $\frac{5}{9}$ and $\frac{7}{12}$ **d** $\frac{11}{15}$ and $\frac{13}{20}$

5 Express each pair as fractions with a common denominator and use your
  results to decide which fraction is the greater.
  a $\frac{3}{4}$ and $\frac{5}{7}$ **b** $\frac{2}{3}$ and $\frac{7}{10}$ **c** $\frac{3}{8}$ and $\frac{5}{12}$ **d** $\frac{4}{15}$ and $\frac{3}{10}$

6 Fred is working on an old steam engine using a $\frac{5}{8}$ inch spanner and
  an $\frac{11}{16}$ inch spanner. Which spanner has the greater measurement?

7 The road up Hairpin Hill has a gradient of $\frac{3}{10}$. The road to Misty Moor has a gradient
  of $\frac{1}{4}$. Which hill has the greater gradient? (Which is the bigger fraction?)

8 Mr Simpson pays $\frac{3}{20}$ of his salary into a pension fund. Mrs Simpson pays $\frac{2}{15}$ of hers
  into her pension fund. Which of them pays the greater fraction of their salary towards
  their retirement?

Brainstormers

1 Express each group of three fractions so they have a common denominator.

   a $\frac{1}{2}, \frac{1}{4}, \frac{1}{8}$ b $\frac{1}{4}, \frac{1}{6}, \frac{1}{8}$ c $\frac{2}{3}, \frac{4}{5}, \frac{7}{8}$

2 List each group of three fractions in order of size, greatest first.

   a $\frac{1}{4}, \frac{1}{2}, \frac{1}{3}$ b $\frac{5}{6}, \frac{13}{15}, \frac{4}{5}$

---

7 Switching between fractions, decimals and percentages

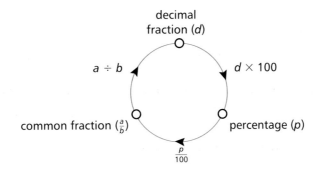

Example 1   Write 0·35 as:

   a a percentage
   b a common fraction in its simplest form.

   a $0·35 = (0·35 \times 100)\% = 35\%$
   b $35\% = \frac{35}{100} = \frac{7}{20}$ (dividing numerator and denominator by 5)

Example 2   Change 8% to:

   a a common fraction in its simplest form
   b a decimal fraction.

   a $8\% = \frac{8}{100} = \frac{2}{25}$ (dividing both the numerator and denominator by 4)
   b $8\% = 8 \div 100 = 0·08$

Example 3   Express $\frac{3}{4}$ as:

   a a decimal fraction
   b a percentage.

   a $3 \div 4 = 0·75 \Rightarrow \frac{3}{4} = 0·75$
   b $0·75 \times 100\% = 75\%$

4 In the morning Ursula works for $4\frac{1}{2}$ hours. After lunch she does another $3\frac{3}{4}$ hours. How long does she work altogether?

5 Sally and Simon both catch salmon.
Simon's salmon weighs $8\frac{1}{4}$ pounds.
Sally's weighs $12\frac{1}{2}$ pounds. How much heavier is Sally's fish?

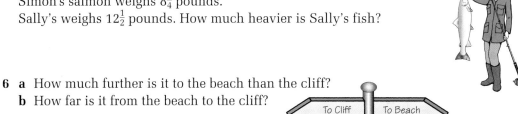

6 **a** How much further is it to the beach than the cliff?
   b How far is it from the beach to the cliff?

To Cliff $\frac{7}{8}$ mile   To Beach $2\frac{1}{4}$ miles

7 Over the year the interest rate at Borders Bank has increased from $2\frac{3}{4}\%$ to $4\frac{1}{8}\%$. Calculate the increase in the rate.

8 The table shows how many hours Sharon worked last week.
Find her total hours for the week.

Day	Mon	Tue	Wed	Thu	Fri
Hours worked	$7\frac{1}{2}$	$7\frac{1}{2}$	$8\frac{1}{4}$	$7\frac{3}{4}$	$6\frac{3}{4}$

9 Sam has to move $4\frac{1}{2}$ tonnes of sand. So far he has moved $1\frac{7}{10}$ tonnes. What weight of sand is left?

10 Lorna has worked at Massive Micros for $6\frac{1}{4}$ years.
Andy has been there for $\frac{11}{12}$ of a year.
How much longer has Lorna been employed at the computer company?

Challenge

Copy and complete this magic square.
Each row, column and diagonal has the same total.

1		3
	$2\frac{1}{2}$	
2		

Brainstormers

a The sum of three fractions is 1. Each has a numerator of 1 but the denominators are all different. Can you find the three fractions?
b Find four fractions whose sum is 1.
Again each numerator has to be 1 and the denominators all different.
(There is more than one answer.)

9 Multiplying fractions

A square of side 1 unit is split into fifths vertically and
quarters horizontally.

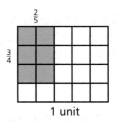

The shaded rectangle has area $= l \times b = \frac{2}{5} \times \frac{3}{4}$

We can see that this is $\frac{6}{20}$ of the square.

Thus $\frac{2}{5} \times \frac{3}{4} = \frac{6}{20} = \frac{3}{10}$

1 unit

> To multiply fractions, multiply the numerators and denominators separately.

Example 1 Calculate $\frac{1}{2} \times \frac{1}{4}$.

$$\frac{1}{2} \times \frac{1}{4} = \frac{1 \times 1}{2 \times 4} = \frac{1}{8}$$

Example 2 Calculate $\frac{4}{5} \times \frac{3}{8}$.

$$\frac{4}{5} \times \frac{3}{8} = \frac{4 \times 3}{5 \times 8} = \frac{12}{40} = \frac{3}{10}$$

Exercise 9.1

1 Calculate:

  a $\frac{1}{2} \times \frac{1}{6}$ **b** $\frac{1}{3} \times \frac{1}{5}$ **c** $\frac{3}{5} \times \frac{1}{2}$ **d** $\frac{3}{4} \times \frac{3}{5}$

  e $\frac{5}{6} \times \frac{1}{2}$ **f** $\frac{4}{7} \times \frac{2}{3}$ **g** $\frac{7}{10} \times \frac{3}{4}$ **h** $\frac{5}{8} \times \frac{3}{8}$

2 Calculate, expressing the answer in its simplest form:

  a $\frac{2}{3} \times \frac{1}{2}$ **b** $\frac{1}{4} \times \frac{2}{3}$ **c** $\frac{3}{4} \times \frac{2}{3}$ **d** $\frac{3}{8} \times \frac{1}{3}$

  e $\frac{5}{6} \times \frac{2}{5}$ **f** $\frac{7}{10} \times \frac{5}{8}$ **g** $\frac{8}{9} \times \frac{3}{4}$ **h** $\frac{4}{5} \times \frac{5}{12}$

3 A jar holds $\frac{1}{2}$ a litre. Salima pours $\frac{1}{5}$ of the contents into a glass.
What fraction of a litre is poured into the glass? (What is $\frac{1}{5}$ of $\frac{1}{2}$?)

4 A forest covers $\frac{2}{5}$ of a hectare. $\frac{1}{4}$ of the
wooded area is oak.
Calculate the area of oak trees.

5 A lesson lasts for $\frac{3}{4}$ of an hour. $\frac{1}{3}$ of the
lesson has passed.
What fraction of an hour has passed?

6 A rectangular field measures $\frac{2}{3}$ km by $\frac{3}{8}$ km.
Calculate the area of the field in km².

7 Ben's coal bunker holds $\frac{4}{5}$ of a tonne. It is $\frac{5}{8}$ full.
What weight of coal is in the bunker?

8 Robert reckons he's a good golfer. $\frac{9}{10}$ of his tee shots hit the fairway
and $\frac{5}{6}$ of his shots from the fairway hit the green.
Calculate the fraction of the holes where he hits the fairway and
the green.

9 Diane spends 5 months of the year working abroad. Of this time $\frac{4}{5}$ is spent in Europe. What fraction of the year does she spend working in Europe?

10 **a** Which is greater, $\frac{1}{2} \times \frac{1}{4}$ or $\frac{1}{3} \times \frac{1}{3}$?   **b** By how much?

Example 3   Calculate $1\frac{1}{4} \times 6$.
$$1\frac{1}{4} \times 6 = \frac{5}{4} \times \frac{6}{1} = \frac{5 \times 6}{4 \times 1} = \frac{30}{4} = \frac{15}{2} = 7\frac{1}{2}$$

Example 4   Find $\frac{3}{4}$ of $3\frac{1}{3}$. (Note: 'of' means '$\times$')
$$\frac{3}{4} \text{ of } 3\frac{1}{3} = \frac{3}{4} \times \frac{10}{3} = \frac{30}{12} = \frac{5}{2} = 2\frac{1}{2}$$

Exercise 9.2

1 Calculate, simplifying where possible:

   a $1\frac{1}{2} \times 3$ **b** $1\frac{1}{3} \times 2$ **c** $2\frac{1}{2} \times 4$ **d** $2\frac{1}{4} \times 3$

   e $2 \times 1\frac{3}{4}$ **f** $3 \times 1\frac{2}{3}$ **g** $4 \times 1\frac{5}{6}$ **h** $8 \times 1\frac{1}{4}$

2 Calculate, simplifying where possible:

   a $\frac{1}{2}$ of $1\frac{1}{3}$ **b** $\frac{1}{2}$ of $1\frac{3}{5}$ **c** $\frac{1}{2}$ of $3\frac{1}{7}$ **d** $\frac{1}{3}$ of $1\frac{1}{2}$

   e $\frac{1}{3}$ of $2\frac{1}{10}$ **f** $\frac{1}{4}$ of $2\frac{2}{5}$ **g** $\frac{2}{3}$ of $1\frac{7}{8}$ **h** $\frac{3}{4}$ of $2\frac{2}{9}$

   i $\frac{2}{5} \times 2\frac{1}{2}$ **j** $\frac{3}{8} \times 3\frac{1}{3}$ **k** $\frac{5}{6} \times 2\frac{1}{10}$ **l** $\frac{9}{10} \times 5\frac{5}{6}$

3 Calculate, simplifying and writing as a mixed number where possible:

   a $1\frac{1}{2} \times 1\frac{1}{4}$ **b** $1\frac{1}{3} \times 1\frac{2}{5}$ **c** $2\frac{1}{2} \times 1\frac{2}{3}$ **d** $1\frac{3}{4} \times 2\frac{1}{3}$

   e $1\frac{1}{2} \times 1\frac{1}{3}$ **f** $1\frac{1}{4} \times 1\frac{3}{5}$ **g** $1\frac{4}{5} \times 2\frac{1}{2}$ **h** $2\frac{1}{4} \times 3\frac{1}{3}$

   i $4\frac{1}{2} \times 1\frac{1}{9}$ **j** $2\frac{5}{8} \times 2\frac{2}{3}$ **k** $1\frac{1}{6} \times 1\frac{2}{7}$ **l** $3\frac{3}{4} \times 2\frac{4}{5}$

4 A rectangular factory door measures 8 m by $2\frac{1}{2}$ m. Calculate the area of the door.

5 A race track is $4\frac{1}{2}$ km long. Amy has run $\frac{1}{3}$ of it. How far has she run?

6 On each of the seven days of the week Lenny spends $\frac{3}{4}$ of an hour exercising. How long is this altogether?

7 Overtime is at time and a half of the basic rate. Joe works $2\frac{1}{2}$ hours of overtime. How many hours at the basic rate is this equal to?

8 An approximation for the circumference of a circle is $3\frac{1}{7} \times$ diameter. Use this formula to calculate the circumference of a circle with diameter 7 cm.

9 Pete runs at $7\frac{1}{2}$ km/h. How far does he run in $1\frac{1}{3}$ hours? (Distance = Speed $\times$ Time)

10 Water flows through a pipe at the rate of $1\frac{1}{4}$ litres per second. Calculate the volume of water that flows through the pipe in $6\frac{2}{3}$ seconds.

Brainstormer

Wanda is considering two types of window for her house.

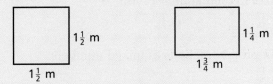

$1\frac{1}{2}$ m

$1\frac{1}{2}$ m

$1\frac{1}{4}$ m

$1\frac{3}{4}$ m

a Compare the perimeters of the two windows.

b Which window has the greater area? By how much?

◀◀ RECAP

Fractions

You should be able to:

- find a fraction of a quantity

    Example   Calculate $\frac{3}{10}$ of £9.

    $\frac{1}{10}$ of £9 = 90p; $\frac{3}{10}$ of £9 = 90p × 3 = £2·70

- find equivalent fractions

    Example   Write $\frac{4}{8}$ in its simplest form. $\frac{4}{8} = \frac{4 \times 1}{4 \times 2} = \frac{1}{2}$

- work with improper fractions and mixed numbers

    Example $\frac{9}{2} = 4\frac{1}{2}$

- add, subtract and multiply fractions, including mixed numbers

Percentages

You should be able to:

- find a percentage of a quantity

    Example   Calculate 15% of £70.

    10% of £70 = £7; 5% of £70 = £3·50; 15% of £70 = £7 + £3·50 = £10·50

- express an amount (A) as a percentage of a given quantity (B)

    Example   Express a mark of 17 out of 20 as a percentage.

    $\frac{17}{20} \times 100 = 17 \div 20 \times 100 = 85\%$

Fractions, decimals and percentages

You should be able to:

- change between fractions, decimals and percentages

    Example $\frac{3}{4} = 0·75 = 75\%$

1 Find:

   a $\frac{1}{4}$ of £12   **b** $\frac{3}{8}$ of £48

2 Write these fractions in their simplest form:

   a $\frac{3}{6}$ **b** $\frac{12}{18}$ **c** $\frac{20}{25}$

3 **a** Express these improper fractions as mixed numbers:

      i $\frac{7}{3}$ **ii** $\frac{15}{8}$

   b Express these mixed numbers as improper fractions:

      i $4\frac{1}{4}$ **ii** $3\frac{5}{6}$

4 Calculate:

   a 10% of £9   **b** 5% of £70   **c** 4% of £800   **d** 75% of £18

5 Express these test marks as percentages:

   a Maths 9 out of 10

   b English 15 out of 25

   c History 27 out of 40

6 Copy and complete the table, writing fractions in their simplest form.

Fraction	$\frac{1}{5}$			$2\frac{3}{10}$		
Decimal		0·8			3·625	
Percentage			45%			112%

7 Calculate and simplify where possible:

   a $\frac{1}{4}+\frac{1}{4}$ **b** $\frac{3}{8}+\frac{1}{3}$ **c** $\frac{5}{6}-\frac{1}{6}$ **d** $\frac{3}{4}-\frac{1}{5}$

   e $2\frac{1}{2}+3\frac{1}{4}$ **f** $1\frac{2}{3}+4\frac{7}{10}$ **g** $4\frac{3}{4}-2\frac{1}{2}$ **h** $3\frac{3}{8}-1\frac{5}{6}$

8 Calculate and simplify where possible:

   a $\frac{3}{4}$ of $\frac{1}{2}$ **b** $\frac{4}{5}\times\frac{3}{8}$ **c** $\frac{2}{5}$ of $3\frac{1}{3}$ **d** $1\frac{1}{3}\times1\frac{1}{8}$

9 Rosie's annual salary is £32 000.
Her bank will lend her $3\frac{1}{4}$ of her annual salary to buy a house.
Calculate the amount the bank will lend to her.

10 Mr Wells receives a gas bill for £85·60 + VAT at 5%.
Calculate:

   a the VAT   **b** his total bill.

8 Coordinates and the straight line

A grid system makes describing position easier.

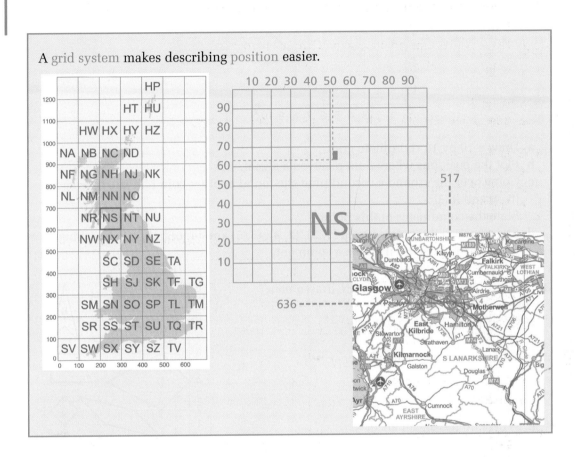

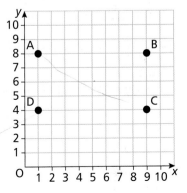

1 Review

◀◀ **Exercise 1.1**

1 A(1, 8), B, C and D are the vertices of a rectangle.
  a Give the coordinates of
    i B   **ii** C   **iii** D.
  b The diagonals of the rectangle intersect at E.
    What are the coordinates of E?
  c Where is:
    i the midpoint of AB
    ii the midpoint of BC?
  d (5, 0) is the point F.
    What kind of shape is
    i AFB   **ii** AFE?

2 Sam uses a metal detector to hunt for old coins. She sets up a grid.
She gets a signal at (0, 4), (7, 5), (9, 2), (8, 0) and (10, 6).

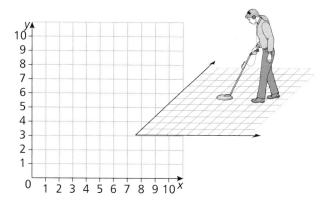

a Draw a 10 by 10 coordinate grid.
b Plot the positions where Sam received a signal.
c Going over the ground a second time she found another coin halfway between (0, 4) and (8, 0).
State the coordinates of this point.
d She searched the points (0, 2), (1, 3), (2, 4), (3, 5) and (4, 6) but found nothing.
i Plot the points.　**ii** Make a comment.

3 Seven different quadrilaterals are drawn on a coordinate grid.
a Quadrilateral A is a rectangle.
Name the other shapes.
b Where are the vertices of:
i the rhombus
ii the square
iii the parallelogram?
c Where do the diagonals of
i the kite
ii the V-kite intersect?

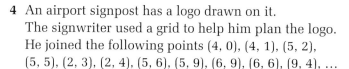

d The points (7, 4) and (10, 4) can be joined to form one side of the trapezium.
What points can be joined to form the side parallel to this?

4 An airport signpost has a logo drawn on it.
The signwriter used a grid to help him plan the logo.
He joined the following points (4, 0), (4, 1), (5, 2), (5, 5), (2, 3), (2, 4), (5, 6), (5, 9), (6, 9), (6, 6), (9, 4), ...
a Can you complete the list to draw the logo?
b The frame round the logo can be drawn by joining the points:
(1, 0), (0, 1), (5, 10), (6, 10), ...
Complete the list.

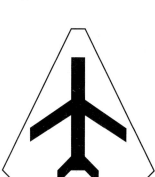

2 Going in all directions

All points plotted on the grid so far have involved going to the right and then going up.
We can also find points to the left of the y axis and under the x axis.

This grid has been split into four regions by the axes.
These regions are called **quadrants**.

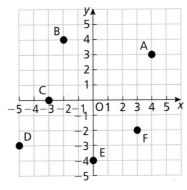

A(4, 3) is in the first quadrant.
B(−2, 4) … 2 left, 4 up … is in the second quadrant.
C(−3, 0) … 3 left, 0 up … is between the second and third quadrants.
D(−5, −3) … 5 left, 3 down … is in the third quadrant.
E(0, −4) … 0 left, 4 down … is between the second and third quadrants.
F(3, −2) … 3 right, 2 down … is in the fourth quadrant.

Exercise 2.1

1 a Plot each of the following points:

A(3, 5), B(0, 4), C(−2, 5), D(−5, 0), E(−4, −3), F(0, −2), G(4, −4), H(3, 0), O(0, 0)

   b Say in which quadrant the point lies, or between which quadrants the point lies.

2 a Name the points in the second quadrant.
   b Which points lie between the second and third quadrants?
   c Which points have the same x coordinate?
   d Which points have the same y coordinate?
   e Which points have their x coordinate and y coordinate equal?
   f M is a point with the same x coordinate as A, and the same y coordinate as F.
      What are the coordinates of M?
   g BFMN are the vertices of a square.
      What are the coordinates of N?

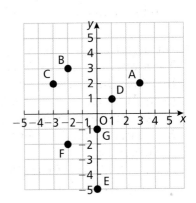

3 P(3, 2), Q(3, −4), R(−5, −4) and S are the vertices of a rectangle.
  a What are the coordinates of S?
  b T is the midpoint of the side PQ. State its coordinates.
  c V is the midpoint of the side QR. What are the coordinates of V?
  d W is where the diagonals of the rectangle cross.
     Give the coordinates of W.
  e P, Q, V and W form the vertices of a quadrilateral. What kind of quadrilateral is it?

Challenge

1 Pat drew a rectangle KLMN.
  K is the point (3, −4).
  Some of the coordinates have been smudged by
  Pat's leaking pen.

  If you know that the sides are parallel to the
  axes, can you figure out the missing coordinates?

2 Pat drew a second rectangle.
  Again, the sides are parallel to the axes.
  The diagonals intersect at T(−1, −2).

  What are the coordinates of Q, R and S?

Exercise 2.2

1 Sam was working with her metal detector at a
  new site.
  a She picked up signals at A(1, −5), B(−4, 2)
     and C(−3, −1).
     Plot these points on a grid.
  b She found a £2 coin at the point with
     coordinates which add up to −2.
     Which of the three points is that?
  c She found an old tin can at the point in the fourth quadrant.
     Which of the three points is this?

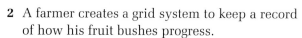

2 A farmer creates a grid system to keep a record
  of how his fruit bushes progress.
  a The bushes at A(1, 3), B(−4, 3), C (−2, −1)
     and D(3, −1) wither. Plot these points.
  b The bush halfway between A and D needs
     pruned. State its coordinates and call it E.
  c The bush halfway between C and E is first to flower.
     What are the coordinates of this point?

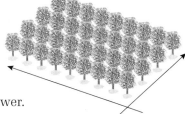

3 A(5, 1), B(−3, 5), C(−5, 1) and D are the vertices of the rectangle ABCD.
  a Plot A, B and C on a grid.
  b To get from B to C we must go 4 down and … left.
     How many squares to the left?
  c The instructions for getting from B to C are the same instructions as for getting
     from A to D. What are the coordinates of D?
  d Where do the diagonals of ABCD cross?
  e Plot the midpoints of the sides of the rectangle.
     What sort of quadrilateral do you get when you join these midpoints?

4 Jeff takes a photograph of a comet one Sunday night.
  He marks a grid on the photo and notes the points A, B,
  C and D, the positions of the comet on each of the
  previous Sundays.

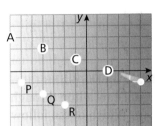

  a A is the point (−7, 3).
     State the coordinates of the points B, C and D.
  b State the position of the comet when the photo was
     taken.
  c Assume the comet will keep moving as it has been.
     Where will it be next Sunday?
  d When the comet was at B, a planet was spotted at P. When the comet was at C, the
     planet was at Q. Assuming the planet keeps moving like this, where will it be seen
     next Sunday?

---

3 Naming the grid lines

In the diagram we can see a set of points all lying in
a straight line.
This line is parallel to the x axis. The coordinates of
the points are:
(−5, 3), (−2, 3), (−1, 3), (0, 3), (1, 3), (3, 3), (4, 3).
Note that every point has a y coordinate of 3.

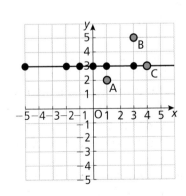

The point A has a y coordinate of 2 (less than 3).
It is below the line.
The point B has a y coordinate of 5 (more than 3).
It is above the line.
The point C has a y coordinate of 3. It is on the line.

We refer to this line as the line $y = 3$.
We say that $y = 3$ is the **equation** of the line.

In a similar way, the line passing through (−5, −2), (−2, −2), (−1, −2) is
called $y = -2$.

4 Through the origin

Example 1
Consider the set of points $(-3, -6)$, $(-2, -4)$,
$(-1, -2)$, $(0, 0)$, $(1, 2)$, $(2, 4)$.

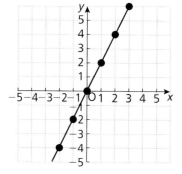

We can see that:
- they lie on a straight line
- the line passes through the origin $(0, 0)$
- in each case the y coordinate is double the x coordinate.

We say that the equation of this line is $y = 2x$.

For the point $(2, 3)$ ... y is less than double x ... the point is below the line.
For the point $(2, 4)$ ... y is double x ... the point is on the line.
For the point $(2, 5)$ ... y is more than double x ... the point is above the line.

Example 2   Draw the line with equation $y = 3x$.

Step 1   Draw a table with a set of convenient x values.

x	-1	0	1	2

Step 2   Calculate the y values using the equation.

x	-1	0	1	2
$y = 3x$	-3	0	3	6

Step 3   Plot the points $(-1, -3)$, $(0, 0)$, $(1, 3)$, $(2, 6)$.

Step 4   Extend the line beyond the plotted points.

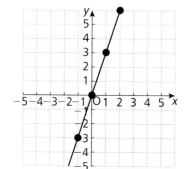

Note that:
- we have a straight line
- the line passes through the origin $(0, 0)$
- in each case the y coordinate is three times the x coordinate.

Exercise 4.1

1 For each set of points:
   i plot the set   **ii** suggest the equation of the line which passes through the points.
   a $(-1, -4)$, $(0, 0)$, $(1, 4)$, $(2, 8)$
   b $(-1, -5)$, $(0, 0)$, $(1, 5)$, $(2, 10)$
   c $(-1, -6)$, $(0, 0)$, $(1, 6)$, $(2, 12)$

2 a Plot the points $(-2, -1)$, $(0, 0)$, $(2, 1)$, $(4, 2)$ and draw a line through them.
  b Why would $y = \frac{1}{2}x$ be a suitable equation to describe the line?
  c Plot the points $(-3, -1)$, $(0, 0)$, $(3, 1)$, $(6, 2)$ and draw a line through them.
  d What is the equation of this line?

3 Copy and complete the table to help you draw the line with equation $y = \frac{1}{4}x$.

x		-4	0	4	8
$y = \frac{1}{4}x$					

4 a Copy and complete the table to help you draw the line with equation $y = x$.
  b Give the coordinates of two other points on this line.

x		-4	0	2	4
$y = x$		-4			

  c Say whether the following points are above, on or below the line.
  i $(16, 16)$ **ii** $(23, 24)$ **iii** $(45, 44)$

5 a Copy and complete the table to help you draw the line with equation $y = -2x$.
  b Give the coordinates of two other points on this line.

x		-2	-1	0	1	2
$y = -2x$		4				

  c In what way does this line differ from every other one drawn in section 4 so far?
  d Say whether the following points are above, on or below the line.
  i $(16, -33)$ **ii** $(23, -46)$ **iii** $(45, -80)$

6 a Draw the line $y = x$ (see question **4**).
  b Copy and complete the table to help you draw the line with equation $y = -x$ on the same grid.

x		-2	-1	0	1	2
$y = -x$		2				

  c At what angle do the two lines cross?
  d Draw the square with coordinates $(4, 4)$, $(4, -4)$, $(-4, -4)$ and $(-4, 4)$.
  e What is the connection between the two lines and the square?

Exercise 4.2

1 A rectangle has diagonals which lie on the lines $y = 2x$ and $y = -2x$.
One vertex is $(2, 4)$.
  a Draw the lines.
  b Draw the rectangle.
  c Give the coordinates of the other three vertices.
  d What is the length and breadth of the rectangle?

2 a Draw the square whose diagonals lie on the lines $y = \frac{1}{2}x$ and $y = -2x$ and which has $(2, -4)$ as a vertex.
  b Give the coordinates of the other vertices.

3 A wind farm is laid out so that two lines of windmills form the diagonals of a square.

Using a coordinate grid to make a map of the farm, these diagonals lie on $y = -3x$ and $y = \frac{1}{3}x$.

a Draw the two lines.

b One vertex of the square is (9, 3). Find the other vertices.

c Find the midpoints of the sides of the square.

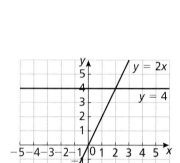

4 a Draw a coordinate grid ($-5 \leqslant x \leqslant 5$ and $-5 \leqslant y \leqslant 5$).

b Use it to help you find where:

   i $y = 3$ meets $y = -3x$ **ii** $y = 4$ meets $y = -2x$

   iii $x = -1$ meets $y = 4x$ **iv** $x = 1$ meets $y = 5x$

c Name three lines which meet at:

   i (1, 3)   **ii** (1, 4)   **iii** (1, −4).

5 a Make a copy of the diagram opposite.

b Where does the line $y = 4$ cross the line $y = 2x$?

c A rectangle 8 units tall by 4 units wide has diagonals which cross at the origin.

One side lies on $y = 4$.

On what lines do the other sides lie?

d One diagonal lies on $y = 2x$.

On which line does the other diagonal lie?

e What are the coordinates of the four vertices?

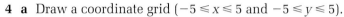

Investigation

In some of the questions above, the diagonals of squares lay on two lines.

a At what angle do the diagonals of a square intersect?

b If the two lines have equations of the form $y = ax$ and $y = bx$ what is the connection between a and b?

5 Other lines

During a Time-team dig, the positions of a set of standing stones are recorded.

To do this, a set of axes is marked out on the ground.

The coordinates of one row of stones can be seen in the table.

x	−1	0	1	2	3
y	2	4	6	8	10

Notice that in each case the y coordinate is double the x coordinate plus 4:

$y = 2x + 4$

Drawn onto a grid, we see that the stones lie in a straight line.

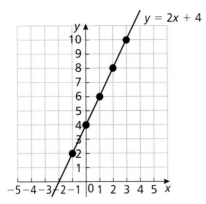

We call this line $y = 2x + 4$.
We say the equation of the line is $y = 2x + 4$.

Example   The diggers spot another line of stones.
The line has the equation $y = 3x - 2$.
Draw the line.

Step 1   Make a table.

x				
y				

Step 2   Make up some easy x coordinates.

x	0	1	2	3
y				

Step 3   Use the equation, $y = 3x - 2$,
to calculate the y coordinates.

x	0	1	2	3
y	−2	1	4	7

Step 4   Plot the points.

Step 5   Draw a line through them.

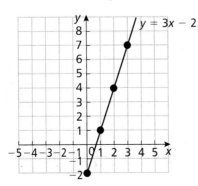

Note that for every point on the line $y = 3x - 2$.

4 The sides of a triangle lie on the three lines $y = 7$, $x = -2$ and $y = 2x + 3$.

   a Draw the three lines using a suitable grid.

   b Write down the coordinates of the vertices of the triangle.

   c What kind of triangle is it?

   d Which of the following points lie outside the triangle?

     i $(-3, 4)$ **ii** $(-1, 5)$ **iii** $(0, 6)$ **iv** $(1, 6)$ **v** $(1, 3)$ **vi** $(2, 8)$

5 Another triangle has sides lying on the lines $y = 3x$, $y = x$ and $y = 9$.

   a Draw the triangle.

   b List the coordinates of its vertices.

   c What kind of triangle is it?

Challenge

A right-angled triangle has its right angle at the origin.
One side lies on the line $y = 2$. Another lies on the line $y = \frac{1}{2}x$.
Can you draw the triangle?
On what line does the third side lie?
What are the vertices of the triangle?

---

6 Shaping up

As shown above, we can describe a shape by saying on what lines the sides lie.

Example   A quadrilateral has its sides lying on the lines $y = 2x + 4$, $y = 6$, $y = 2$
           and $y = 8 - x$.

         a Draw the quadrilateral.

         b Give the coordinates of its vertices.

a Make tables of values.

$y = 2x - 4$				$y = 6$			$y = 2$			$y = 8 - x$		
x	−1	0	3	**x**	0	3	**x**	0	3	**x**	0	3
y	2	4	10	**y**	6	6	**y**	2	2	**y**	8	5

Two points are enough for each line, but three act
as a check. Draw the lines.

b The vertices are the points $(-1, 2)$, $(1, 6)$, $(2, 6)$
and $(6, 2)$.

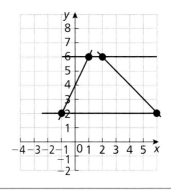

Exercise 6.1

1 The diagram shows how the sides of a rhombus lie on
the lines $y = 2x$, $y = -2x$, $y = 2x + 8$ and $y = -2x + 8$.
  a Pair off the equations to show the parallel sides.
  b Which of the four lines pass through $(2, 4)$ and $(0, 0)$?
  c What are the equations of the lines on which the
diagonals lie?
  d What are the coordinates of the point where the
diagonals intersect?
  e Where do $y = 2x$ and $y = -2x + 8$ intersect?

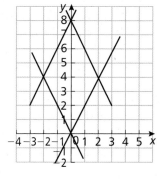

2 The sides of a kite lie on $y = x$, $y = 8 - x$, $y = -2x$ and
$y = 2x + 8$.
  a Two of the lines are already drawn. Which two?
  b Copy and complete the diagram to find the kite.
  c State the coordinates of its vertices.
  d On which lines do the diagonals lie?
  e On which line is the axis of symmetry of the kite?

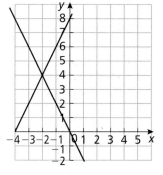

3 The sides of a parallelogram lie on the lines
$y = 2x + 7$, $y = 2x - 2$, $y = -x + 7$ and $y = -x - 2$
  a Match up each side of ABCD with its equation.
  b What is the equation of the line on which the diagonal
BD lies?

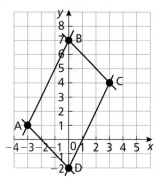

4 A trapezium is contained within the lines $y = -2x$,
$y = \frac{1}{3}x + 1$, $y = \frac{1}{3}x + 4$ and $x = 3$.
  a Draw the lines on a grid like this.
  b Which pair of lines are parallel?
  c Give the coordinates of the vertices of the trapezium
in the first quadrant.
  d Where do the parallel sides cut the y axis?

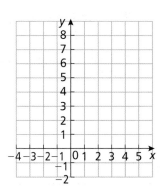

171

7 Best-fitting line

A teacher compared the class marks for maths and physics by making a scatter graph.

First she made a table of data:

Student	1	2	3	4	5	6	7	8	9	10	11	12	13	14	15	16	17	18	19	20
Maths	31	21	65	60	51	92	75	84	39	36	10	20	57	68	15	86	41	28	64	71
Physics	29	40	79	59	59	90	63	85	40	46	19	18	68	59	22	72	48	36	67	72

Each pair of marks is treated like coordinates.
Each point represents a different student.

From this a scatter graph is formed.

One student, Peter, sat his physics exam but missed the maths.
Peter scored 54 in physics.
The teacher wants to estimate his maths mark.

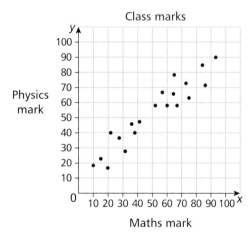

To help her she draws a line through the 'cloud' of points. This line follows the general trend of the points and leaves roughly the same number of points above as below it. The line is referred to as the **line of best fit**. We can use it to find what maths score matches up with a physics score of 54.

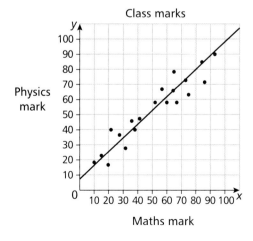

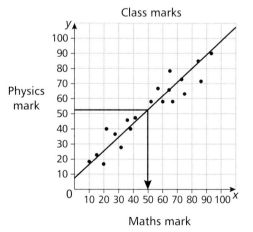

The teacher estimated that Peter could have got 50 for his maths.

Exercise 7.1

1 Use tracing paper to help you find the line of best fit for each scatter graph.
   Use the line to estimate the value of the score which should be paired with the given score.

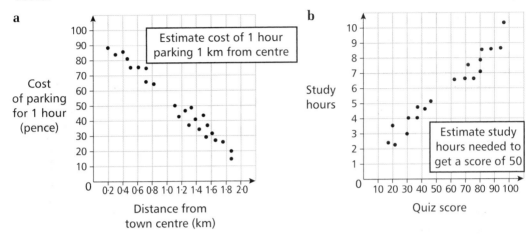

2 Ten farms were surveyed in 2000 and again in 2004. The number of sheep in the flocks were recorded. The table records the data found.

Farm	1	2	3	4	5	6	7	8	9	10
Flock in 2000	5	10	15	20	30	32	35	40	40	48
Flock in 2004	15	20	20	27	30	34	34	35	40	42

   a Make a chart similar to the one shown.

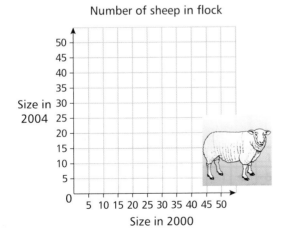

   b Plot points to represent each farm.
   c Draw a line of best fit.
   d Use your line to estimate the size of flock in 2004 of a farm that had a flock of 25 sheep in 2000.

Example 2

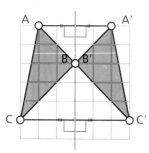

A'B'C' is the image of ABC.

PQ'R' is the image of PQR.

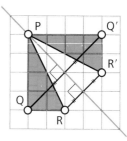

We can treat a mirror as an axis of symmetry, 'measuring' in it by imagining a mirror ruler.

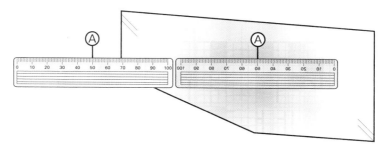

A pin, A, is 5 cm away from the surface of the mirror.
Its image, A', is 5 cm from the surface of the mirror … from the inside.

Exercise 2.1

1 Copy and complete each image so that it has mirror symmetry about the given axis.

a

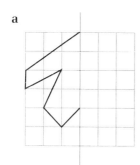

b

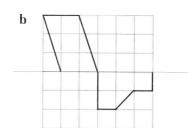

c

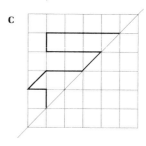

2 A point is 10 cm from an axis of symmetry. How far is it from its image?

A •————— 10 cm —————⌐————————————• A'

3 Abbie read a book in the corner by the mirror.

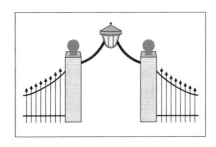

   a From the tip of her head, P, to the mirror is 112 cm.
How deep is the image of P in the mirror?

   b Q, the tip of her foot, is touching the mirror.

      i What is the distance from Q to the mirror surface?

     ii What is the distance from the image of Q to the surface of the mirror?

    iii What can be said about a point and its image if the point is on the axis of symmetry?

   c From R to its image is 100 cm.
How far is R from the surface of the mirror?

   d The back of the chair, ST, is 97 cm long.
How long is its image in the mirror?

   e $\angle$STR is 130°.
How big is the image angle?

4 A gateway has been designed to have an axis of symmetry.

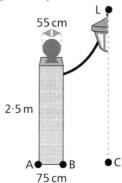

   a The gateway is 200 cm wide.

      i How far is the point B from the axis of symmetry?

     ii How far is the point A from the axis of symmetry?

    iii How far is the point A from its image?

   b One pillar is 2·5 m tall. How tall is the other pillar?

   c The diameter of the ball on the left-hand side is 55 cm.
What is the radius of the ball on the other side?

   d There is a light at L. $\angle$LAB = 72°.

      i What is angle $\angle$LA'B'?   **ii** What is angle $\angle$ALA'?

5 Nature provides many examples of symmetry.
Look at the points marked on the fly.
RT is an axis of symmetry and R is the point where the front edges of the fly meet.

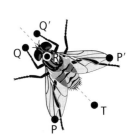

   a The distance between P and its image on the fly is 14 mm.
How far is the axis from P?

   b The distance between Q and the axis of symmetry is 4 mm.
How far apart are Q and its image?

   c $\angle$PRT = 32°. What is the size of $\angle$PRP'?

2 Name the ratio, $\sin x°$, $\cos x°$ or $\tan x°$, highlighted in each diagram.

a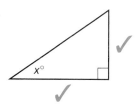

b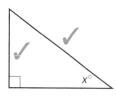

c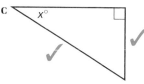

d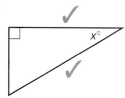

e

f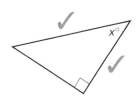

3 $\sin x° = \dfrac{a}{c}$. In a similar way write down:

   a $\cos x°$ **b** $\tan x°$ **c** $\sin y°$ **d** $\cos y°$ **e** $\tan y°$.

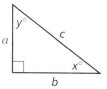

4 $\tan R = \dfrac{ST}{RT}$. Write down:

   a $\sin R$ **b** $\cos R$ **c** $\sin S$ **d** $\cos S$ **e** $\tan S$

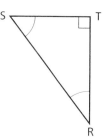

5 Write these numbers correct to 1 decimal place.

   a $2·47$ **b** $3·6283$ **c** $0·315$ **d** $37·28$ **e** $61·25$ **f** $45·361$

6 Write these numbers correct to 3 significant figures.

   a $0·6528$ **b** $0·376\,25$ **c** $0·677\,48$ **d** $8·267\,295$ **e** $3·145$ **f** $0·978\,16$

7 Use your calculator to find these values correct to 3 significant figures.

   a $\sin 73°$ **b** $\sin 68°$ **c** $\cos 52°$ **d** $\cos 27°$ **e** $\tan 36°$ **f** $\tan 56°$

8 $\sin A = \frac{5}{8}$. Using a calculator:

         $A = 38·682\,187\,45\ldots$

         $\Rightarrow \angle A = 38·7°$ to 1 decimal place

$\sin^{-1}$

Find the size of B, C and D if:

   a $\sin B = \frac{4}{7}$ **b** $\cos C = \frac{2}{9}$ **c** $\tan D = \frac{11}{6}$

9 Copy and complete each problem. Part **a** has been done for you.

a

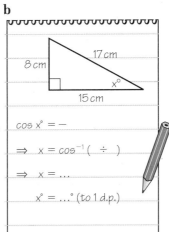

5 m, 3 m, 4 m, $x°$

$\sin x° = \dfrac{3}{5}$

$\Rightarrow\ x = \sin^{-1}(3 \div 5)$

$\Rightarrow\ x = 36{\cdot}8699\ldots$

$x° = 36{\cdot}9°\ (\text{to 1 d.p.})$

b

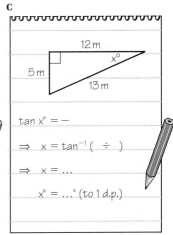

17 cm, 8 cm, 15 cm, $x°$

$\cos x° = -$

$\Rightarrow\ x = \cos^{-1}(\ \div\ )$

$\Rightarrow\ x = \ldots$

$x° = \ldots°\ (\text{to 1 d.p.})$

c

12 m, 5 m, 13 m, $x°$

$\tan x° = -$

$\Rightarrow\ x = \tan^{-1}(\ \div\ )$

$\Rightarrow\ x = \ldots$

$x° = \ldots°\ (\text{to 1 d.p.})$

10 Copy and complete parts **b** and **c**.

a

6 cm, d cm, 32°

$\sin 32° = \dfrac{d}{6}$

$\Rightarrow\ d = 6\sin 32°$

$d = 3{\cdot}2\ \text{cm}\ (\text{to 1 d.p.})$

(6) (sin) (32) (=)

b

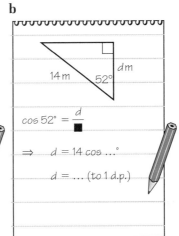

14 m, d m, 52°

$\cos 52° = \dfrac{d}{\blacksquare}$

$\Rightarrow\ d = 14\cos \ldots°$

$d = \ldots\ (\text{to 1 d.p.})$

c

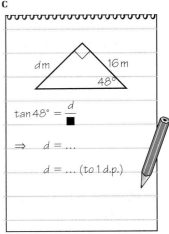

d m, 16 m, 48°

$\tan 48° = \dfrac{d}{\blacksquare}$

$\Rightarrow\ d = \ldots$

$d = \ldots\ (\text{to 1 d.p.})$

11 This 4 metre long ladder is safe if its foot is less than 2·2 metres from the wall.

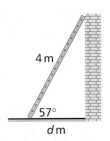

4 m, 57°, d m

  a Find out if the ladder is safe in two ways:
   i Scale drawing and measurement
    Use the scale: 1 cm to 50 cm.
   ii Trigonometry
    Use the cosine ratio.
  b Which method is more accurate?
  c Is accuracy important? Why?

5 a How high is the cliff?
  b What is the shortest possible length
     of rope that will stretch from the top
     of the cliff to the boat?

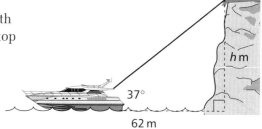

37°

62 m

h m

6 Steve, a trick-cyclist, hopes to
   clear the row of barrels.
   Calculate the angles $x°$ and $y°$ in
   the ramps.

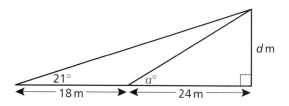

18 m   3 m $x°$ 25·2 m $y°$ 25 m

7 Calculate:
   a d
   b angle $a°$.

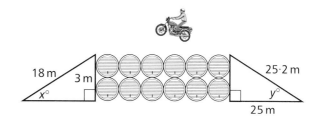

21°   18 m $a°$ 24 m d m

---

3 Getting trigonometry into shape

We can use trigonometry to calculate lengths and angles in many shapes.
But remember, we need to find a right-angled triangle!

Exercise 3.1

Give answers correct to 1 decimal place, unless told otherwise.

1 *The rectangle and square.*
   a Calculate the value of x.
   b i What is the size of $\angle ABE$?
      ii Calculate the length of AE.
      iii What is the length of the diagonals
         of square ABCD?

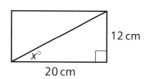

12 cm $x°$ 20 cm

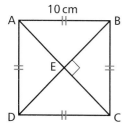

10 cm   A   B   E   D   C

9 Copy and complete each problem. Part **a** has been done for you.

a

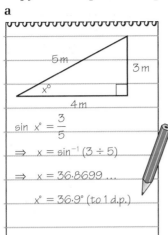

$\sin x° = \dfrac{3}{5}$

$\Rightarrow x = \sin^{-1}(3 \div 5)$

$\Rightarrow x = 36.8699\ldots$

$x° = 36.9°$ (to 1 d.p.)

b

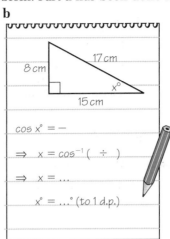

$\cos x° = -$

$\Rightarrow x = \cos^{-1}(\ \div\ )$

$\Rightarrow x = \ldots$

$x° = \ldots°$ (to 1 d.p.)

c

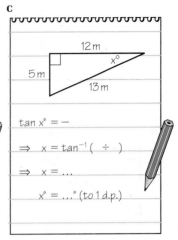

$\tan x° = -$

$\Rightarrow x = \tan^{-1}(\ \div\ )$

$\Rightarrow x = \ldots$

$x° = \ldots°$ (to 1 d.p.)

10 Copy and complete parts **b** and **c**.

a

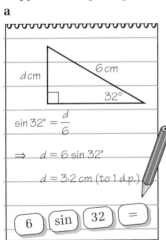

$\sin 32° = \dfrac{d}{6}$

$\Rightarrow d = 6 \sin 32°$

$d = 3.2$ cm (to 1 d.p.)

$\boxed{6}\ \boxed{\sin}\ \boxed{32}\ \boxed{=}$

b

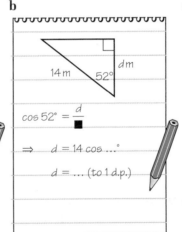

$\cos 52° = \dfrac{d}{\blacksquare}$

$\Rightarrow d = 14 \cos \ldots°$

$d = \ldots$ (to 1 d.p.)

c

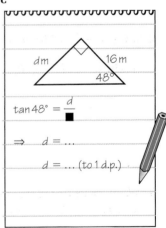

$\tan 48° = \dfrac{d}{\blacksquare}$

$\Rightarrow d = \ldots$

$d = \ldots$ (to 1 d.p.)

11 This 4 metre long ladder is safe if its foot is less than 2·2 metres from the wall.

a Find out if the ladder is safe in two ways:
   i Scale drawing and measurement
      Use the scale: 1 cm to 50 cm.
   ii Trigonometry
      Use the cosine ratio.

b Which method is more accurate?

c Is accuracy important? Why?

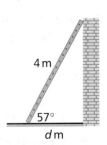

12 What is the 3-figure bearing of B from A in each diagram?

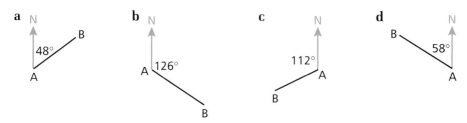

a **b** **c** **d**

13 What is the 3-figure bearing of A from B in each diagram?

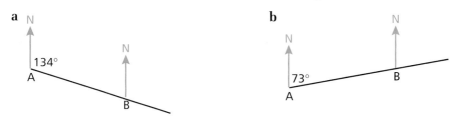

a **b**

---

2 Problem solving

When using trigonometry to help you solve problems:
- look for a right-angled triangle
- examine the data given to help you decide which ratio to use
- give your answer to the degree of accuracy requested.

Example
George was 280 m from the foot of the Eiffel tower.
He had to look up through an angle of 47° to see the top.
How high is the tower to the nearest metre?

You know an angle.
You know the length of the adjacent side; you want
the length of the opposite side.

SOH CAH TOA … Use the tangent ratio.

$$\tan 47° = \frac{h}{280}$$
$$\Rightarrow \quad h = 280 \tan 47°$$
$$\Rightarrow \quad h = 300{\cdot}263\,238\,8\ …$$

The tower is 300 m tall, to the nearest metre.

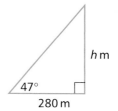

Exercise 2.1

1 Calculate the value of d and x in the diagrams, correct to 1 decimal place.

a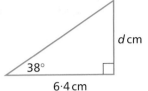

b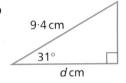

c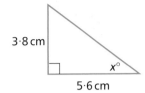

d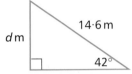

e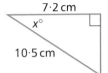

f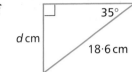

g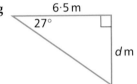

h

i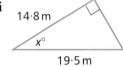

2 Calculate the height of each building.

a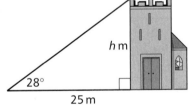

b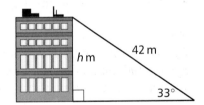

3 How wide is the river?

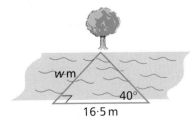

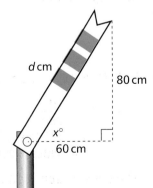

4 A signal on the railway line slopes at x° to the horizontal.
  a Calculate the value of x.
  b Use Pythagoras' theorem to calculate the value of d.

5 a How high is the cliff?
  b What is the shortest possible length
    of rope that will stretch from the top
    of the cliff to the boat?

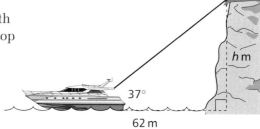

6 Steve, a trick-cyclist, hopes to
  clear the row of barrels.
  Calculate the angles $x°$ and $y°$ in
  the ramps.

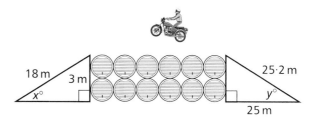

7 Calculate:
  a d
  b angle $a°$.

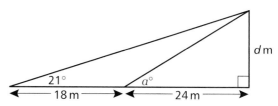

3 Getting trigonometry into shape

We can use trigonometry to calculate lengths and angles in many shapes.
But remember, we need to find a right-angled triangle!

Exercise 3.1

Give answers correct to 1 decimal place, unless told otherwise.

1 *The rectangle and square.*
  a Calculate the value of *x*.
  b i What is the size of $\angle$ABE?
    ii Calculate the length of AE.
    iii What is the length of the diagonals
      of square ABCD?

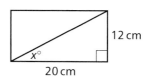

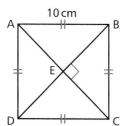

2 *The isosceles triangle.*
  a Calculate the length of:
    i RU
    ii ST.

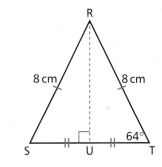

  b Calculate x.
    (You will need to make a
    right-angled triangle.)

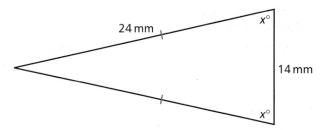

3 *The kite and rhombus.*
  a In the kite, calculate:
    i   PT
    ii TR
    iii ST
    iv the lengths of the diagonals to
        the nearest centimetre.

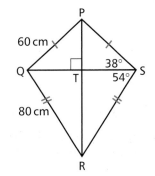

  b In the rhombus calculate the value of:
    i x
    ii y
    iii the longer diagonal
    iv the shorter diagonal.

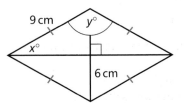

4 *The parallelogram and trapezium.*
  a Calculate the height of the
    parallelogram, XY.

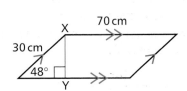

  b Calculate:
    i   the height of the trapezium, h
    ii the angle marked $x°$.

5 *The circle.*

    a ST is a tangent to the circle.

        i Calculate the radius OT.

        ii Use Pythagoras' theorem to help
            you calculate OS.

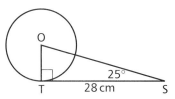

    b Calculate:

        i the chord CB

        ii the diameter AB.

Exercise 3.2

1 Calculate the angle the slope of the roof makes
with the horizontal.

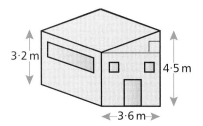

2 Calculate:

    a the height of the roof, h m

    b the slope of the roof, $a°$

    c the width of the house, w m.

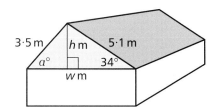

3 The slant height of the cone is 28 cm.
The angle between the sloping edge and the base is 65°.
Calculate:

    a the height, h cm, of the cone

    b the radius of the base of the cone, r cm, in two
different ways.

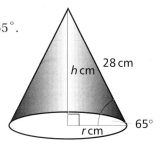

4 Land, sea and air

Remember: directions can be described using 3-figure bearings.

A 3-figure bearing is an angle measured from the north in a clockwise direction.

Examples

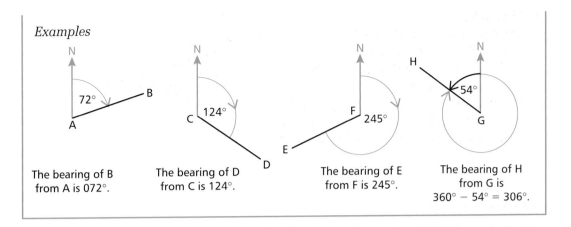

The bearing of B
from A is 072°.

The bearing of D
from C is 124°.

The bearing of E
from F is 245°.

The bearing of H
from G is
360° − 54° = 306°.

Exercise 4.1

1 The *Merry Mate* sails on a course of 065° for
32 km from the harbour H to the island at I.
Calculate:
   a how far east (x km)
   b how far north (y km)
   the island is from H.

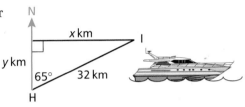

2 The *Saucy Sue* sails on a course of 290°
for 26 km from port P to port Q.
Calculate:
   a how far west
   b how far north
   the boat is from P.

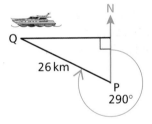

3 A plane flies north-east for 750 km from
A to B.
It then changes course to south-east and
flies a further 480 km from B to C.
   a What kind of triangle is △ABC?
   b Calculate the bearing of C from A.
   c Calculate the distance AC.

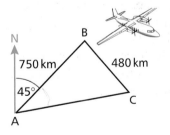

4 '1 in 12' means that the road rises one metre
for each 12 metres of road.
Calculate the angle between the road and
the horizontal in each case.

 a 1 in 12
 b 1 in 15
 c 1 in 20
 d 1 in 10

5 Gina follows the path up Haddow Hill which is 300 metres high.

a From A to B, a horizontal distance of 120 m, her height above sea level increases by 100 m vertically.
Calculate her angle of climb, $x°$.

b Calculate Gina's angle of climb
  i   from B to C
  ii from C to D.

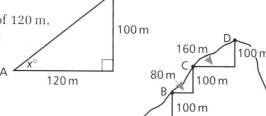

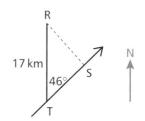

6 A ship is 17 km south of an oil-rig, and is following a course of 046°.

a What is the size of $\angle RST$ when the ship is closest to the oil-rig?

b How close to the oil-rig does the ship get?

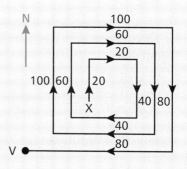

Challenge

Air–sea search

Oscar Delta Foxtrot is searching for a missing vessel. It starts at X and makes a 'square search', flying N, E, S, W on lines 20 km apart. It finds the vessel at V, at the end of a line.

a Make a scale drawing of the square search, using a scale of 1 cm to 10 km. Start from X at the centre of your page.

b Measure the distance and bearing (three figures, clockwise from the north) of V from X.

c Check your answers by trigonometry.

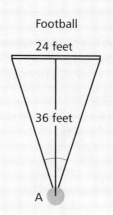

Investigation

Is it easier to score from the penalty spot at football or hockey?

Calculate the angles at A and B to compare the shooting angles.
What do you find?
Are there other factors to think about?

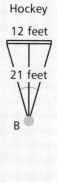

5 Angles of elevation and depression

If you are looking up at an object then the angle between the horizontal and your line of sight is called the angle of elevation of the object.

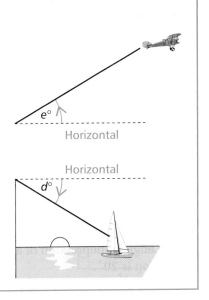

If you are looking down at an object then the angle between the horizontal and your line of sight is called the angle of depression of the object.

Exercise 5.1

1 The diagram shows a block of high-rise flats close to sea cliffs.

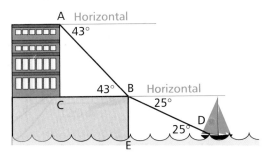

a Write down the angle of elevation from:
  i B to the top of the flats at A
  ii D to the top of the cliff at B.
b Write down the angle of depression from
  i the top of the flats, A, to the top of the cliff, B
  ii B to the boat at D.
c Write down the size of: i ∠BAC   ii ∠DBE.

2 A picture of the Greenside Tor is shown.
  a What is the size of the angle of depression from the top of the hill, T, to the bottom of the hill at R?
  b What is the size of ∠TRS?
  c Calculate the height, h m, of the Greenside Tor.

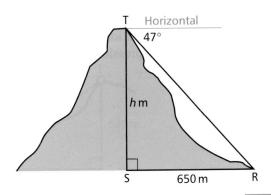

6 a What is the angle of depression from the aircraft to the top of the hill?

b The plane flies horizontally for another 100 m towards the hill.
What will be the angle of depression then?

c By how much has the angle of depression changed?

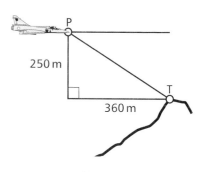

7 A galleon for the film *Pirates on the Move* is 16·4 km from the harbour as shown.

a What is the bearing from the boat at B to the harbour at H?

b How far north of the boat is the harbour?

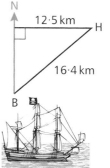

8 Which picture is longer? By how much?

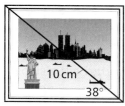

Exercise 6.2

1 Calculate the angle of elevation from P to the top of each building.

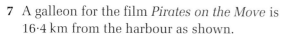

2 Using right-angled triangles ABC and ADC, calculate the length of the traffic jam BD.

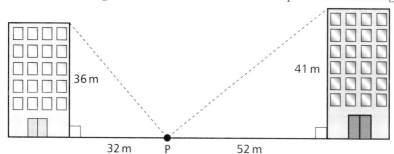

3 The angle of elevation from Tom to the kite is 36°.

   a How high is the kite flying?

   b The kite itself is built as shown.
      How long are the sticks which form its diagonals?

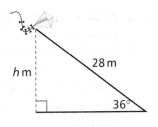

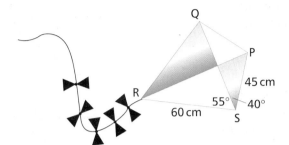

4 Two wrecks are at the bottom of the sea at A and B.
   A search boat is at C.

   a Calculate the angle of depression from C to B.

   b Use Pythagoras' theorem to find the depth of the
      water.

   c The angle of depression from C to A is 63°.
      Calculate the distance between the two wrecks A and B.

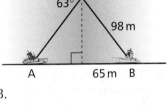

5 Two boats at E and F are 8·6 km apart.
   The boat at F is 5·7 km west of the boat at E.
   Calculate the bearing of F from E.

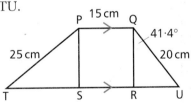

6 PQUT is a trapezium with PQ parallel to TU.
   PQRS is a square of side 15 cm.

   a Calculate the size of ∠PTS.

   b Calculate the length of RU.

   c Find the perimeter of PQUT.

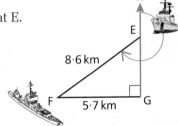

Practical exercise

1 Copy and complete the table.
   Use a calculator and give your answers correct to 1 decimal place.

$x°$	0	10	20	30	40	50	60	70	80	90
$y = \sin x°$	0	0·2	0·3	0·5						
$y = \cos x°$	1	1	0·9							
$y = \tan x°$	0	0·2	0·4							

2 a On 5 mm squared paper draw the graph of $y = \sin x°$.

b On the same diagram draw the graph of $y = \cos x°$.

c Use your graph to find the value of x for which $\sin x = \cos x$.

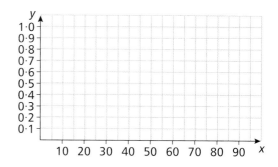

3 a On 5 mm squared paper draw the graph of $y = \tan x°$.

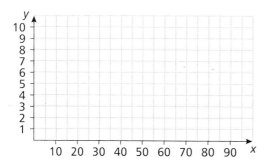

b Copy and complete the tables, giving your answers to the nearest whole number.

$x°$	80	81	82	83	84	85	86	87	88	89
$y = \tan x°$										

$x°$	89·2	89·4	89·6	89·8	89·9	89·99	89·999
$y = \tan x°$							

c What happens to $\tan x°$ as x approaches 90?

7 The gradient of a slope

The ski-jumps at Lake Placid have different slopes or gradients.

We define the gradient of a slope between two points as:

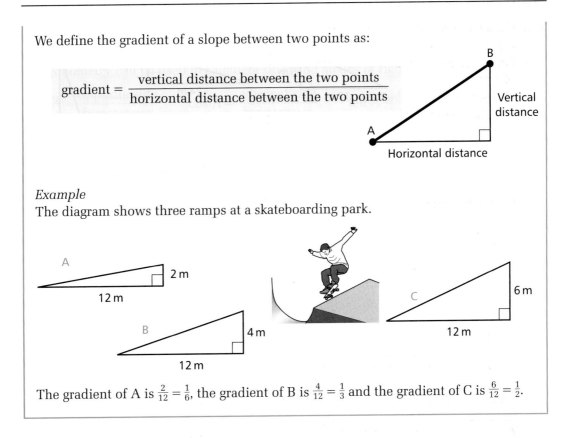

$$\text{gradient} = \frac{\text{vertical distance between the two points}}{\text{horizontal distance between the two points}}$$

Example
The diagram shows three ramps at a skateboarding park.

The gradient of A is $\frac{2}{12} = \frac{1}{6}$, the gradient of B is $\frac{4}{12} = \frac{1}{3}$ and the gradient of C is $\frac{6}{12} = \frac{1}{2}$.

Exercise 7.1

1 Write down the gradient of each line.

a — A, B, C triangle: 4 m (A to C), 1 m (B to C)

b — P, Q, R triangle: 6 m (P to R), 4 m (Q to R)

c — S, T, V triangle: 8 m (S to V), 1 m (T to V)

d — L, W, K triangle: 5 m (W to K), 5 m (L to K)

2 Make use of the grid to help you measure the gradient of each line.

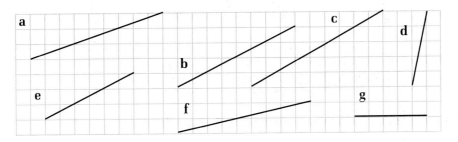
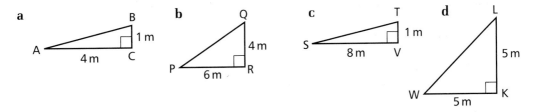

11 3-D shapes

The design of a car involves many people. All of these people must have a good understanding of 3-D shapes and 3-D space, and be able to recognise 3-D shapes from 2-D representations.

1 Review

◀◀ Exercise 1.1

1 Name each 2-D shape.

a   b    c   d

e   f 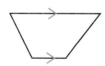   g

2 State what type each triangle is.

a   b   c 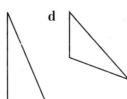   d   e   f

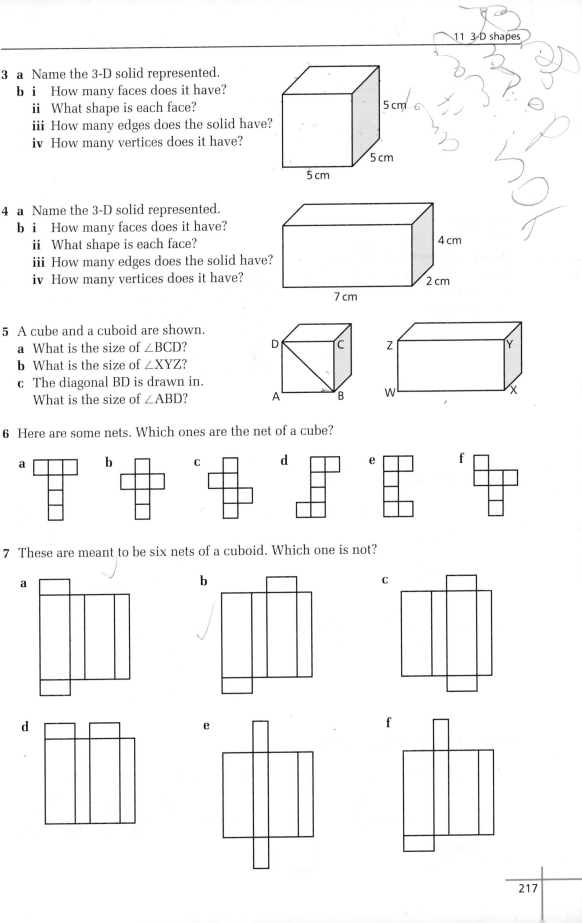

3 a Name the 3-D solid represented.
b i How many faces does it have?
ii What shape is each face?
iii How many edges does the solid have?
iv How many vertices does it have?

5 cm

5 cm

5 cm

4 a Name the 3-D solid represented.
b i How many faces does it have?
ii What shape is each face?
iii How many edges does the solid have?
iv How many vertices does it have?

4 cm

2 cm

7 cm

5 A cube and a cuboid are shown.
a What is the size of $\angle$BCD?
b What is the size of $\angle$XYZ?
c The diagonal BD is drawn in.
What is the size of $\angle$ABD?

D C Z Y

A B W X

6 Here are some nets. Which ones are the net of a cube?

a **b** **c** **d** **e** **f**

7 These are meant to be six nets of a cuboid. Which one is not?

a **b** **c**

d **e** **f**

8 Calculate:

i the volume   **ii** the surface area of each 3-D shape.

a
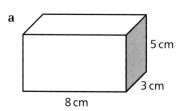
5 cm
3 cm
8 cm

b
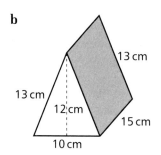
13 cm
13 cm
12 cm
15 cm
10 cm

c
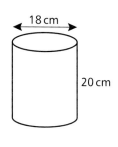
18 cm
20 cm

9 Calculate the length of the unknown side in each right-angled triangle.

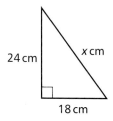
24 cm
x cm
18 cm

20 mm
y mm
52 mm

---

2 Prisms

Reminders   A prism is a solid which has a constant cross-section. Wherever you cut it, parallel to the base, you get a shape congruent to the base.

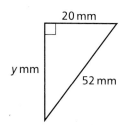

This diagram shows a **triangular** prism but there are many types of prisms. Each prism takes its name from the shape of the base.

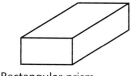
Rectangular prism
(Cuboid)

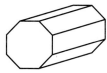
Octagonal
prism

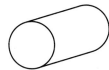
Circular prism
(Cylinder)

A **face** is a surface of a solid.
An **edge** is the line formed where two faces meet.
A **vertex** is formed at the meeting point of edges.
We speak about one vertex and two or more **vertices**.

Exercise 2.1

1 Spot the prisms and name them.

a 　　**b** 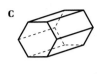　　**c** 　　**d**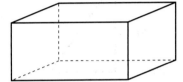

e 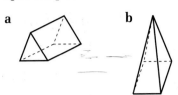　　**f** 　　**g**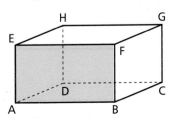

2 Look at this solid.
It has a constant cross-section. It is a prism.

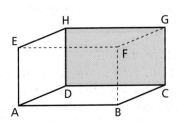

  a What shape is the cross-section?
  b What type of prism is the solid?
  c What name is more commonly used for this solid?
  d Find two other ways in which this solid fits the
     definition of a prism.

3 a What shape is the base of this prism?

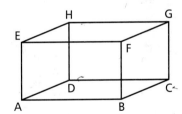

  b What type of prism is it?
  c What name is more commonly used for this prism?

4 A 2-D representation of a cuboid is shown.

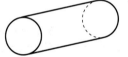

  a ABCD is a face.
     Name another face which is congruent to face ABCD.
  b Name a face which is congruent to:
     i CDHG　　**ii** ADHE.
  c Name three other edges which are the same length as:
     i BC　　**ii** BF　　**iii** CD.
  d Name three other edges that are parallel to AB.
  e Name the three edges which meet at vertex D.

Be careful with 2-D representations. They can be ambiguous!
Which face is closer, ABFE or DCGH?
Shading and dotted lines help.

5 The end of this prism is an isosceles triangle.

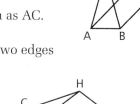

  a How many faces does the triangular prism have?
  b Name the two triangular faces.
  c Name the two rectangular faces which are congruent.
  d Name the other face.
  e Name three other edges which are the same length as AC.
  f Name two other edges which are parallel to BE.
  g What can you say about the length of BE and the two edges which are your answer to **f**?

6 a What shape is face ABCDE and face FGHIJ?
  b Is this solid a prism?
  c Name the type of solid.

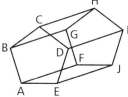

---

3 Pyramids

A pyramid is a solid defined by a base and a point, called an **apex**, not on the base.

Edges run from each vertex of the base to the apex.

The pyramid takes its name from the name of the base.

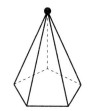

Triangle-based pyramid (tetrahedron)   Square-based pyramid   Pentagon-based pyramid

---

Exercise 3.1

1 a How many faces does this pyramid have?
  b Name the square face.
  c Name the triangular faces.
  d Name the apex.

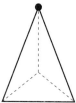

2 Look at pyramid UVWXYZ.
  a What shape is its base?
  b What type of pyramid is it?
  c How many triangular faces does it have?
  d Name the triangular faces.

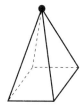

3 How many
  a triangular faces
  b edges
  does a hexagon-based pyramid have?

4 A cone is a pyramid with a circular base.
  How many
  a faces
  b edges
  c vertices
  does it have?

5 The team coach lays out cones to practise ball control.

  a When each cone is lifted there is a mark left in the grass.
    What shape is that mark?
  b The ball is a 3-D solid. What is its mathematical name?

6 This is a square-based pyramid whose apex is
  not directly above the centre of the base.
  Instead it is directly above M.
  a Name the edges which meet at O.
  b Which of these edges is the longest?

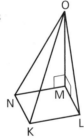

Challenge

A certain 2-D representation makes it easier to count faces, vertices and edges.
This type of representation can be called a **basal view** as you have to imagine holding
the solid and viewing it with X-ray eyes through the base of the shape.

For a **prism**, consider one end 'inside' the other, for example:

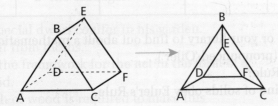

9 The table shows income tax rates for different taxable incomes.

  a On a taxable income of £45 000 how much is taxed at

   i 10%   **ii** 22%   **iii** 40%?

  b Gordon's tax allowance is £5350.
  His total annual income is £38 400.
  Copy and complete:

Taxable income	Rate of tax
£0–£2020	10%
£2020–£31 400	22%
over £31 400	40%

> Taxable income £...
>
> Tax at 10% rate = 10% of £... = £...
>
> Tax at 22% rate = 22% of £... = £...
>
> Tax at 40% rate = 40% of £... = £...
>
> Total tax payable   = £...

10 Copy and complete this bank statement.

		STATEMENT		
Date	Paid out	Paid in	Balance
4 Apr			145·00
10 Apr		53·70	
15 Apr	138·30		
10 Apr	76·69		
28 Apr		247·64	

11 The Burnside Building Society offers 5% p.a. interest on savings accounts.
Calculate the interest on:

  a £80 invested for 1 year

  b £200 invested for 4 years (interest taken out at the end of each year)

  c £700 invested for 3 months

  d £12 000 invested for 9 months.

Revising Chapter 4   Similarity

1 The first hole at Jan's golf club is 400 metres due north.
On her first shot at the hole, Jan hit the ball 240 metres on
a bearing of 070°. Her second shot landed in the hole.

  a Make an accurate drawing of what happened.

  b What bearing did Jan's second shot take?

  c How far did she hit her second shot?

2 An overhead projector projects enlarged images onto a screen.

  a On acetate, a triangle has one side measuring 5 cm.
  On the screen, the corresponding side has a length of 60 cm.
  What is the scale factor of the enlargement?

  b On the screen, one of the other sides of the triangle measures 84 cm.
  What was the length of the corresponding side on the acetate?

REVISE

3 The scale of a map is 1 : 20 000.
   On the map the distance between two towns is 3 cm.
   What is the actual distance in kilometres between these towns?

4 Two rectangles are similar.
   The smaller rectangle has a length of 6 cm and a breadth of 4 cm.
   The length of the larger rectangle is 10 cm.
   Calculate the breadth of this rectangle.

5 The area of a right-angled flower bed is 600 cm².
   Another similar triangular flower bed has an area of 2400 cm².
   One side of the smaller triangle has a length of 30 cm.
   What is the length of the corresponding side of the larger triangle?

6 Tanice and Stacey walked on a bearing of 120° for 2·5 km.
   They then turned and walked for a further 1·5 km on a
   bearing of 240°.
   a Make an accurate drawing of their route.
   b How far are they from their starting point?

Revising Chapter 5   Formulae

1 If $a = 2$ and $b = 9$ find the value of:
   a $b - 5$ **b** $6a$ **c** $2a + 11$ **d** $b - a$ **e** $50 - 5b$ **f** $9a - 2b$
   g ab **h** b^2 **i** $4ab$ **j** $3a^2$ **k** $ab - 3a$ **l** $11a - ab$

2 **a** $R = \dfrac{5 + Q}{2}$; find R if $Q = 7$.   **b** $C = a - \sqrt{b}$; find C if $a = 12$ and $b = 9$.
   c $M = (K - 2)^2$; find M if $K = 7$.   **d** $f = u - \frac{1}{2}r$; find f if $u = 17$ and $r = 7$.

3 The cost, £C, of hiring a minibus is given by the formula:

$$C = 50 + 0{\cdot}25M + 3P$$

   where M is the number of miles travelled and P is the
   number of passengers, including the driver.
   Heaton Park School hired a minibus for a 230 mile round
   trip for a group of 17 pupils with their teacher driving.
   How much did the minibus cost?

4 **a i** Find a formula that calculates the perimeter, P m, of
         this painting from the length, x metres, and the
         height, y metres.
      ii Find P if $x = 2{\cdot}3$ and $y = 1{\cdot}7$.
   b i Find a formula for the total weight, T kg, if each
         bottle weighs w kg, the beaker weighs z kg and the
         tray weighs t kg.
      ii Calculate T if $w = 9{\cdot}5$, $z = 5{\cdot}5$ and $t = 3{\cdot}5$.

REVISE

7 The length of each pencil in a pencil tub was measured in centimetres.

   10 11 11 12 13 14 14 15 16 16 16 16

   a Calculate **i** the range in lengths   **ii** the median length.
   b An old 5 cm pencil is added to the tub.
      Calculate the new **i** range in lengths   **ii** median length.
   c Which measure was most affected by the addition of this one piece of data?

8 a On a coordinate grid draw the lines:
      i $y = x$ **ii** $x = 4$ **iii** $y = 1$
   b Shade the region trapped by the three lines.
   c What kind of shape is it?

9 Calculate:
   a $-6 + 2$ **b** $-3 \times (-5)$ **c** $3 \times (-4) \times 2$

10 The bearing from A to B is $127°$.
    What is the bearing from B to A?

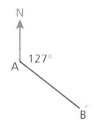

11 Straw B is shorter than Straw A.
    a Form an inequation to describe this situation.
    b Solve the inequation.
    c If x is a positive whole number, find the
       length of each straw.

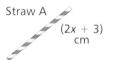

Straw A $(2x + 3)$ cm $(4x - 1)$ cm   Straw B

12 Solve these equations by first removing the brackets:
    a $4(x - 2) = x + 4$ **b** $6(2x - 1) = 5(x + 3)$

 Test A Part 2

1 Drew has to calculate how much paint he will need to decorate a room.
   The room is rectangular. The floor measures $4·1$ metres by $3·8$ metres.
   The ceiling is $2·25$ metres high.

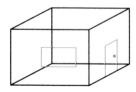

   a Calculate:
      i the area of the ceiling
      ii the area of the four walls (pretend there are no doors or windows)
      iii the total area to be painted.
   b One litre of the paint that has been chosen covers an area of $6·8$ m².
      Calculate how much paint is required.

2 Four Red Kites were released at Doune in Stirlingshire.
They have radio transmitters attached to them so that they can be monitored.

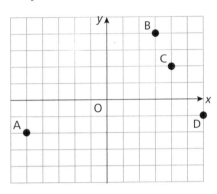

Their position after one day is shown on the coordinate diagram.
Doune is situated at the origin and each square on the diagram has a side of 1 km.
Calculate the distance from Doune to each Red Kite.

3 Andrew has made a decked area in front of his house.
It is rectangular and is 4·1 metres long.
To strengthen it he has put a length of wood
diagonally underneath the deck. This piece of wood
is 4·9 metres long.
What is the width of the decked area?

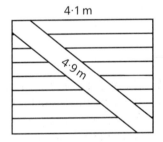

4 Wendy's parents have bought her a playhouse.
It is made by joining plastic rods together to make the
framework.
The walls and roof of the house are made of plastic
sheeting which is laid over the framework.
   a Make a list of how many rods of each length are
      required.
   b Calculate the altitude of triangle XYZ.
   c Calculate the area of △XYZ.
   d Work out the total area of plastic sheeting needed.
      (Remember: no base!)

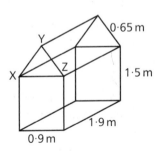

5 The sales staff at Country Caravans are paid a basic
salary plus commission of 2% of their sales.
Gary's basic salary is £1280 per month.
   a How much commission is he given in a month
      when his sales total £45 000?
   b How much, in total, should he expect to earn in a
      year if this is a typical month?

6 In this children's climbing frame, the right-angled triangles are similar.
The rectangles are also similar.

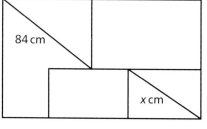

   a The reduction scale factor for the triangles is $\frac{2}{7}$.
   What is the length of the corresponding side, x cm, of the smaller triangle?

   b The area of the larger rectangle is 7700 cm². The reduction scale factor of the smaller rectangle is $\frac{1}{5}$.
   What is the area of the smaller rectangle?

7 Jane makes phone calls costing £0·528, £1·346, £0·254 and £2·736.
Calculate the mean cost of these calls.

8 Gill is making HP repayments on a TV set.
The table shows the total amount she has repaid and the number of months.

Number of months	1	2	3	4	5	6
Amount repaid	£35	£70	£105	£140	£175	£210

   a Draw a graph to illustrate the table.

   b Does the amount repaid vary directly with the number of months?
   How does the graph show this?

   c The HP plan lasts for 9 months. How much does Gill repay in this time?

9

> Distance = Speed × Time

Calculate the distance travelled in:

   a $\frac{3}{4}$ hour at 36 km/h

   b $2\frac{1}{2}$ hours at $2\frac{2}{3}$ km/h.

10 The table shows how much Tragic Travel Insurance Plc charges one person for insurance. The cost depends on destination and length of stay.

No. of days	UK (£)	Europe (£)	Worldwide (£)
1–3	8·25	14·50	30·50
4–6	9·75	16·80	36·70
7–9	11·52	22·60	39·45
10–17	14·83	24·85	42·50
18–25	18·56	26·90	45·37
26–35	22·85	30·25	48·52
each extra week	5·30	8·25	15·78

Mr and Mrs Curtis take their three children to Hong Kong for a 3 week holiday.
The children receive a 40% discount.
Calculate the cost of insuring the family.

REVISE

11 a Write an equation for this situation.
    b Solve the equation to find his number.

I'm thinking of a number. I add 7 to it then multiply the answer by 9 to get 234. Whats my number?

12 Complete this cross-number puzzle.

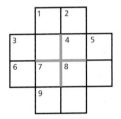

Across
1 $5x - 92 = x$
3 $7x = 360 - x$
4 $8x + 92 = 2x + 284$
6 $738 - x = 8x$
8 $6x = 209 - 5x$
9 $224 + 3x = 19x$

Down
1 $14x - 325 = x$
2 $264 + 7x = 15x$
3 $25x = 1248 - x$
5 $12x + 10 = 5x + 213$
7 $336 - 2x = 14x$
8 $x = 126 - 8x$

 Test B Part 1

1 Eric is making a skeleton model of a cuboid.
The cuboid is 15 cm by 12 cm by 7 cm.
    a What is the total length of straw that he will need?
    b He will need a piece of plasticine at each vertex.
       How many pieces will he need?

2 Ann works from Monday to Friday. She starts at 8.30 am.
She has lunch from 12.30 till 1.15.
She stops work at 5 pm.
How many hours does she work in:
    a a day   **b** a week?

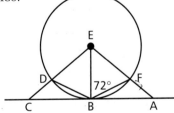

3 Calculate:
    a 10% of 45 kg   **b** 50% of 750 ml   **c** 25% of 5000 tonnes
    d 75% of 240 litres   **e** 40% of 70 days   **f** 15% of 240 hours.

4 This diagram shows a wheel-clamping device.
    a $\angle$FBE is 72°. What size is $\angle$BFE?
    b Find the size of $\angle$BEF.
    c What size is $\angle$EBA? Why?
    d Calculate $\angle$BAE.

5 Round each number to 2 decimal places:
    a 4·576   **b** 11·249   **c** 17·956

6 Calculate the time between:
    a 11 47 and 19 35   **b** 20 15 and 03 55

REVISE

7 **a** A ruler measures 30 cm.
Express 30 cm as fraction of 1 metre in its simplest terms.
b A car weighs 480 kg.
Express 480 kg as a fraction of a tonne in its simplest terms.
c A TV programme lasts for 30 minutes.
Express 30 minutes as a fraction of 1 day in its simplest terms.

8 The amount of VAT Sam pays on his gas bill ($£V$) varies directly as the pre-VAT charge ($£C$).
When $C = £60$, $V = £3$.
a Find a formula for V in terms of C.   **b** Calculate V when $C = £80$.

9 A line has the equation $y = 2x + 1$.
a Copy and complete the table to find four points on this line.
b Plot the points and draw the line.
c Which of the following points lie on the line?
   i $(5, 11)$ **ii** $(21, 10)$ **iii** $(60, 121)$

x		−1	0	1	2
$y = 2x + 1$					

10 Calculate:
a $5 - (-3)$ **b** $-7 - (-1)$ **c** $2 - (-4) - 8$

11 **a** Complete these by finding the missing factors:
   i $5x^2 = 5x \times \dots$ **ii** $2ab = 2b \times \dots$ **iii** $6mn = 2n \times \dots$
b Factorise fully:
   i $8x - 16$ **ii** $16 - 24y$ **iii** $4ab - 6$

12 **a** $K = 35 - a^2$ Calculate K if $a = 5$.
b $Q = \sqrt{R} + 2$ Calculate Q if $R = 49$.
c $M = \dfrac{4mn}{3}$ Calculate M if $m = 6$ and $n = 5$.
d $x = \dfrac{10}{a - b}$ Calculate x if $a = 25$ and $b = 5$.

Test B Part 2

1 A tent has dimensions as shown.
a Calculate the length of sloping edge AB.
b Calculate the area of sloping face ABCD.
c Work out the total area of canvas required to make the tent. (Don't include the floor.)
d Work out the area required for the plastic ground sheet.

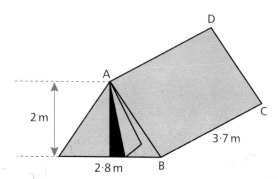

2 a Calculate the volume of this tin of beans.

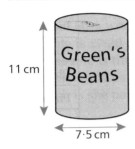 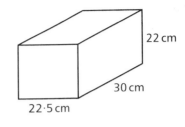

11 cm

Green's Beans

7·5 cm

22 cm

30 cm

22·5 cm

b The tins are stacked in boxes like the one shown.
What is the volume of the box?
c How many tins would fit into the box?
d What is the total volume of these tins?

3 a Calculate the normal price of the tent, including VAT.
b In a sale there is a discount of $\frac{1}{3}$.
What is the sale price?

TENT
£300
+ VAT @ 17·5%

4 Shona, Kirsty and Fiona set off for a hill walk.
They walked for 1·5 km on a bearing of 315°.
Then, following a bearing of 190°, they walked for a further 5 km.
a Make an accurate drawing of their route.
b What bearing would they need to follow to get back to where they started?
c How far are they away from their starting point?

5 Jean is making a pie chart to show how the pupils in her form get to school.

Method	Number of degrees in pie chart
Walk	120°
Car	96°
Bus	84°
Cycle	60°

What fraction of the class:
a walk **b** come by car **c** catch a bus **d** cycle to school?
Express your answers in their simplest form.

6 The formula $C = \frac{5}{9}(F - 32)$ converts degrees Fahrenheit to degrees Celsius.
Use the formula to convert these temperatures to degrees Celsius:
a 32 °F **b** 212 °F **c** 104 °F **d** −13 °F

7 Max, a car salesman, is paid a basic weekly wage of £210.
He earns 2% commission on the value of his sales.
In one week he sells cars for £2600, £850, £5345 and £3695.

a How much commission does he earn this week?
b Calculate his total pay for the week.
c If this is a typical week in terms of sales, estimate his annual wage.

REVISE

6 £1·56, £3·48, £4·20, total £9·24

7 £8·74

8 a £198·94   **b** £8·94

9 a £1·50, £1·60   **b** Bestbuy

Page 43 Exercise 3.1

1 a £1000   **b** £1370

2 a £10 140   **b** £14 016

3 £1500

4 a £200   **b** £10 400

5 a £405   **b** £21 060

6 a £1083·33   **b** £250

7 a £175·50   **b** £9126

Page 43 Exercise 3.2

1 a £3120   **b** £16

2 a £2000   **b** £2350

3 a £5280   **b** £7800

4 a £893·25   **b** £90·50

5 a City Cleaners   **b** £10·88

6 a £262·50   **b** £300

7 a £2495·50   **b** £687·50

8 a i £290·63   **ii** £236·25   **b** £2827·76

Page 45 Investigation

a £174·60

Page 45 Exercise 4.1

1 £7·30

2 £200·49

3 £17 553·12

4 a £20   **b** £420

5 a £55·80   **b** £1915·80

6 20p, £5·20; 24p, £8·24; 20p, £10·20; 90p, £18·90

7 a 57p   **b** £10·07   **c** £362·52

8 a £1200   **b** £31 200   **c** £2600

9 a i £19   **ii** £15·80   **b i** £399   **ii** £331·80
   c i £64   **ii** £67·20

10 a £9270   **b** £10 300

Page 47 Exercise 5.1

1 a 7·5 h   **b** 37·5 h

2 38 h

3 38·75 h

4 a 8, 7·5, 8, 7·25, 6·75   **b** 37·5 h

Page 48 Exercise 5.2

1 £13

2 £11, £12, £12·50, £15·60, £17·70, £19·36

3 a £6   **b** £7·50   **c** £8·40
   d £13·05   **e** £17·25

4 a £5   **b** £7·50   **c** £10·50
   d £8·75   **e** £13·25

5 a £8   **b** £6   **c** £7·60
   d £10·80   **e** £15·20

6 a £11·50   **b** £57·50

7 a £47·60   **b** £10·20   **c** £57·80

8 a £322   **b** £57·50   **c** £379·50

Page 49 Exercise 6.1

1 £105

2 £130

3 £3·50

4 £80

5 £85

6 a £88   **b** £20 240

7 a £100   **b** £175

8 £8400

Page 50 Exercise 6.2

1 £2·40

2 £160

3 a £300   **b** £925

4 £26·80

5 a £217·50   **b** £126   **c** £343·50

6 a £90   **b** 45

7 Kevin, £30

Page 51 Exercise 7.1

1 a £222   **b** £291·80   **c** £465·12

2 a £31   **b** £260·40   **c** £458·35

3 a £216   **b** £262   **c** £297·75

4 a £443·17   **b** £115·39   **c** £327·78

5 a £2114·43   **b** £656·74   **c** £1457·69

6 a £59·77   **b** £310·43   **c** £252·29

Page 53 Exercise 8.1

1 a No   **b** £0

2 a Yes   **b** £10 055

3 a £455   **b** £7955   **c** £19 630

4 £10 255; £19 505; £33 092; £4689

5 a £5   **b** 10%

6 a £13 000   **b i** £2020   **ii** £10 980

7 £36 145

8 a £40 150
   b i £2020   **ii** £29 380   **iii** £8750

9 £1255, £1255, £0, £0; £12 755, £2020, £10 735, £0;
   £19 970, £2020; £17 950, £0; £35 255, £2020,
   £29 380, £3855

Page 55 Exercise 8.2

1 a Taxable income is less than £2020   **b** £200

2 £158·50

3 a £202, £935, £1137
   b £202, £5020·40, £5222·40

4 a £202   **b** £20 880
   c £4593·60   **d** £4795·60

5 a £21 560   **b** £202
   c £4298·80   **d** £4500·80

6 £1000, £100, £0, £100; £6255, £202, £931·70,
   £1133·70;
   £17 255, £202, £3351·70, £3553·70; £26 981,
   £202, £5491·42, £5693·42

7 £6665·60

8 a £1400   **b** £8065·60

9 £32 105·60

Page 57 Exercise 9.1

1 **a** Cosmic CDs   **b** £24·86   **c** 98765432

3 **a** £99·73   **b** £74·73   **c** £450·58

   d £430·83   **e** £430·83

4 **a** £10·00 DR, £30·00, £50·00

   b £20·00, £50·00 DR, £50·00

   c £48·00 DR, £35·00, £34·00 DR

   d £14·00, £5 DR, £63·00

5 **a** £45·26   **b** £40·48 DR   **c** £432·99

   d £352·99   **e** £352·99

6 **a** £1970·99   **b** £1207·17   **c** £664·09

   d £61·61 DR   **e** £61·61 DR

Page 59 Brainstormer

20 Aug is £0·80 DR balance or £27·60 paid out

Page 59 Exercise 10.1

1 £75

2 £1960

3 **a** £309   **b** £36

4 **a** £261·25   **b** £421·25   **c** £246·25

5 **a** £4107·50   **b** £3257·50   **c** £3443·95

6 £12

7 £280

8 **a** £1·50   **b** £35   **c** £175   **d** £750

9 **a** £3·60   **b** £18

10 **a** £21·60   **b** £172·80

Page 61 Exercise 10.2

1 £24

2 £120

3 **a** £390   **b** £1170

4 **a** £5·40   **b** £43·20

5 **a** £4   **b** £200   **c** £250   **d** 96p

6 Zoe, 50p

7 **a** £990   **b** £5940

8 **a** £562·50   **b** £2250

9 **a** £288   **b** £24   **c** £192

10 **a** £15   **b** 80p   **c** £180   **d** £2080

Page 63 Revise

1 **a** £2207   **b** £13 242

2 **a** £625   **b** £90

3 **a** £15·72   **b** £47·16

4 **a** 8·5, 8·5, 8, 7·25, 7·25

   b 39·5 h

5 £532·25, £36·45, £63·55 DR

6 **a** £400   **b** £2400

7 £323

8 **a** £944·40

   b i £24 554·40   **ii** £2046·20

9 **a** £522·55

   b £133·47

   c £389·08

10 **a** £16 855   **b i** £2020   **ii** £14 835

11 **a** £202   **b** £21 680

   c £4769·60   **d** £4971·60

4 Similarity

Page 65 Exercise 1.1

1 **a** N, NE, E, SE, S, SW, W, NW

   b 000°, 045°, 090°, 135°, 180°, 225°, 270°, 315°

2 **a** 35°   **b** 102°   **c** 175°

3 **a i** 050°   **ii** 230°

   b i 235°   **ii** 055°

   c i 160°   **ii** 340°

4

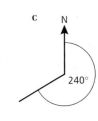

Page 66 Exercise 2.1

1 **a** 6 cm   **b** 3 m

2 **a** 3 cm   **b** 450 feet

3 **a** 1.5 km   **b** 1 km   **c** 5·75 km

4 **a** 5·5 m, 4 m   **b** 5·5 m, 1·5 m   **c** £252

5 **a** 1·2 km, 0·8 km   **b** 0·05 cm   **d** 500 m

6 **a** 30 miles, 65 miles, 60 miles   **b** 3 h 52·5 min

7 1 cm represents 2 m

8 1 cm represents 80 m

Page 68 Exercise 3.1

1 **a** 6 m   **b** 10 m   **c** 16 m

2 **a** 1.5 km   **b** 3.5 km   **c** 2.75 km

3 25 m, 1 cm represents 5m; 30 m, 1 cm rep. 10 m;
   750 m, 1 cm rep. 150 m; 2 km, 1 cm rep. 500 m

4 1 : 1500, 1 cm rep. 15 m; 1 : 400, 1 cm rep. 4 m;
   1 : 30 000, 1 cm rep 300 m; 1 : 25 000, 1 cm rep.
   250 m; 1 : 25 000, 1 cm rep. 250 m

5 40 cm, 20 cm, 10 cm, 4 cm

6 1 : 200 000

7 **a** 6 cm   **b** 1 : 135

8 1 : 160

9 1 : 1350

Page 70 Exercise 4.1

1 pupil's own drawings

2 **c** 7·5 km

3 **b** 2·5 km

4 **b** 590 m

5 **b** 6·73 km

6 **b** 325·6 miles

Page 71 Exercise 4.2

1 **a** 050°, 30 km   **b** 110°, 2·75 km

   c 240°, 1 km   **d** 320°, 3 km

   e 250°, 3·9 km   **f** 350°, 400 m

2 **a i** 170°, 400 m, 050°, 300 m

     ii 240°, 1·5 km, 120°, 1·08 km

   b i 122°, 195°   **ii** 302°, 015°

3 **a** 275°   **b** 127·5 km   **c** 110°

c i (5, 8)

   ii (9, 6)

d i isosceles triangle

   ii obtuse-angled triangle

2 a/b/d i

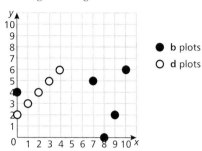

● **b plots**
○ **d plots**

c (4, 2)

d ii These points lie in a straight line

3 a B V-kite, C rhombus, D kite, E trapezium,
   F parallelogram, G square

   b i (1, 7), (4, 8), (4, 6), (7, 7)

   ii (8, 2), (9, 3), (10, 2), (9, 1)

   iii (2, 0), (4, 2), (8, 3), (6, 1)

   c i (2, 4)   **ii** (9, 7)

   d (8, 6), (10, 6)

4 a (9, 3), (6, 5), (6, 2), (7, 1), (7, 0), (6, 1), (5, 1)

   b (11, 1), (10, 0)

Page 159 Exercise 2.1

1 a

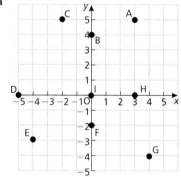

   b A (1st), B (1st/2nd), C (2nd), D (2nd/3rd),
   E (3rd), F (3rd/4th), G (4th), H (4th/1st),
   O (all four)

2 a B, C   **b** none

   c B, F and G, E   **d** A, C

   e D, F   **f** M(3, −2)

   g N(3, 3)

3 a (−5, 2)   **b** (3, −1)

   c (−1, −4)   **d** (−1, −1)

   e trapezium

Page 160 Challenge

1 L(3, 2), M(−5, 2), N(−5, −4)

2 Q(3, −1), R(−5, −1), S(−5, −3)

Page 160 Exercise 2.2

1 a

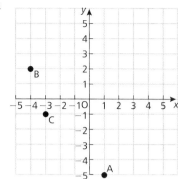

   b B   **c** A

2 a

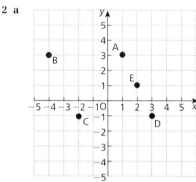

   b E(2, 1)   **c** (0, 0)

3 a

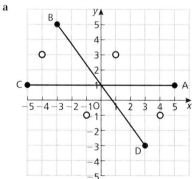

   b 2   **c** (3, −3)

   d (0, 1)   **e** rhombus

4 a B(−4, 2), C(−1, 1), D(2, 0)

   b (5, −1)

   c (8, −2)

   d (2, −5)

Page 162 Exercise 3.1

1 a $y = 5$ **b** $y = -1$ **c** $y = -3$

2 a $y = 0$

   b x axis

3 a i below   **ii** on   **iii** above   **iv** above

   b i above   **ii** above   **iii** below   **iv** on

   c i above   **ii** above   **iii** above   **iv** below

4 a/b

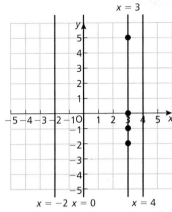

x = 3

x = -2 x = 0   x = 4

c x = 3
e y axis

5 a (4, 3) **b** (24, 6) **c** (-4, -1) **d** (0, 0)
6 a i left **ii** right **iii** right **iv** on
　　b i on **ii** left **iii** right **iv** left
　　c i left **ii** on **iii** right **iv** on
7 a x = -2 **b** west **c** east
　　d y = -1 **e** (-2, -1)
　　f i north
　　　 ii south

Page 163 Exercise 3.2

1 a

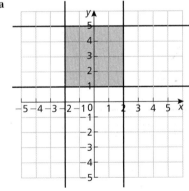

c square **d** (-2, 1), (-2, 5), (2, 1), (2, 5)

2 a

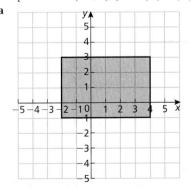

b x = -2, x = 4, y = -1, y = 3

3 a

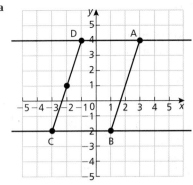

b C(-3, -2), D(-1, 4)

4 a

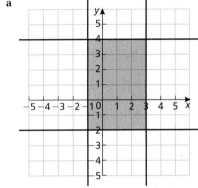

b (-1, -2), (-1, 4), (3, -2), (3, 4)
c yes, from equations
d within, outside, within, neither
5 a rock, branch
　　b (4, -2), (4, -5)

Page 164 Exercise 4.1

1 i pupil's own diagrams
　　ii a y = 4x **b** y = 5x **c** y = 6x
2 a pupil's own diagram
　　b each point on the line, each y coordinate is
　　　 half the corresponding x coordinate
　　c pupil's own diagram
　　d $y = \frac{1}{3}x$
3 -1, 0, 1, 2; pupil's own diagram (line passing
　　through (0, 0) and (8, 2))
4 a 0, 2, 4 **b** (5, 5), (6, 6)
　　c i on **ii** above **iii** below
5 a 2, 0, -2, -4
　　b (3, -6) (4, -8)
　　c slopes down to right
　　d i below **ii** on **iii** above
6 a pupil's own diagram
　　　 (line passing through (0, 0) and (2, 2)
　　b 1, 0, -1, -2
　　c 90°
　　d pupil's own diagram
　　e lines are the diagonals of the square

285

Page 165 Exercise 4.2

1 a/b pupil's own diagram

  c $(-2, 4), (-2, -4), (2, -4)$

  d 4 units by 8 units

2 a

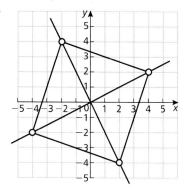

  b $(4, 2), (-2, 4), (-4, -2)$

3 a

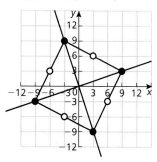

  b $(-3, 9), (-9, -3), (3, -9)$

  c $(6, -3), (3, 6), (-6, 3), (-3, -6)$

4 a pupil's own diagram

  b i $(-1, 3)$ **ii** $(-2, 4)$

   iii $(-1, -4)$ **iv** $(1, 5)$

  c i $y = 3, x = 1, y = 3x$

   ii $x = 1, y = 4, y = 4x$

   iii $x = 1, y = -4, y = -4x$

5 a pupil's own diagram

  b $(2, 4)$

  c $y = -4, x = 2, x = -2$

  d $y = -2x$

  e $(2, 4), (2, -4), (-2, 4), (-2, -4)$

Page 166 Investigation

a $90°$ **b** $a \times b = -1$

Page 168 Exercise 5.1

1 a i $(0, 1), (1, 3), (2, 5), (3, 7)$

   ii pupil's own drawing

  b i $(0, -1), (1, 2), (2, 5), (3, 8)$

   ii pupil's own drawing

  c i $(0, 2), (1, 3), (2, 4), (3, 5)$

   ii pupil's own drawing

  d i $(0, -1), (1, 0), (2, 1), (3, 2)$

   ii pupil's own drawing

2 a $(0, 3), (1, 5), (2, 7), (3, 9)$

  b/c pupil's own drawing

3 a i $(0, 1), (2, 2), (4, 3), (6, 4)$

   ii pupil's own drawing

  b i $(0, -1), (3, 0), (6, 1), (9, 2)$

   ii pupil's own drawing

  c i $(0, 2), (4, 3), (8, 4), (12, 5)$

   ii pupil's own drawing

4 a/b $(0, 3), (2, 4), (4, 5), (6, 6)$

  c pupil's own drawing

  d ii $(10, 8)$

5 a i $(0, 8), (1, 6), (2, 4), (3, 2)$

   ii pupil's own drawing

  b i $(0, 10), (1, 7), (2, 4), (3, 1)$

   ii pupil's own drawing

  c i $(0, 6), (1, 5), (2, 4), (3, 3)$

   ii pupil's own drawing

6 a/b

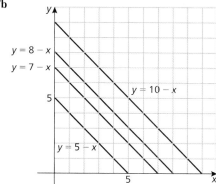

Page 169 Investigation

a pupil's own drawing

b i $(2, 4)$ **ii** $(1, 4)$

c i no   **ii** parallel lines

d pupil's own drawings

e same coefficient of x

Page 169 Exercise 5.2

1 a below   **b** on   **c** above   **d** on

  e above   **f** below   **g** above   **h** on

  i below

2 a south   **b** north

  c $25 + 7 = 32$ **d** 37

3 a pupil's own drawing, line passing through

    $(9, -2), (0, 1), (3, 0)$

  b below

  c i line passing through $(0, 6), (-3, 0)$

   ii $(-3, 2)$

4 a/b lines giving triangle with vertices

    $(-2, -1), (-2, 7), (2, 7)$

  c right-angled

  d i, v, vi

5 a/b lines giving triangle with vertices

    $(0, 0), (3, 9), (9, 9)$

  c obtuse-angled

Page 170 Challenge

Lines giving triangle with vertices
$(0, 0)$, $(-1, 2)$, $(4, 2)$; $y = -2x$

Page 171 Exercise 6.1

1 a $y = 2x$ and $y = 2x + 8$; $y = -2x$ and $y = -2x + 8$
  b $y = 2x$ **c** $x = 0$, $y = 4$
  d $(0, 4)$ **e** $(2, 4)$
2 a $y = 2x + 8$, $y = -2x$
  b/c kite with vertices $(0, 0)$, $(-2, 4)$, $(0, 8)$, $(4, 4)$
  d $x = 0$, $y = 4$ **e** $y = 4$
3 a AB: $y = 2x + 7$; BC: $y = -x + 7$; CD: $y = 2x - 2$;
  DA: $y = -x - 2$
  b $x = 0$
4 a pupil's own drawing, 4 lines passing through
    i $(0, 0)$ and $(-1, 2)$
    ii $(0, 1)$ and $(3, 2)$
    iii $(0, 4)$ and $(3, 5)$
    iv $(3, 0)$ and $(3, 6)$
  b $y = \frac{1}{3}x + 1$ and $y = \frac{1}{3}x + 4$
  c $(3, 2)$, $(3, 5)$ **d** $(0, 1)$, $(0, 4)$

Page 173 Exercise 7.1

1 a 55p   **b** 5·5 h
2 a/b/c

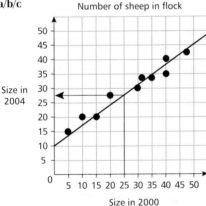

Number of sheep in flock

  d 28 sheep
3 a/b/c

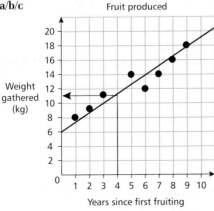

Fruit produced

  d 11 kg

4 a/b/c

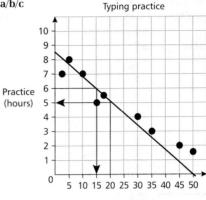

Typing practice

d i 15 **ii**   5 hours

Page 176 Revise

1 a/c pupil's own drawing
    b $(5, -1)$ **d** 1st   **e** 2nd
2 a/b pupil's own drawing
    c rectangle with vertices
      $(3, 4)$, $(3, -2)$, $(-5, 4)$, $(-5, -2)$
3 a $-5, -3, -1, 1$
    b line passing through $(-1, -5)$ and $(2, 1)$
4 a i line passing through $(0, 0)$ and $(1, 3)$
    ii line passing through $(0, 8)$ and $(8, 0)$
    iii line passing through $(0, 6)$ and $(2, 7)$
  b i $y = 3x$ **c ii** $y = 8 - x$
  d $(2, 6)$
5 a/b

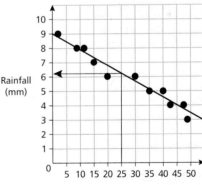

Rainfall across Scotland

  c 6 mm

9 Symmetry

Page 178 Exercise 1.1

1 a pupil's own drawings
  b it has two axes of symmetry

2

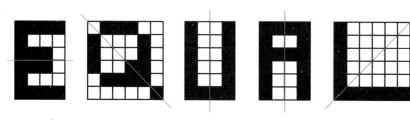

3

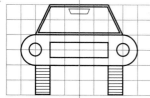
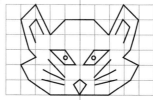

4 a B, C, D, E, H, I, K, O, X
b A, H, I, M, O, T, U, V, W, X, Y
c O, Q, L

5 a

b

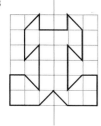
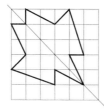
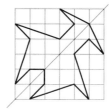

6

LOOK ON
THE BRIGHT
SIDE OF LIFE

Page 180 Exercise 2.1

1 a

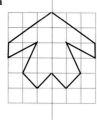

b

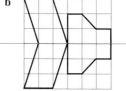

c

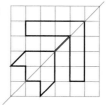

2 20 cm

3 a 112 cm   **b i** 0 cm   **ii** 0 cm   **iii** image is on axis
  c 50 cm   **d** 97 cm   **e** 130°

4 a i 100 cm **ii** 175 cm **iii** 350 cm
  b 2·5 m   **c** 27·5 cm
  d i 72°   **ii** 36°

5 a 7 mm   **b** 8 mm   **c** 64°

Page 182 Exercise 2.2

1 a

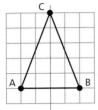

b

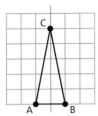

c

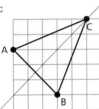

2 a pupil's own drawing   **b** 46 mm
   c i 75°   **ii** symmetry
3 a 32 mm   **b** 51° and 78°

4 a

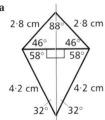

b

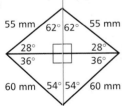

c

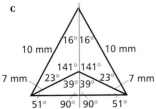

5 a trapezium
   b axis does not go through vertices
   c i 90°   **ii** 90°   **d** parallel
6 a i 56 cm
     ii

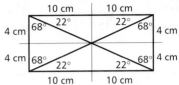

   b i 88 cm
     ii

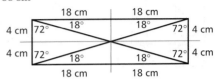

   c i 80 cm
     ii

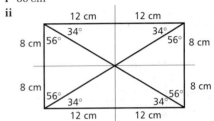

   d i 32 cm
     ii

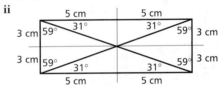

7 a rhombus   **b** they pass through vertices
8 a square   **b**

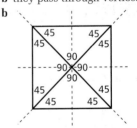

Page 186 Exercise 3.1
1 a pupil's own drawing
   b all points on it have an x coordinate of 3
   c A′(5, 4), B′(4, 3), C′(3, 5)
2 a A′(8, 2), B′(5, 6), C′(4, 1)
   b It is its own image.
3 a pupil's own drawing
   b i (8, 5)   **ii** (3, 0)
   c (5, 2)   **d** (5, 2)   **e** same point
4 a all points have a y coordinate of 5
   b/c(i) pupil's own drawing
   c ii (1, 8), (4, 7), (6, 5), (7, 4)
   d i (6, 5)   **ii** (6, 5) same

5 a/b/d

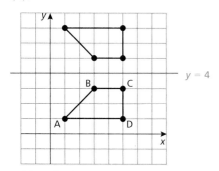

c AD and BC

e still parallel

6 a/b

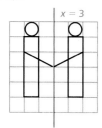

c i (0, 3)   **ii** (3, 2)

iii (2, 2)   **iv** (4, 1)

v (5, 3)   **vi** (5, 0)

d i $x = a$ **ii** $y = 6 - b$

7 a/b

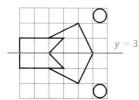

c i (5, 5)   **ii** (5, 6)

iii (4, 1)   **iv** (4, 5)

v (5, 4)   **vi** (3, 3)

d i $y = b$ **ii** $x = 6 - a$

Page 188 Exercise 3.2

1 a (0, 0), (1, 1), (2, 2), etc.

b

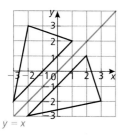

c (−2, −3), (2, 1), (3, −2)

d the point (x, y) has an image (y, x)

2 a (0, 0), (1, −1), (2, −2), etc

b

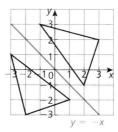

c (−3, 1), (1, −2), (−2, −3)

d the point (x, y) has an image $(−y, −x)$

3 a i (0, 0), (0, 1), (0, 2)

ii y axis

iii x axis

b/c/d

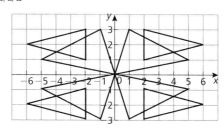

Page 189 Challenges

1 Shortest distance will be obtained by reflecting C in riverbank; shortest distance is AC′, a distance of 25 metres when measured.

2 Aim at reflection of target in cushion, a point 16 cm along cushion from the point on the cushion nearest the cue ball.

Page 190 Exercise 4.1

1 a i 2   **ii** twice   **iii** 180°

b i 3   **ii** 3 times   **iii** 120°

c i 4   **ii** 4 times   **iii** 90°

d i 5   **ii** 5 times   **iii** 72°

e i 6   **ii** 6 times   **iii** 60°

f i 7   **ii** 7 times   **iii** $\dfrac{360°}{7}$

2 a i D

ii CD

iii equal

b ∠CEB

c ∠DBA

3 17·4 cm

4 a 5

b 72°

c 100 cm

d pentagon

5 a

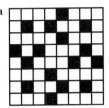

b

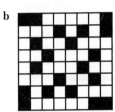

c

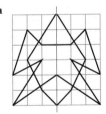

6 a DS

b AO has rotated through 180° to get to OD

c AP is image of BQ after 60° rotation clockwise

d ∠AMB = 60°, ∠MBN = 20°, ∠BNM = 100°

Page 194 Revise

1 a   **b**

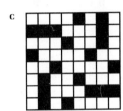

2 a i Q   **ii** RP   **iii** ∠QRP

b i 7 cm   **ii** 34°

c 2 cm

3 a BD

b

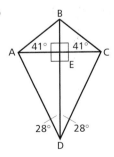

c 19·4 cm

4 a/b/c

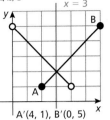

A′(4, 1), B′(0, 5)

d (3, 2)

5 a 3   **b** 60°   **c** 24 cm

10 Trigonometry

Page 195 Exercise 1.1

1

Triangle	Opposite side	Adjacent side	Hypotenuse
△CDE	ED	CD	CE
△FGH	FH	GH	FG
△JKL	JK	KL	JL
△MNP	MP	MN	NP
△QRS	RS	QR	QS
△TUV	TV	TU	UV

2 a $\tan x°$ **b** $\sin x°$ **c** $\sin x°$
  d $\cos x°$ **e** $\tan x°$ **f** $\cos x°$

3 a $\dfrac{b}{c}$ **b** $\dfrac{a}{b}$ **c** $\dfrac{b}{c}$

  d $\dfrac{a}{c}$ **e** $\dfrac{b}{a}$

4 a $\dfrac{ST}{SR}$ **b** $\dfrac{TR}{SR}$ **c** $\dfrac{TR}{SR}$

  d $\dfrac{ST}{SR}$ **e** $\dfrac{TR}{ST}$

5 a 2·5   **b** 3·6   **c** 0·3
  d 37·3   **e** 61·3   **f** 45·4

6 a 0·653   **b** 0·376   **c** 0·677
  d 8·27   **e** 3·15   **f** 0·978

7 a 0·956   **b** 0·927   **c** 0·616
  d 0·891   **e** 0·727   **f** 1·48

8 a ∠B = 34·8°

  b ∠C = 77·2°

  c ∠D = 61·4° (all answers correct to 1 d.p.)

9 b $\cos x° = \frac{15}{17} \Rightarrow x = \cos^{-1}(15 \div 17)$
    $\Rightarrow x = 28·0724...; x° = 28·1°$
    (to 1 d.p.)

  c $\tan x° = \frac{5}{12} \Rightarrow x = \tan^{-1}(5 \div 12)$
    $\Rightarrow x = 22·6198...; x° = 22·6°$
    (to 1 d.p.)

Answers

10 b $\cos 52° = \frac{d}{14} \Rightarrow d = 14\cos52°;$
$\quad d = 8·6$ (to 1 d.p.)
c $\tan 48° = \frac{d}{16} \Rightarrow d = 16\tan48°;$
$\quad d = 17·8$ (to 1 d.p.)

11 a i By scale drawing and measurement d is about 2·2 m, so strictly speaking the ladder is not safe as d is not less than 2·2 m
ii using trigonometry, d is 2·1786... m which is less than 2·2 m so the ladder is safe
b using trigonometry is more accurate as all measurements are subject to error; your measurements here were only accurate to the nearest mm
c yes, where health and safety are involved accuracy is very important

12 a 048°   **b** 126°   **c** 248°   **d** 302°
13 a 314°   **b** 253°

Page 199 Exercise 2.1

1 a 5·0 cm   **b** 8·1 cm   **c** 34·2°
d 9·8 m   **e** 46·7°   **f** 10·7 cm
g 3·3 m   **h** 47·0°   **i** 40·6°
2 a 13·3 m   **b** 22·9 m
3 13·8 m
4 a 53·1°   **b** 100 cm
5 a 46·7 m
b 77·7 m (77·6 m won't quite reach the boat)
6 $x° = 9·6°, y° = 7·2°$
7 a $d = 16·1$ m   **b** $a° = 33·9°$

Page 200 Exercise 3.1

1 a 31·0°
b i 45°   **ii** 7·1 cm   **iii** 14·1 cm
2 a i 7·2 cm   **ii** 7·0 cm   **b** 73·0°
3 a i 36·9 cm   **ii** 64·7 cm   **iii** 47 cm
iv PR = 102 cm, QS = 95 cm
b i 41·8°   **ii** 96·4°
iii 13·4 cm   **iv** 12 cm
4 a 22·3 cm   **b i** 23·5 cm   **ii** 47·2°
5 a i 13·1 cm   **ii** 30·9 cm
b i 3·6 cm   **ii** 10·6 cm

Page 202 Exercise 3.2

1 19·9°
2 a 2·9 m   **b** 54·6°   **c** 6·2 m
3 a 25·4 cm
b 11·8 cm using both trigonometry and Pythagoras' theorem

Page 203 Exercise 4.1

1 a 29·0 km   **b** 13·5 km
2 a 24·4 km   **b** 8·9 km
3 a Right-angled at B
b ∠BAC = 32·6° so the bearing is 078°, to the nearest degree
c 890·4 km
4 a 4·8°   **b** 3·8°   **c** 2·9°   **d** 5·7°

5 a 39·8°   **b i** 51·3°   **ii** 32·0°
6 a 90°   **b** 12·2 km

Page 204 Challenge

85 km, 045°

Page 204 Investigation

The angle at A is 37°, the angle at B is 32°. There is a wider shooting angle in football, but the penalty spot is nearer the goal in hockey. The width of the goal and the height of the crossbar are other things that need to be considered. How good the goalkeepers are and how good the players are at taking penalties are also important!

Page 205 Exercise 5.1

1 a i 43°   **ii** 25°   **b i** 43°   **ii** 25°
c i 47°   **ii** 65°
2 a 47°   **b** 47°   **c** 697·0 m
3 21·1 m
4 32·6°
5 a 20°; Z-angles (alternate angles) because of parallel lines
b 29·1 m
6 44·1 m
7 300·7 m
8 a 41·4°   **b** 35·2°   **c** 35·2°

Page 207 Exercise 6.1

1 a 6·1 cm   **b** 4·2 cm   **c** 7·1 cm
2 a 39°   **b** 37°   **c** 67°
3 The second flagpole by 0·1 m (the heights are 7·8 m and 7·9 m)
4 The second road by 1·1 m (the widths are 12·0 m and 13·1 m)
5 49·9°
6 a 34·8°
b 43·9°
c it has increased by 9·1°
7 a 050°   **b** 10·6 km
8 The second picture by 0·4 cm (the lengths are 7·9 cm and 8·3 cm)

Page 208 Exercise 6.2

1 48·4° and 38·3°
2 BC = 1537·7 m, CD = 1071·1 m, so BD = 2608·8 m
3 a 16·5 m
b ST = 34·5 cm, PT = 28·9 cm, RT = 49·1 cm; therefore, the diagonals are 69·0 cm and 78·0 cm
4 a 48·5°
b 73·3 m
c 37·4 + 65 = 102·4 m
5 222°
6 a 36·9°
b 13·2 cm
c perimeter = 108·2 cm

Page 209 Practical exercise

1

$x°$	0	10	20	30	40	50	60	70	80	90
$y = \sin x$	0	0·2	0·3	0·5	0·6	0·8	0·9	0·9	1·0	1·0
$y = \cos x$	1	1	0·9	0·9	0·8	0·6	0·5	0·3	0·2	0
$y = \tan x$	0	0·2	0·4	0·6	0·8	1·2	1·7	2·7	5·7	

2a/b

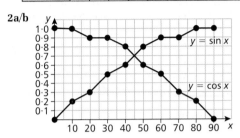

c $\sin x = \cos x$ for $x = 45$

3 a

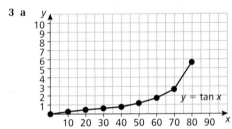

b

$x°$	80	81	82	83	84	85	86	87	88	89
$y = \tan x$	6	6	7	8	10	11	14	19	29	57

$x°$	89·2	89·4	89·6	89·8	89·9	89·99	89·999
$y = \tan x$	72	95	143	286	573	5730	57 296

c $\tan x°$ gets bigger as x approaches 90, becoming very large as x becomes very close to 90.

Page 211 Exercise 7.1

1 a $\frac{1}{4}$ **b** $\frac{2}{3}$ **c** $\frac{1}{8}$ **d** $\frac{1}{1}$ or 1

2 a $\frac{1}{3}$ **b** $\frac{1}{2}$ **c** $\frac{5}{9}$ **d** $\frac{5}{1}$ or 5

   e $\frac{1}{2}$ **f** $\frac{2}{9}$ **g** $\frac{0}{5}$ or 0

3 a $\frac{3}{4}$ **b** $\frac{5}{12}$ **c** $\frac{7}{24}$ **d** $\frac{35}{12}$

4 a 0·9   **b** 2·3   **c** 0·4

5 pupil's own diagrams

6 a 0·4   **b** 0·4

7 a 0·2   **b** 0·2

Page 214 Revise

1 a 4·2 cm   **b** 7·4 cm   **c** 7·0 cm

2 a 43°   **b** 36°   **c** 74°

3 7·4 m

4 11·9 m (63·81 m − 51·95 m)

5 $\angle PQR = \angle PRQ = 72°$; $\angle QPR = 36°$

6 a 75·5 km   **b** 101·6 km

7 32·2°   **8** 50·8 m

9 a $\frac{1}{2}$ **b** $\frac{3}{2}$

11 3-D shapes

Page 216 Exercise 1.1

1 a square   **b** rectangle
   c triangle   **d** parallelogram
   e rhombus   **f** trapezium
   g kite

2 a isosceles   **b** equilateral
   c right-angled   **d** obtuse-angled
   e acute-angled   **f** right-angled isosceles

3 a cube
   b i 6   **ii** square   **iii** 12   **iv** 8

4 a cuboid
   b i 6   **ii** rectangle   **iii** 12   **iv** 8

5 a 90°   **b** 90°   **c** 45°

6 a, b, c, d and **f**

7 d is not the net of a cuboid

8 a i 120 cm³   **ii** 158 cm²
   b i 900 cm³   **ii** 660 cm²
   c i 5089 cm³   **ii** 1640 cm²

9 $x = 30, y = 48$

Page 219 Exercise 2.1

1 a triangular prism   **c** hexagonal prism
   f pentagonal prism   **g** octagonal prism

2 a rectangle
   b rectangular prism   **c** cuboid
   d front to back, right to left, top to bottom

3 a circle
   b circular prism   **c** cylinder

4 a EFGH
   b i ABFE   **ii** BCGF
   c i FG, EH and AD
   ii CG, DH, AE
   iii GH, FE, BA
   d EF, CD, GH   **e** AD, CD, HD

5 a 5   **b** ABC and DEF
   c BEFC and ADFC   **d** ABED
   e BC, EF and DF   **f** AD, CF
   g they are the same length

6 a pentagon   **b** yes
   c pentagonal prism

Page 220 Exercise 3.1

1 a 5
   b ABCD
   c ABE, BCE, CDE and ADE
   d E

2 a pentagon
   b pentagon-based pyramid
   c 5
   d UVZ, VWZ, WXZ, XYZ, YUZ

3 a 6   **b** 12

4 a 2   **b** 1   **c** 1

5 a circle   **b** sphere

6 a MO, NO, KO, LO   **b** KO

Page 221 Challenge

1 a pupil's own diagrams

 b 5, 6, 9, 2; 6, 8, 12, 2; 7, 10, 15, 2;
  8, 12, 18, 2; 9, 14, 21, 2

2 a pupil's own diagrams

 b 4, 4, 6, 2; 5, 5, 8, 2; 6, 6, 10, 2;
  7, 7, 12, 2; 8, 8, 14; 2

Page 223 Exercise 4.1

1 a 12 **b** 8

2 a i 3 **ii** 2 **iii** 4 **b** 6

3 a 12·8 m **b** 21 m

4 4·2 m

5 a 12 **b** 6 **c** 12

6 a 10 **b** 5 **c** 10

7 a 6 **b** 28 min

Page 224 Exercise 4.2

1 a 6·28 m **b** 54·8 m **c** £29·62

2 4 cm **3** 15 cm **4** 22·2 m

Page 225 Exercise 5.1

1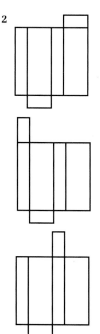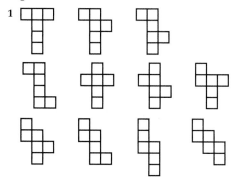

2

3 a triangular prism

 b 1·8 cm, 1·8 cm, 0·9 cm

 c pupil's drawing of net of triangular prism

4 a cylinder

 b they are the same

 c any net where the two circles are directly
  opposite

5 a pupil's drawings of two nets of square-based
  pyramid

 b i 20 cm **ii** 48 cm

6 a All the same length **b** equilateral

 c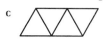

7 a cube **b** tetrahedron

 c pentagonal prism **d** triangular prism

 e cuboid **f** square-based pyramid

Page 227 Exercise 5.2

1 a cuboid **b** 780 cm² **c** 1 000 cm³

2 a 129 mm by 86 mm by 43 mm

 b one net is:

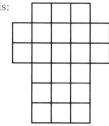

Each small
square has a
side of 43 mm

3 a 2904 cm² **b** 10 648 cm³

4 175 cm²

5 a 1200 cm³ **b** 13 cm **c** 840 cm²

6 a 15·6 cm² **b** 249 cm³ **c** 319·2 cm²

7 a pupil's scale drawing

 b 22 cm, 24 cm, 24 cm

 c 21·3 cm **d** 1420 cm² (3 s.f.)

8 a 3 **b** 268 cm²

9 a cylinder **b** 137 cm³

 c 15·7 cm **d** 149 cm²

10 a A **b i** 215 cm³ **ii** 211 cm²

Page 231 Revise

1 a i square-based pyramid **ii** 5, 8, 5

 b i hexagonal prism **ii** 12, 18, 8

 c i cuboid **ii** 8, 12, 6,

 d i triangular prism **ii** 6, 9, 5

 e i triangle-based pyramid (tetrahedron)
  ii 4, 6, 4

2 a PQ, LM, ON **b** PL, SO, RN

 c PLOS **d** pupil's own drawings

3 a cylinder **b** triangular prism **c** cuboid

4 Any three from:

 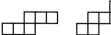

5 a hexagonal prism
  b not a prism
  c cuboid (rectangular prism)
6 a 39 cm   **b** 6·24 m   **c** 8880 cm^2
7 6

12 Chapter revision

Page 233 Revising Chapter 1
1 a 45 cm^2 **b** 49 cm^2 **c** 60 cm^2
  d 12 cm^2 **e** 45·5 cm^2
2 a 27·5 cm^2 **b** 9 cm^2 **c** 48 cm^2
3 a 5280 cm^2 **b** 3850 cm^2 **c** 1430 cm^2
4 a 192 210 m^2 **b** 19·221 hectares

Page 234 Revising Chapter 2
1 a i 252 cm^3 **ii** 282 cm^2
  b i 400 cm^3 **ii** 400 cm^2
2 a 200 cm^3 **b** 150 cm^3
  c 3500 cm^3 **d** 85 000 cm^3
3 a i 3240 cm^3 **ii** 1714 cm^2
  b i 5376 cm^3 **ii** 2441 cm^2
4 a 15 cm^2 **b** 225 cm^3
  c 6·5 cm   **d** 300 cm^2
5 a 330 cm^2 **b** 442 ml

Page 235 Revising Chapter 3
1 £9672
2 a £47·95   **b** £239·75
3 a £930   **b** £19 530
4 a £15·20   **b** £11·40   **c** £9·50
5 a i £22·50   **ii** £180
  b i £17·50   **ii** £87·50
6 a £60   **b** £234
7 a 7 hours 15 minutes
  b 36 hours 15 minutes
8 a £494·61   **b** £165·94   **c** £328·67
9 a i £2020   **ii** £29 380   **iii** £13 600
  b £33 050, £202, £6463·60, £660,
    total £7325·60
10 £198·70, £60·40, £16·29 DR, £231·35
11 a £4   **b** £40   **c** £8·75   **d** £450

Page 236 Revising Chapter 4
1 a pupil's own drawing   **b** 325°   **c** 390 m
2 a 12   **b** 7 cm
3 0·6 km   **4** $6\frac{2}{3}$ cm   **5** 60 cm
6 a pupil's own drawing   **b** 2·2 km

Page 237 Revising Chapter 5
1 a 4   **b** 12   **c** 15   **d** 7
  e 5   **f** 0   **g** 18   **h** 81
  i 72   **j** 12   **k** 12   **l** 4
2 a $R = 6$ **b** $C = 9$ **c** $M = 25$ **d** $f = 13\frac{1}{2}$
3 £161·50
4 a i $P = 2x + 2y$ or $P = 2(x + y)$ **ii** 8
  b i $T = 2w + z + t$ **ii** $T = 28$

5 a 40, 80, 120, 160, 200, 240   **b** $C = 40H$
  c straight line graph passing through
    (0, 0), (1, 40), (2, 80), etc.
6 a 4, 15, 26, 37, 48   **b** 246
7 a 5, 11, 17, 23, 29   **b** $M = 6n - 1$
  c $6 \times 1 - 1 = 5$, $6 \times 2 - 1 = 11$, $6 \times 3 - 1 = 17$,
    $6 \times 4 - 1 = 23$, $6 \times 5 - 1 = 29$ **d** 233

Page 238 Revising Chapter 6
1 a $m = 8$ **b** $a = 3$ **c** $x = 1$
2 a $3(m - 9) = 30$, $m = 19$
  b $2(n + 12) = 28$, $n = 2$
3 a i $6x + 10 + 2x + 3x + 5 = 180$
    ii $x = 15$
    iii 100°, 30°, 50°
  b i $55 - x + 3x + 2x + 5 = 180$
    ii $x = 30$
    iii 25°, 90°, 65°
4 a $x = \frac{1}{2}$ **b** $m = 4$ **c** $k = 3$
  d $x = 5$ **e** $x = 9$ **f** $w = 11$
5 a i $30(3x + 10) = 25(4x + 8)$
    ii $x = 10$
    iii 40 cm × 30 cm; 48 cm × 25 cm
  b i $3(4x - 1) = 2(x + 1)$ **ii** $x = \frac{1}{2}$
    iii 3 m × 1 m; $1\frac{1}{2}$ m × 2 m
6 a i $x \geqslant 3$ **ii** 3 or 4
  b i $x < \frac{1}{2}$ **ii** $-2, -1$ or 0
  c i $x \leqslant 2$ **ii** $-2, -1, 0, 1$ or 2
  d i $x > 3$ **ii** 4
  e i $x \geqslant 2$ **ii** 2, 3 or 4
  f i $x < 1$ **ii** $-2, -1$ or 0
7 a $t - 7 < -6$
  b $t < 1$, temperature in Crail is colder than 1 °C

Page 239 Revising Chapter 7
1 a £1·25   **b** £3·60   **c** 48 litres
  d 200 m   **e** 5850 tonnes
2 a £5·80   **b** 32p   **c** £2·50
  d £555   **e** £112
3 a 60%   **b** 55%   **c** 60%   **d** 1·5%
4 a 2100   **b** 6300
5 a £22·50   **b** £397·50
6 a i $\frac{15}{8}$ **ii** $\frac{33}{5}$ **b i** $11\frac{1}{2}$ **ii** $4\frac{3}{4}$
7 a i $\frac{4}{5}$ **ii** $\frac{2}{3}$
  b For example: $\frac{6}{10}$ and $\frac{9}{15}$
8 $\frac{1}{4}, \frac{7}{10}, \frac{1}{5}, \frac{3}{8}, \frac{19}{200}, \frac{3}{500}$;
  0·25, 0·7, 0·2, 0·375, 0·095, 0·006;
  25%, 70%, 20%, 37·5%, 9·5%, 0·6%
9 a $\frac{2}{3}$ **b** $\frac{11}{24}$ **c** $\frac{31}{40}$
  d $\frac{2}{3}$ **e** $\frac{1}{20}$ **f** $\frac{1}{8}$
  g $\frac{1}{14}$ **h** $\frac{4}{9}$ **i** $\frac{3}{8}$
10 a 7   **b** $6\frac{1}{3}$ **c** $2\frac{4}{15}$
  d $2\frac{3}{8}$ **e** 4   **f** $7\frac{1}{2}$

Page 240 Revising Chapter 8

1 a /b

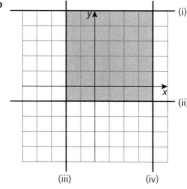

c (4, 5), (4, −1), (−2, −1), (−2, 5)

2 a 1, 4, 7, 10

b

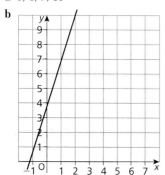

3 a 8, 4, 2, 0

b

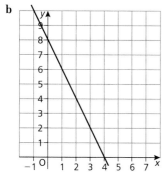

4 a

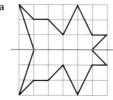

b y = 2x   **c** y = 10 − x

5 a/b

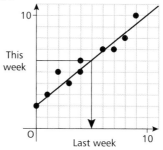

c 5

Page 241 Revising Chapter 9

1

a   **b**

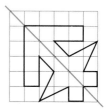

2 a i W   **ii** WX   **iii** angle XYZ
  b i 9 cm   **ii** 88°   **iii** 4 cm
3 a 4   **b** ∠EFG, ∠HIJ, ∠KLA   **c** 36 cm

Page 242 Revising Chapter 10

1 a 3·3 cm   **b** 7·3 cm
2 a 35°   **b** 40°   **c** 50°
3 a 11·3 m   **b** 12·3 m
4 a 281·2 m   **b** 9°
5 a 052°   **b** 9·3 km
6 31°
7 pupil's own diagrams

Page 243 Revising Chapter 11

1 a triangular prism   **b** cuboid
  c square-based pyramid   **d** sphere
2 a AB, BE, ED, AD, CF   **b** BC   **c** AD, BE
3 a cuboid   **b** 7 cm   **c** 3 cm
4 a 18·8 cm   **b** 235·6 cm²   **c** 292 cm²
5 20·1 m

13 Preparation for assessment

Page 245 Test A (Non-calculator)

1 £7·72, £7·47, £1·78, £16·97
2 a 75%   **b** 40%   **c** 67·5%
3 a 6·4   **b** 15·7   **c** 20·0
4 a 2 h 40 min   **b** 7 h 22 min
5 a 25%   **b** 20%
6 a white 15, striped 6, pink 9
  b i white   **ii** striped
7 a i 6 cm   **ii** 14 cm
  b i 11 cm   **ii** 14 cm   **c** range

8 a/b

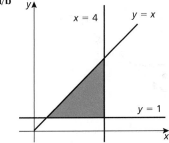

c triangle

9 a −4 **b** 15 **c** −24

10 307°

11 a $4x − 1 < 2x + 3$

b $x < 2$

c A 5 cm, B 3 cm

12 a $x = 4$ **b** $x = 3$

Page 246 Test A (Calculator)

1 a i 15·58 m² **ii** 35·55 m² **iii** 51·13 m²

b 7·52 litres

2 A 5·4 km, B 5 km, C 4·5 km, D 6·1 km

3 2·7 m

4 a $4 × 0·9$ m, $5 × 1·9$ m, $4 × 1·5$ m, $4 × 0·65$ m

b 0·47 m **c** 0·21 m² **d** 11·29 m²

5 a £900 **b** £26 160

6 a 24 cm **b** 308 cm²

7 £1·216

8 a

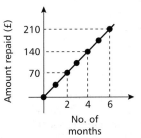

b yes, graph is a straight line passing through the origin

c £315

9 a 27 km **b** 6·67 km

10 £172·41

11 a $9(x + 7) = 234$

b $x = 19$

12

	2	3		
4	5	3	2	
8	2	1	9	
	1	4		

Page 249 Test B (Non-calculator)

1 a 136 cm **b** 8

2 a 7 h 45 min **b** 38 h 45 min

3 a 4·5 kg **b** 375 ml **c** 1250 tonnes

d 180 litres **e** 28 days **f** 36 hours

4 a 72° **b** 36°

c 90°, AC is a tangent to the circle **d** 54°

5 a 4·58 **b** 11·25 **c** 17·96

6 a 7 h 48 min **b** 7 h 40 min

7 a $\frac{3}{10}$ **b** $\frac{12}{25}$ **c** $\frac{1}{48}$

8 a $V = \frac{1}{20} × C$ **b** £4

9 a −1, 1, 3, 5

b pupil's own diagram

c (5, 11), (60, 121)

10 a 8 **b** −6 **c** −2

11 a i x **ii** a **iii** $3m$

b i $8(x − 2)$ **ii** $8(2 − 3y)$ **iii** $2(2ab − 3)$

12 a $K = 10$ **b** $Q = 9$ **c** $M = 40$ **d** $x = \frac{1}{2}$

Page 250 Test B (Calculator)

1 a 2·44 m **b** 9·03 m²

c 23·67 m² **d** 10·36 m²

2 a 486·0 cm³ **b** 14 850 cm³

c 24 **d** 11 663·2 cm³

3 a £352·50 **b** £235

4 b 027° **c** 4·3 km

5 a $\frac{1}{3}$ **b** $\frac{4}{15}$ **c** $\frac{7}{30}$ **d** $\frac{1}{6}$

6 a 0 °C **b** 100 °C **c** 40 °C **d** −25 °C

7 a £249·80 **b** £459·80 **c** £23 909·60

8 a 60 **b i** $\frac{1}{3}$ **ii** $\frac{1}{12}$

c pie chart with angles 66°, 48°, 120°, 96°, 30°

9 a 3 minutes **b** 2 minutes **c** 2·9 minutes

10 a 136° **b** 73·4 km

11 £875

12 423 cm³

Page 253 Test C (Non-calculator)

1 a £10·80 **b** £32·40

2 a $\frac{5}{6}$ **b** $\frac{5}{8}$ **c** $\frac{1}{6}$

d $1\frac{1}{12}$ **e** $2\frac{9}{10}$ **f** $2\frac{3}{4}$

3

```
135 \ 45    47 / 133
        88
    92 X 92
        88
133 / 47    45 \ 135
```

4 a 500 **b** 500 **c** 0·005

5 3 h 15 min

6 a 40% **b** 40%

7 a 40 cm **b** 12 cm

8 a 12, 6, 3, 0

b

(0, 12)

(4, 0)

9 a −5 **b** 4 **c** 6

10 a 12 cm   **b** 23°   **c** 11 cm

11 a 50, 75, 100, 125

    b $C = 25m$

    c straight line graph passing through (0, 0),
(1, 25), (2, 50), etc.

12 a i $x + 2 + 2x + 1 + 3x = 36$

     ii $x = 5\frac{1}{2}$

     iii £7·50, £12, £16·50

    b i $5y - 2 + 6y + 8y + 9 = 45$

     ii $y = 2$

     iii £8, £12, £25

Page 255 Test C (Calculator)

1 a 8961 cm^2 **b** $0·8961 \text{ m}^2$

2 a Triangular prism   **b** 60°

   c $367·2 \text{ cm}^3$ **d** $386·1 \text{ cm}^3$

3 a $0·81 \text{ m}^2$ **b** £6·47   **c** $0·05 \text{ m}^3$ **d** £6

4 a i £80   **ii** 20%   **b** loss of 12%

5 £300

6 a i 0·75   **ii** 75%

    b i 0·33   **ii** 33·33%

    c i 0·29   **ii** 28·57%

    d i 1·7   **ii** 170%

7 a 44 cm

    b 220 cm

    c 11 cm

8 a i £114   **ii** £93·75

    b i £108·30   **ii** £89·06

9 a\c

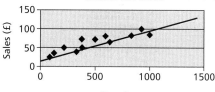

Sales of hot drinks

    b positive correlation

    d approx. £80

    e approx. 100

10 a 400   **b** 300   **c** 17, 25, 29

    d 300   **e** slightly below

11 a i $P = 2m + n$ **ii** $P = 7·13$

    b i $P = 2a + 2b$ **ii** $P = 776$

12 a $a = 6$ **b** $k = 5$

    c $y = 5$ **d** $x = 7$

Page 257 Test D (Non-calculator)

1 a -4 **b** -10 **c** 8

2 64

3 a £423·73   **b** £106·78   **c** £316·95

4 a $V = 3·5R$ **b** $V = 21$ volts

5 Alistair gets £240, Murray gets £40

6 $3\frac{3}{4}$ km/h

7 The soccer team ticket

8 1 in 4

9 a Minutes in car park

```
0 | 2 4 5 7
1 | 1 3 3 4 7 8
2 | 0 0 1 1 2 5 6 8 9
3 | 0 1 1 2 3 3 5 7
4 | 0 0 1 1 2 2 3 4 4
```

$n = 36$ 2|1 represents 21 minutes

    b 28·5 minutes

10 a First fortnight

     i 9·7 mm   **ii** 10 mm   **iii** 4 mm;
second fortnight

     i 10·6 mm   **ii** 11 mm   **iii** 3 mm

    b The second fortnight was wetter – the mean
and median rainfall were higher. There was
rain on each day of both fortnights, between
8 and 12 mm during the first fortnight and
between 9 and 12 mm during the second
fortnight.

11 a $a > -8, b < -1$ **b** $c < -8, d < -1$

12 a i $6(m + 4)$ **ii** $3(24 - n)$

     iii $8(3 + ab)$ **iv** $x(2x + 1)$

    b i $8(y + 2)$ **ii** $7(w + 2)$

Page 259 Test D (Calculator)

1 a 25°   **b** 7·6 m

2 4·3 m

3 a Triangular prism   **b** $134·4 \text{ cm}^3$

   c 5·2 cm   **d** $220·8 \text{ cm}^2$

4 a 540 euro   **b** £42·90

5 80 cm

6 a i $\frac{2}{25}$ **ii** 0·08   **b i** $\frac{9}{10}$ **ii** 0·9

    c i $\frac{13}{20}$ **ii** 0·65   **d i** $\frac{1}{200}$ **ii** 0·005

7 a i $\frac{1}{25}$ **ii** 0·04

    b i £32   **ii** £1200   **iii** £8

8 1173 units

Charges (£)	73·31
Standing charge	5·71
Sub total	79·02
VAT	3·95
Total due	82·97

9 42·5 m

10 a   **b** (8, 3)

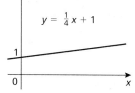

$y = \frac{1}{4}x + 1$

11 a 7, 10, 13   **b** $M = 3d + 1$

    c $3 \times 1 + 1 = 4, 3 \times 2 + 1 = 7, 3 \times 3 + 1 = 10,$
$3 \times 4 + 1 = 13$

    d 472

12 £139 250

Page 261 Test E (Non-calculator)

1 £180 profit

2 a £2·80   **b** £8·55   **c** £465   **d** £1250

3 a straight line passing through (0, 0) and (100, 80)

   b it's a straight line and it passes through (0, 0)

   c $E = 0·8W$

   d 60 mm

4 a i $8·21 \times 10^2$

     ii $6·432 \times 10^3$

     iii $4·71 \times 10^{-4}$

   b i 36 000   **ii** 0·0021

5 £7·50

6 £20

7 a i $\frac{1}{10}$ **ii** 10%   **b i** $\frac{1}{50}$ **ii** 2%

   c i $4\frac{1}{4}$ **ii** 425%   **d i** $3\frac{3}{200}$ **ii** 301·5%

8 a 12

   b

Households using 'Scour'		
After		Before
	0	2 3 4 5
8 4	1	0 1 4 8
9 6 5 3 1	2	1 1 2 3 5 6
9 8 7 4 3 3 3 1 0	3	1 2 2 3 5
4 1 1 0	4	1
$n = 20$		$n = 20$
2	1 represents 21 households	

   c yes, largest number of scores now in the thirties rather than the twenties

9

a 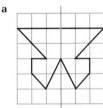   **b**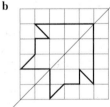

10 a 5

   b DEF, GHI, JKL, MNO

   c 42·5 cm

11 a 21   **b** 27   **c** 17   **d** 1

   e 5   **f** 14   **g** 28

12 a i 1, 2, 3, 6   **ii** 1, 2, 4, 8

     iii 1, 2, 3, 6, 9, 18   **iv** 1, 23

   b i 6   **ii** 6

   c i $4(2ab - 3)$ **ii** $4(3x - 4y)$

     iii $n(2m - n)$

Page 263 Test E (Calculator)

1 a 400 m   **b** 6·45 m/s

2 a 90°   **b** 45°   **c** 2·83 cm, 4 cm

3 2488 litres

4 a £3536   **b** £42 432

5 a £476   **b** £184

6 5 h 36 min

7 0·75 m²

8 a $180   **b** £55·56

9 a i $\frac{2}{7}$ **ii** $\frac{1}{7}$ **iii** $\frac{4}{7}$ **iv** 1

   b i 53   **ii** 365   **iii** 0·145

10 a

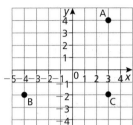

   b right-angled   **c** 9·2 units   **d** 0.86   **e** 41°

11 a (left to right, top to bottom) 9, 18, 27, 234, 531; 12, 21, 30, 237, 534; 5, 14, 23, 230, 527

   b i nth term $= 9n + 3$

     ii nth term $= 9n - 4$

   c i nth term $= 8n - 4$

     ii 980

12 $15(7x + 3) = 6(19x + 3); x = 3$

Page 265 Test F (Non-calculator)

1 a 16   **b** 24   **c** $1\frac{4}{15}$

   d $1\frac{5}{6}$ **e** $\frac{5}{9}$

2 a 15 min   **b** 1 hour

   c return (only 10 min compared to 15 min)

   d 25 min

3 a £10·35   **b** £41·40

4 a i 3 m   **ii** $\frac{9}{16}$ m²   **b i** 9 m   **ii** $4\frac{1}{2}$ m²

5 36°

6 a 2 : 7   **b** 1 : 3·5

7 a 20   **b** 11

8 a $\frac{1}{4}$ **b** $\frac{7}{10}$

9 a i Z   **ii** XY   **iii** $\angle$ZXY

   b i 2·5 cm   **ii** 70°   **iii** 6 cm

10 a pupil's own scale drawing

   b i 25 km   **ii** 102° or 103°

11 a $S \leqslant 60$ **b** $w + 3 > 9$ **c** $m \geqslant 6·5$

12 a $x = 7$ **b** $n = 3$ **c** $x = 6$

   d $y = 3$ **e** $a = 7$ **f** $x = 7$

Page 267 Test F (Calculator)

1 a 0·9 m²   **b** 0·45 m²   **c** £5·74

2 2·12 m (to 3 s.f.)

3 a 16·3 cm (to 3 s.f.)

   b 158 cm² (to 3 s.f.)

   c 151 cm³ (to 3 s.f.)

4 (top to bottom, left to right) $\frac{1}{4}$, 0·25, 25%; $\frac{1}{5}$, 0·2, 20%; $\frac{1}{20}$, 0·05, 5%; $\frac{7}{10}$, 0·7, 70%; $\frac{4}{25}$, 0·16, 16%; $\frac{3}{5}$, 0·6, 60%; $\frac{2}{3}$, 0·67, $66\frac{2}{3}$%; $\frac{1}{8}$, 0·125, $12\frac{1}{2}$ %; $2\frac{9}{25}$, 2·36, 236%

5 a £5·80

   b £10 556 (assuming he works 52 weeks!)

6 a 425 km

　b 75 min

7 a £ 12 800

　b £202

　c £2371·60

　d £2573·60

8 a 37 pence

　b £279·72

　c £14 545·44

　　(assuming she works 52 weeks!)

9 a 2·75 m

　b 8·46 m

10 a

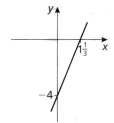

b above; (7, 17) lies on the line

11 The pyramid by 1·2 cm³ to 1 d.p.
(66·67 cm³ and 65·45 cm³)

12 a $C = 3n + 1$ 　**b** 1306